COLUMBUS ON HIMSELF

Columbus

ON HIMSELF

FELIPE
FERNÁNDEZ-ARMESTO

Hackett Publishing Company, Inc.
Indianapolis/Cambridge

14 13 12 11 10   1 2 3 4 5 6 7

For further information, please address
    Hackett Publishing Company, Inc.
    P.O. Box 44937
    Indianapolis, Indiana 46244-0937

    www.hackettpublishing.com

Cover design by Abigail Coyle
Printed at Sheridan Books, Inc.

The title-page lettering by Sebastian Carter is adapted from the type of the
great Complutensian Polyglot Bible of 1514

Library of Congress Cataloging-in-Publication Data
Fernández-Armesto, Felipe.
  Columbus on himself / by Felipe Fernández-Armesto.
    p. cm.
  Originally published: London : Folio Society, 1992.
  Summary: Presents Columbus's self-perception and personal history, as far as
possible, in his own words.
  ISBN 978-1-60384-133-7 (pbk.) — ISBN 978-1-60384-134-4 (cloth)
  1. Columbus, Christopher. 2. Explorers—America—Biography.
3. Explorers—Spain—Biography. 4. America—Discovery and exploration—
Spanish. I. Columbus, Christopher. II. Title.
  E111.F364 2010
  970.01'5092—dc22
  [B]   2009040714

CONTENTS

MAPS

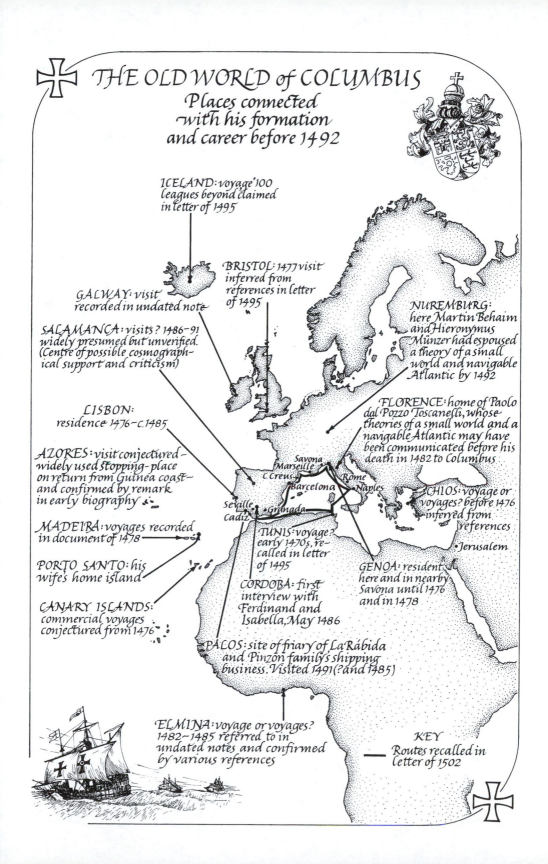

THE OLD WORLD of COLUMBUS
Places connected with his formation and career before 1492

ICELAND: voyage '100 leagues beyond' claimed in letter of 1495

BRISTOL: 1477 visit inferred from references in letter of 1495

GALWAY: visit recorded in undated note

NUREMBURG: here Martin Behaim and Hieronymus Münzer had espoused a theory of a small world and navigable Atlantic by 1492

SALAMANCA: visits? 1486–91 widely presumed but unverified. (Centre of possible cosmographical support and criticism)

LISBON: residence 1476–c.1485

FLORENCE: home of Paolo dal Pozzo Toscanelli, whose theories of a small world and a navigable Atlantic may have been communicated before his death in 1482 to Columbus

AZORES: visit conjectured – widely used stopping-place on return from Guinea coast – and confirmed by remark in early biography

Savona
Marseille
C.Creus
Barcelona
Rome
Naples
Seville
Cadiz
Granada

CHIOS: voyage or voyages? before 1476 inferred from references

Jerusalem

MADEIRA: voyages recorded in document of 1478

TUNIS: voyage? early 1470s, recalled in letter of 1495

GENOA: resident here and in nearby Savona until 1476 and in 1478

PORTO SANTO: his wife's home island

CORDOBA: first interview with Ferdinand and Isabella, May 1486

CANARY ISLANDS: commercial voyages conjectured from 1476

PALOS: site of friary of La Rábida and Pinzon family's shipping business. Visited 1491 (?and 1485)

ELMINA: voyage or voyages? 1482–1485 referred to in undated notes and confirmed by various references

KEY
—— Routes recalled in letter of 1502

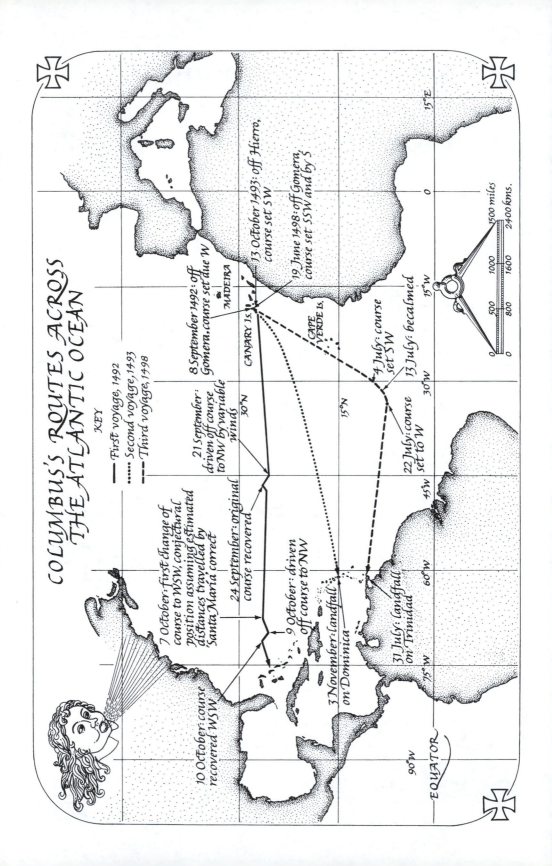

COLUMBUS'S ROUTES ACROSS THE ATLANTIC OCEAN

KEY
—— First voyage, 1492
· · · · · Second voyage, 1493
– – – Third voyage, 1498

8 September 1492: off Gomera, course set due W

13 October 1493: off Hierro, course set SW

19 June 1498: off Gomera, course set SSW and by S

MADEIRA

CANARY IS.

CAPE VERDE Is.

4 July: course set SW

13 July: becalmed

22 July: course set to W

21 September: driven off course to NW by variable winds

24 September: original course recovered

7 October: first change of course to WSW; conjectural position assuming estimated distances travelled by 'Santa Maria' correct

9 October: driven off course to NW

10 October: course recovered WSW

3 November: landfall on Dominica

31 July: landfall on Trinidad

30°N

15°N

90°W

75°W

60°W

45°W

30°W

15°W

0

15°E

EQUATOR

500   1000   1500 miles
800   1600   2400 kms.
0

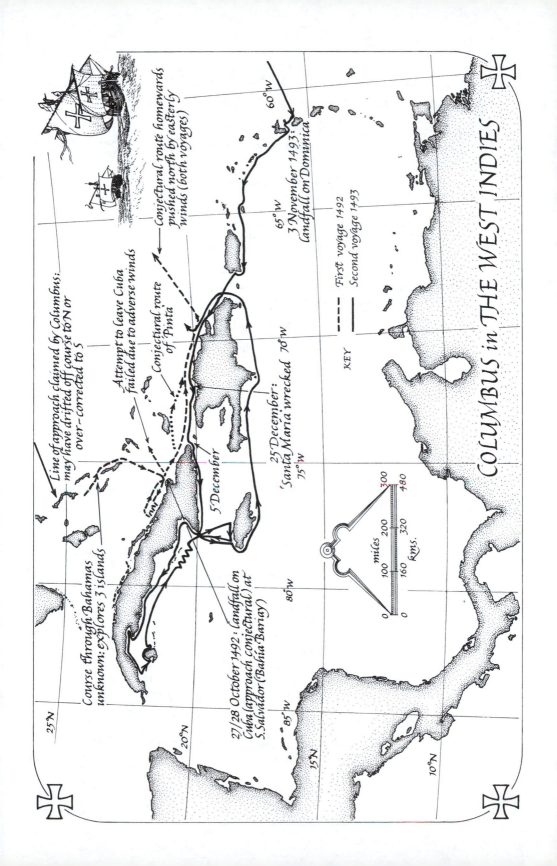

COLUMBUS in THE WEST INDIES

Line of approach claimed by Columbus:
may have drifted off course to N or
over-corrected to S

Course through Bahamas
unknown: explores 3 islands

Attempt to leave Cuba
failed due to adverse winds

Conjectural route
of Pinta

Conjectural route homewards
pushed north by easterly
winds (both voyages)

3 November 1493:
landfall on Dominica

5 December

25 December:
'Santa Maria' wrecked

27/28 October 1492: landfall on
Cuba (approach conjectural) at
S.Salvador (Bahía Bariay)

KEY

First voyage 1492
Second voyage 1493

25°N

20°N

15°N

10°N

60°w

65°w

70°w

75°w

80°w

85°w

miles
0   100   200   300
0   160   320   480
kms.

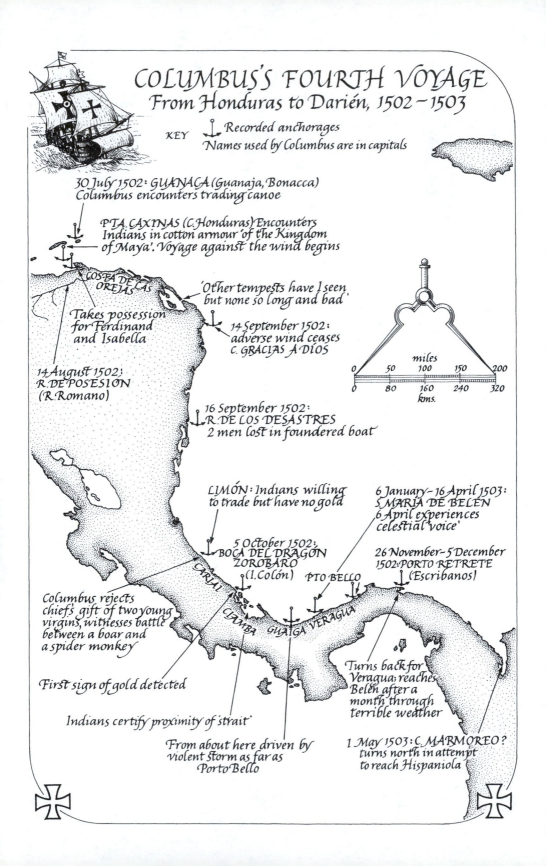

COLUMBUS'S FOURTH VOYAGE
From Honduras to Darién, 1502–1503

KEY ⚓ Recorded anchorages
Names used by Columbus are in capitals

30 July 1502: GUANACA (Guanaja, Bonacca)
Columbus encounters trading canoe

PTA. CAXINAS (C. Honduras) Encounters
Indians in cotton armour 'of the Kingdom
of Maya'. Voyage against the wind begins

COSTA DE LAS
OREJAS

'Other tempests have I seen
but none so long and bad'

Takes possession
for Ferdinand
and Isabella

14 September 1502:
adverse wind ceases
C. GRACIAS A DIOS

14 August 1502:
R. DE POSESION
(R. Romano)

miles
0   50   100   150   200
0   80   160   240   320
kms.

16 September 1502:
R. DE LOS DESASTRES
2 men lost in foundered boat

LIMÓN: Indians willing
to trade but have no gold

6 January – 16 April 1503:
S. MARIA DE BELEN
6 April experiences
celestial 'voice'

5 October 1502:
BOCA DEL DRAGON
ZOROBARO
(I. Colón)

PTO BELLO

26 November – 5 December
1502: PORTO RETRETE
(Escribanos)

CARIAI

CHAMBA   GUAIGA VERAGUA

Columbus rejects
chief's gift of two young
virgins, witnesses battle
between a boar and
a spider monkey

Turns back for
Veragua: reaches
Belén after a
month through
terrible weather

First sign of gold detected

Indians certify proximity of 'strait'

From about here driven by
violent storm as far as
Porto Bello

1 May 1503: C. MARMOREO?
turns north in attempt
to reach Hispaniola

ILLUSTRATIONS

PREFACE

As the fifth centenary of the discovery of the New World approaches, biographers are gathering over Columbus's bones. This book is intended to provide an antidote to biographies by presenting Columbus's self-perception and personal history, as far as possible, in his own words. Almost no individual of his time – certainly no other professional mariner – ever wrote so much about himself or revealed so much of himself in his writings. For 'natural' writers like Columbus, with little or no formal education, autobiography is often an irresistible form of self-expression. Despite the loss of much of his output, and his own evasions and suppressions, Columbus's surviving works are an abundant fund of material, which even the most brilliant and sensitive of objective reconstructions could hardly better. Although almost everything Columbus wrote is available in good editions and poor translations, it is remarkable how full and vivid – and, in some respects, how surprising and new – a picture of the man can be yielded by a particular sequence of texts. What I have attempted, in the pages which follow, is to produce such a sequence, justified by rigorous selection, rational arrangement and accurate translation.

In selecting the texts I have adopted two criteria: first, authenticity – for even when the surviving sources have been purged of the many forgeries, Columbus's authentic voice is often muffled or distorted by the interventions of early editors; secondly, relevance: for although almost anything a man commits to paper can reveal something about himself, Columbus has left a great deal of 'business' correspondence and memoranda which are not strictly autobiographical or self-revelatory. I have tried to identify sources which make a direct contribution to the narrative of his life or yield a direct insight into his life and character. Some texts select themselves. Many, however, are included or excluded only on the basis of very nicely balanced judgements. The second chapter, for instance, consists almost entirely of extracts from a work by an early editor of Columbus's writings, known as *El primer viaje* (*The First Voyage*), which in turn derives from a lost work of Columbus's own, entitled *Libro de la primera navegación* (or *Book of the First Navigation*). Much of the material survives only in the form of editorial paraphrases and I decided to exclude these in favour of the relatively few *ipsissima verba* extracts from the original work, eked out with paraphrases only when I felt convinced that the editorial version was particularly close to the original and included material of exceptional importance. The third chapter is monopolised by a letter sometimes branded as inauthentic, but which I include for reasons given below (pp. 101–3). The fourth chapter consists largely of a single document, known as the Torres Memorandum, which, some readers may feel, is relatively weak in the autobiographical and self-revelatory insights which abound elsewhere. However, like most previous compilers of Columbus anthologies, I have felt obliged to include it because it is the only surviving source from Columbus's own hand from the period of his second Atlantic crossing: in any case, careful reading, in the context of the other material presented here, discloses more than a superficial perusal might suggest. Later in the book, a case could be made for including more of Columbus's personal letters, especially to his son. But, as he was a prolix and repetitive writer at the best of times, I have excluded letters which add little or nothing to the picture or which merely reinforce the evidence of those presented here. I hope that the result of the selection – and, in particular, of the decision largely to exclude early editorial paraphrases – is to present the reader for the first time with a Columbus anthology which consists almost entirely of the explorer's own words.

The reader should be aware of one big limitation at the outset. A man is what he reads, and not all his reading is necessarily reflected in his writing. A comprehensive study ought to include more of the marginal annotations Columbus made in the books he read, with the passages from those books which he particularly signalled – usually by means of a pointing hand drawn in the margin. Only a few items of this sort fit into the scheme of the present book, though in the footnotes and passages of commentary I have kept this evidence in mind and quoted or alluded to it where necessary. It demands cautious handling; and its limitations are apparent in much current and recent work, for the present trend in Columbus scholarship is towards ever more relentless exploitation of this material.

Two important recent studies, for instance, have tried to illuminate aspects of Columbus's mental world by identifying themes prominent in his reading. The first* concentrates on passages to which he drew attention in the margins of his copy of the *Historia Rerum Ubique Gestarum* of Pope Pius II. The investigation reveals interests of Columbus's which can be only sparsely documented from his own writings, including, notably, interests in hydrographical theory and the geology of mountains. The most prominent theme, however, is fascination with the Amazon myth. This suggests to the author responsible for these researches that Columbus's motives in exploring the ocean included an ambition to hunt down the land of the Amazons, even though other explanations are possible, such as that Columbus was looking for flattering images of feminine fortitude for his royal patroness, or that he was fascinated by *mirabilia* generally.

The second study* has concentrated on Columbus's better known annotations to the *Imago Mundi* and other works of Cardinal Pierre d'Ailly. Here, the researcher has rightly drawn attention to Columbus's eagerness to highlight material of an eschatological character. The difficulty, however, of dating all but a couple of annotations made during what may have been repeated perusals of the book over a long period of time makes speculative the author's conclusion that Columbus's millenarianism, attested by his own writings only at a later date, was fully formed by 1492.

A further important limitation of the present book is that even after every effort has been made to reproduce Columbus's authentic voice, the influence of his first editor, Bartolomé de Las Casas, cannot be entirely excluded. A vast amount of the surviving material survives only in abstracts or extracts made by Las Casas, and therefore reflects the priorities of the editor as well as the thought of the writer.

Las Casas was guided by two considerations above all. First, he was concerned to fulfil his role as 'protector of the Indians'. He collected material designed to show the inhabitants of the New World in the best possible light, as possessing rational intellects, legitimate polities, natural rights and inherent goodness. He exhorted the Spanish colonists of the New World on their behalf and, apart from an interval spent in a Dominican house of study, he lobbied the court, during a career devoted to Indian welfare, from 1516 (or 1511, by his own account) until his death in 1566. It is probably fair to assume that his role in transmitting so much of Columbus's literary legacy has resulted in the over-representation of the Indians in the surviving material.

Secondly, he had a providential conception of history, according to which the discovery of the New World was ordained at a propitious moment for the salvation of the natives' souls, and Columbus was divinely elected as the instrument of it. In consequence, although he often makes sententious criticisms of his hero – who failed, for example, to perceive the iniquities of slavery and other forms of forced labour – his selections tend to present Columbus in a favourable light. And, while there can be no doubt that Columbus shared a similar notion of the significance of his discoveries and of his own place in the divine scheme of things, it is possible that Las Casas's attitude has resulted in undue prominence for this theme, from too early a date. Everything included in this book and attributable to Las Casas or to another early editor is enclosed in square brackets.

The material is arranged chronologically, in order of the events and periods to which it relates. In most cases, this corresponds to the time at which the texts were written, but in the first chapter, dedicated to Columbus's early life – the period, that is, before his first Atlantic crossing – some remembered or retrospective extracts are included. This is not primarily in order to provide an account of Columbus's life: Columbus's own version, which is refracted, rather than reflected, in the mirror of his self-perception, is in any case not the best source for such an account and is certainly an inadequate source on its own. What this book *can* provide, however – better, perhaps, than any other source – is an unfolding picture of Columbus's image of himself. One of the most durable assumptions made of Columbus is that he was a man almost incapable of intellectual progress, whose mentality was arrested at an early stage of its development, frozen in a set of assumptions to which he clung with unremitting obstinacy for the rest of his life. These assumptions included a confidence amounting to 'certainty' in his 'mission', its providential origins, and its cosmographical significance. Yet, when all the things he wrote about himself are strung together in the order in which he wrote them, it seems to me that a different picture emerges. Though Columbus was the prey of many *idées fixes* of his own, and could be obsessively pig-headed, his self-image was dappled with doubts. His sense of divine purpose grew gradually and fitfully and was born and nourished in adversity; his geographical notions, though they crystallised as time went on, took shape slowly and were surprisingly volatile until after his voyages had begun and, with his reading, had reinforced crucial assumptions with what he took to be 'evidence'.

Columbus was not the uniquely single-minded figure of most accounts, but a man whose mental development proceeded by fits and starts and led, at different times, in different directions.

He is a notoriously difficult writer to translate. His hand was hard to read and much of his work survives only in copies made at one or two removes from the original. The resulting textual problems sometimes defy solution, especially, for instance, in the account of his first explorations in the New World, where the terms for 'south-east' and 'south-west' and 'north-east' and 'north-west' and 'leagues' and 'miles' are often impenetrably confused. Moreover, he wrote a foreigner's Spanish, full of idiosyncratic or inaccurate usages. At times, his language is close to the Mediterranean seamen's macaronic which is known from some odd fragments of fifteenth- and sixteenth-century nautical argot, and of which a version is still spoken today; at times, his meaning has to be inferred from Portuguese or Genoese models or simply divined by informed guesswork. Some of Columbus's practices, especially in the use of botanical, topographical and ornithological terms, were bafflingly slipshod. A translator needs a cast of mind which is capable of embracing a thorough knowledge not only of Columbus's own works but also of the Spanish of the period in general, and particularly of nautical texts, with some knowledge of Portuguese and Italian (especially Genoese) material of a similar character. It is also necessary to be well acquainted with the historical context in order to make sense of many allusions. My own career happens to have given me a grounding in all the relevant fields and to have made me painfully aware of the shortcomings of previous translators, only one of whom seems, to me, to have a strong 'feel' for the meaning of the texts.*

To feel that one understands most of what Columbus was trying to say does not mean, of course, that one renders it in an appropriate style, and here another problem intervenes. Columbus was stylist-ically inconsistent. At times he wrote 'artlessly', the words pouring indiscriminately from his pen in unchecked enthusiasm; yet, for an uneducated man, he was capable at other times of an astonishing degree of rhetorical contrivance. Like all good writers, he could choose his models as suited his purpose, and he shows himself variously a passable master of legal, academic, biblical, chivalric and hermetic discourse. It seems to me, however, that there is always an element of more or less conscious literary creation in Columbus's writings: he always wrote as if striving actively for a literary standard which had to be worked at (the piece of verse translated below,

p. 207–8, is among the works never translated before). He was remarkably sparing, to my mind, in technical seamen's talk, and the swashbuckling translations of S. E. Morison,* for instance – while delightful to read and more accurate than most – therefore fail to convey the character of his prose. I have tried to deal with the problem of style by tackling each document in its own character, while attempting throughout to capture the pretensions of Columbus's work and a sense of his struggle with an imperfectly mastered language. Grammatical solecisms, however, have been eliminated; and in all but the most intractable cases of ambiguity I have plumped for a particular meaning.

Perhaps the least that can be expected of an anthology of Columbus's writings is that it will suggest some sort of answer to the question, 'What was he like?' His attractive traits are balanced by corresponding defects: his affection for his family by his desire to escape the world of restricted social opportunity which they represented; the generosity of his judgements of men by the venom usually drawn forth by better acquaintance. The reader of these pages will probably be happy to have avoided Columbus in the flesh. His tireless self-recommendation must have been wearying to others. His egotism approached the obsessive and his self-righteousness, the paranoid. He was loquacious rather than eloquent and he gives the impression of having wearied enemies into opposition and bored friends into assent.

His religion grew on him. The tradition that he was always intensely religious derives not directly from his own writings, but from those of an early editor and biographer. To judge from his own evidence, his first intense religious experience occurred on his way home from his first voyage, and the conviction that he was an agent of Providence grew on him from then onwards. Similarly, his cosmographical theories did not, perhaps, spring fully armed at the early stage supposed by tradition, but took shape gradually. Not until the time of his third voyage, for instance, does he allude directly to all the sources which are said to have contributed to his first plan for a voyage of Atlantic exploration.

Two features, however, do emerge as constants throughout the period covered by his surviving writings: his empirical epistemology and his social ambitions. He was always an adventurer in the social sense of the word, aiming for acceptance in the world of aristocrats and bureaucrats which dominated the Spanish court. If one were to judge from his own writings alone, one would be tempted to conclude that he acquired bookish culture, and undertook a chivalric escapade by sea, not for their own sake, or in any spirit of scientific enquiry or crusading fervour, but because they were means of social advancement, in a circle to which he aspired, by a route he prized. He saw himself, however, as a figure ennobled not only by acquired learning and the glory of great deeds, but also by practical sagacity. He seems to have believed firmly and consistently that practical wisdom was superior to book-learning and that knowledge could be verified by empirical means alone. He loved to debunk written authority from observed experience and, in defending himself against learned critics, made a virtue of his record as a practical mariner. At the same time, the limitations of this 'scientific' outlook are apparent in his increasing susceptibility to the notion that, as he put it, 'navigation is like a prophetic vision' (below, p. 229). He was profoundly influenced by the millenarian literature common in his day in the Aragonese court and the Franciscan Order; he claimed the revelations of a seer for himself; and he came increasingly to see his self-professed role as an instrument of Providence in the context of a highly egocentric eschatological vision. He led a life of ambition and misery. Frustration usually succeeds high hopes. No one can read his writings in sequence without sensing the growing bitterness and strain. He was almost entirely dependant on his royal patrons and almost entirely disappointed in his hopes; his reproaches against them are a strong theme in his writings, first muted, then daring, then reckless. Most men would have been content with a hundredth part of Columbus's personal achievement; yet he died in wretchedness, promising, from his painful deathbed, a hundredfold more.

I thank Anthony Pagden and Ivon Asquith, who both suggested independently the form the book has ultimately taken, in which footnotes are minimised and the commentary and context are distinguished from Columbus's own words typographically; and Sue Bradbury, a patient patron and enthusiastic editor. Being a teacher is a great education, and I should have overlooked much, perhaps most, of what is of interest in these texts without the help of the pupils who have studied them with me in Oxford over the past ten years: the others will forgive me if I just mention John Hopewell and Alina Gruszka.

POSTSCRIPT

After this book was completed, Professor A. Rumeu de Armas drew my attention to a newly discovered MS, purportedly containing writings of Columbus copied in the eighteenth century, some of which are otherwise unknown. As this collection has no satisfactory history or provenance, I have not added anything from it to the selection made for this book. A fascimile edition is available: *Libro copiador de Cristóbal Colón* (Testimonio, Madrid, 1989).

EDITORIAL NOTE

All passages of text in roman type are by Felipe Fernández-Armesto, while those in bold are Columbus's own writings. The square brackets have been used in three ways: where they enclose bold text they indicate paraphrases of Columbus's own words by Las Casas and other early editors; where italic, the present editor's interpretation of various lacunae in the original, and where roman, editorial explanation and clarification.

The dates used as headings for extracts from 'The First Voyage' and the Log of the Third Voyage are not Columbus's own, but are postulations by early editors.

I

ORIGINS AND EARLY LIFE

History has all the world's best stories and the life of the weaver's son who discovered America could hardly be matched even by the most inventive imagination. Columbus had, perhaps, more influence on mankind than any individual since Muhammad. Despite his humble origins, he rose by dint of spectacular achievements to fame and fortune; he was hailed in his lifetime as a prophet and 'a new apostle'. Yet he died in the misery of embittered frustration.

Though a surprising and challenging figure, Columbus is not a 'mysterious' character in the sense claimed by writers looking for a licence to speculate. On the contrary, thanks largely to his own copious writings, he is better known and more accessible than any comparable figure of his day. Compared with his most obvious contemporary counterparts, Vasco da Gama, who discovered the sea-route to India, and John Cabot, who explored the northern route to the New World, the surviving information about him is vast.

The sources are genuinely sparse, however, for the first forty years or so of his life. His writings survive in substantial amounts only from the time of his first Atlantic crossing in 1492. The periods of his birth, childhood, early navigations and the genesis of his project for a transnavigation of the ocean have to be reconstructed from retrospective glimpses and recollections refracted, or perhaps distorted, by the passage of time and the change of perspective. In this book, which aims to present Columbus as he saw himself, through his own writings, the first chapter has therefore to be of a different kind from the rest, with a relatively small number of fragments of Columbus's own words, embedded in connecting passages and commentary.

Columbus was evasive about his origins and early life. An early biography, attributed to his younger son, suggests that this was out of modesty. He preferred, his biographer alleges, to rise by merit, rather than relying on his illustrious ancestry to define his place in the world.* A concept typical of Renaissance moral philosophy underlies the argument: nobility consists not in ancient lineage but in personal virtue. This was, however, like many Renaissance concepts, one which Columbus did not fully share. His hankering after an illustrious past can be detected in the shadowy claim that 'I am not the first Admiral of my line'.* The most consistent single purpose to which his own life was dedicated was the desire to found a great noble dynasty of his own: the priorities he claimed – the service of God and of the monarchs of Spain, the advancement of science – appear, by comparison, subordinate or ancillary.

Nor was Columbus a man to do anything for reasons of modesty. Even the humility he affected in later life, when he frequented court in a rough Franciscan habit, was of a showy, exhibitionistic kind. He claimed to be divinely inspired – which is a curiously egotistical form of self-effacement. He could never have sensed his vocation without pride, or sustained it without ambition. It was not modesty that made him reticent, perhaps, but shame. His origins were left in the shadows because they were obscure. It is as certain as any knowledge we have from so long ago that the Cristóbal Colón who sailed to the New World in 1492 was the same Cristoforo Columbo who was born in or near Genoa, the son of a weaver named Domenico, probably a little over forty years before. The evidence consists not only in Columbus's repeated, and apparently heartfelt, asseverations of his Genoese provenance, but also in a document of unimpeachable authenticity, in which some of his Genoese kinsfolk declare their intention of sending to Spain, after his rise to fame, to seek his patronage.* This fact helps to convey a sense of the social trajectory of Columbus's life: the restrictive and glutinously clannish circle into which he was born – so typical of late medieval Genoa; the escape into worldly success; the clustering of kinsmen around the fortunate *arriviste*; the role of family provider to which he was committed by his hard-won place in the acceptance world. At the end of his life, Columbus was distributing titles of honour and (largely imaginary) wealth among his brothers. One thinks of Napoleon – another character from an intensely 'tribal' Italian tradition – turning his impoverished siblings into sovereigns. Columbus betrayed the truth about himself when he admitted that the monarchs of Spain had raised him 'from nothing', and made him their 'creature'.*

Apart from his Genoese birth, the only other credible assertion

18

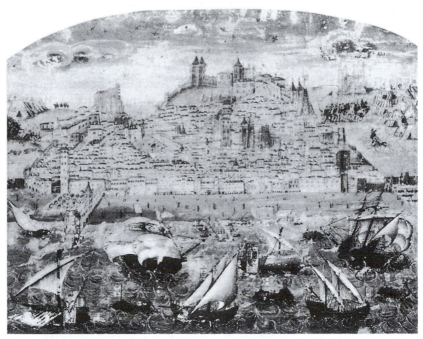

Lisbon: he was welcomed by the Genoese community in the
city, among whom he found friendship and employment

Genoa, 1493: birth place of Columbus

'La Virgen de Cristóbal Colón'.
The kneeling figure is reputedly Christopher Columbus

Columbus made about his early life was that he went to sea at 'a very early age'.* We do not know when – or why – that was. The biography ascribed to his son claims that it was when the future discoverer was fourteen. In 1492, Columbus dated the event twenty-three years previously, if we can trust the transcription of the document. Yet, if the chronology is uncertain, something of the outline of Columbus's early voyages, before the start of his transatlantic career, can be pieced together from a Genoese document which shows that in 1478 he was trading sugar in Madeira for Genoese businessmen, and from his own allusions.

His fullest account occurs in fragments of a letter he wrote to his royal Spanish patrons from his own new-found island of Hispaniola in January, 1495.* The fragments were extracted by Las Casas (see above, p. 11) and it is impossible to reconstruct their context with any certainty. Their content covers, by way of reminiscence, four voyages to widely separated destinations, all of rather remote date by the time they were recalled, united by nothing save the writer's self-congratulatory tone. From these four sparse and disjointed paragraphs, can any coherent picture of Columbus's early voyages be constructed? The answer is yes, but only by painstaking means and with tentative results. Still, while the detailed meanings of the fragments can be teased out of them only with difficulty, their general import is clear. In common with the other evidence, they show what they were evidently intended to show: that Columbus acquired, during the 1470s and the early 1480s, wide experience of navigation, especially in the Atlantic as it was known in his day.

The four fragments have to be understood against the background of the circumstances in which they were written. At the time he wrote them, Columbus's career was threatened by his own failures and by a crisis in his patrons' confidence. He had returned, late in 1494, to the camp he had set up on the island of Hispaniola, after a frustrating voyage of exploration between Cuba and Jamaica. He had searched with increasing desperation for evidence that his discoveries were Asiatic in character and capable of yielding great riches, especially gold. That evidence had eluded him. He had been forced to the conclusion that Cuba had no gold. And he had taken refuge in fantastic devices: exacting from his crew an oath that Cuba was part of the mainland of China; claiming to have sighted the legendary oriental Christian potentate, Prester John; and talking to his men of leaving the islands to circumnavigate the world. In these circumstances, he had good reason to fear the taunts of the enemies who abounded at court and who had claimed from the first that his discoveries would turn out to be useless. His great advantage over those enemies, who were almost all more learned than he, was the extent of his practical knowledge of the world, culled in his career as a navigator. When he wrote to the monarchs, he staked a claim for his own evaluation of his achievements to be respected.

In the first extract, Columbus advanced a claim to have taken part in the corsair warfare waged in the early 1470s by René d'Anjou in an attempt to wrest the Neapolitan throne from its Aragonese occupants.

Fragment of a Letter to Ferdinand and Isabella, Hispaniola, January 1495

It happened to me that King René, who is with God, sent me to Tunis to seize the galleass *Fernandina*, and when I was already off the island of San Pietro, off Sardinia, a brig told me that the said galleass was accompanied by two round ships and a carrack. The men that were with me mutinied at this and determined not to continue the voyage but to return to Marseilles for another ship and more men. Realising that I could not change their minds by force but only by means of some guile, I agreed to their demands and, after altering the way the compass lay, I made sail when it was getting dark. And the next day, as the sun rose, we were beyond Cape Carthage, while they were all sure that we were heading for Marseilles . . .

The episode is unlikely to have been a pure invention, since partisanship of the Angevin pretender cannot have been calculated to endear Columbus to the Spanish monarchs, who had inherited the Aragonese claims. The setting of the tale Columbus tells is the Gulf of the Lion* and the Tyrrhenian Sea – Genoa's home waters, which he had sailed so thoroughly in his youth that he remembered the sailing directions in detail until the last years of his life.* The anecdote may not be true. It has the flavour of a copy-book *sententia*, designed to illustrate a maxim of moral philosophy; but the story-line, according to which he successfully tricked mutinous sailors by tampering with the compass, is typical of the way Columbus liked to see himself. He was equally proud of deceiving his crew on his first transatlantic voyage by tampering with the log, and of intimidating the natives of Jamaica during his last voyage by exploiting an eclipse. Whether strictly true or not, the story should be seen as true to the man and as part of his claim to a sort of natural sagacity with which he felt able to challenge the wisdom of the scholars.

In the second extract, a further fragment of the same letter to Ferdinand and Isabella, Columbus claimed to have sailed into the north-west Atlantic beyond Thule – a name usually employed at the time to designate Iceland.

In the year 1477, in the month of February, I sailed a hundred leagues beyond the island of Thule, the south coast of which is seventy-three degrees north of the equator – not sixty-three degrees, as some men say – and it is not within the line that delimits the western hemisphere according to Ptolemy, but is much further west.* And to this island, which is as big as England, the English travel with merchandise, especially the men of Bristol, and at the time when I went there the sea was not frozen, although there were very big tides, so that twice a day in some places the tide rose twenty-five fathoms high and fell again by the same amount . . .

Columbus was played false by either his memory or his fancy. He muddled the height of the Iceland tides with those of Bristol, where it would have been normal to put in during such a voyage. In his eagerness to show the superiority of practical experience over learned authorities he committed an outrageous howler in estimating Iceland's latitude. The figure of 'a hundred leagues' is no doubt conventional, but whale- or walrus-hunts and fishing expeditions did take mariners 'beyond' Iceland. The voyage to northern waters was common for Mediterranean and Iberian traders; and the Iceland route was much frequented by ships from Bristol such as Columbus might have joined in the course of a trip: Bristolian-Portuguese voyages in partnership are commonly recorded at a slightly later date. Even if he was ascribing to himself experiences which he really knew only by report, there is nothing inherently implausible about the claims advanced.

The third extract takes the form of a truncated sentence in the same letter:

I have been in the King of Portugal's fort of Elmina, which is on the

equator, and so I am a good witness that it is not uninhabitable as they say . . .

This claim – to have sailed south to São Jorge da Mina, near the mouth of the River Volta, where the Portuguese traded in gold from 1482 – is abundantly confirmed: both by recollections recorded by Columbus in marginal annotations to books in his library (as we shall see in a moment), and by the familiarity he showed with equatorial Africa in comparisons and implied comparisons with the New World environment. Again, though Columbus misread his latitude by about five degrees, the point of the extract is clear, despite its brevity: practical wisdom is superior to book-lore.

The point of the last fragment (also from the letter to Ferdinand and Isabella) is less obvious:

It has so happened that I have had to take two ships and leave one of them in Porto Santo to stop a leak, which held her up for one day, and I arrived at Lisbon eight days ahead of her because I was carried by a storm-force wind from the south-west and she encountered no more than a slight wind in the north-north-east, which is adverse . . .

Here, as in the remark about the tides in the second extract, Columbus seems to be emphasising the unpredictability of nature and therefore, perhaps, the power of experience to discern phenomena inaccessible to a learned approach, based on reason and precedent.

The mention of the route between Lisbon and Porto Santo takes us back to a formative period of Columbus's life, in the mid- to late 1470s, when he was engaged in the sugar trade of the Madeira archipelago – a boom enterprise of the period, dominated by rich Genoese, including Columbus's employers, the Centurione family. Porto Santo was a particularly significant place in Columbus's life, because his wife, Doña Felipa Moniz, whom he married probably during the period 1478–80, came from there. As the daughter of the first captain or governor of the island, she was able to bring her husband two inestimable advantages: first, a relatively elevated social position; secondly, access to her father's charts and papers, which, according to Las Casas,* inspired him to investigate Portuguese explorations of the African Atlantic.

How had Columbus achieved this double breakthrough: from

obscure origins to a creditable match, from Mediterranean to Atlantic navigation?

When, on his deathbed, on 19 May 1506, in Valladolid, he added a codicil to his will, in which he made bequests to a number of residents of Lisbon, or to their heirs,* he may have been recalling another early voyage, memorable not for any navigational experience he may have got from it, but because it marked a turning-point in his life: the voyage that took him from Genoa to a new life in Portugal. The date and circumstances are not known for certain: the tradition that Columbus was shipwrecked after a northern-bound trading fleet was attacked by French pirates is early and plausible. An incident which occurred in 1476 broadly fits the terms of the story,* and a date in the mid-1470s, and in any case before 1477, would suit what is known of the chronology of Columbus's career. But whether or not the circumstances of his arrival in Lisbon were as dramatic as tradition claims, the time he spent there was of enormous significance. He was welcomed by the Genoese community in the city, among whom he found friendship and employment. The castaway – if that is what he was – began a long period of habitual residence in Portugal and a lifetime of navigation in the Atlantic. In particular, his new way of life involved sugar buying trips to islands of the Atlantic – certainly to Madeira and Porto Santo and presumably to the Azores and the Canaries – as well as opportunities to make longer journeys into less frequented waters, which may have played a part in influencing him to attempt to explore the remote ocean.

We do not know how or when the project of attempting an Atlantic crossing first took shape in his mind. His writings do suggest, however, that he was making observations which may have been relevant to such a project in the early 1480s and perhaps in the late 1470s. Any theory that the Atlantic was navigably narrow had to depend on three types of argument in its favour: empirical evidence, such as that of flotsam washed up from the farther shore; theoretical argument, based on the claims that the land-mass occupied more of the earth's surface than was commonly supposed, or that the globe was smaller than commonly supposed, or both; and citations from written authorities, especially classical and scriptural ones, in support of the case.

Columbus was to accumulate an extensive and ill-assorted collection of such citations, but the difficulties of dating his perusal of the books from which they were culled make it impossible to say for certain that he was amassing them earlier than 1488. Of his interest in the other two types of argument, however – in transatlantic flotsam and in speculations about the size of the globe – there is evidence in isolated references to voyages he made from Lisbon. These references occur in the marginal annotations Columbus made in books he read. They cannot be dated with any certainty, but it is likely that they refer to journeys made before Columbus transferred his home base to Castile in 1486.

The most interesting, from one perspective, is that in which Columbus records a sighting of allegedly oriental castaways at Galway in Ireland.* The sort of business which took him to Bristol and perhaps to Iceland could well have involved a call at that busy port. The biography attributed to his son mentions such human flotsam among the evidence that induced Columbus to seek an ocean route to the east, though in this source the find is located in the Azores.* The annotation occurs in the margins of the second chapter of Columbus's copy of the *Historia Rerum Ubique Gestarum* by the humanist Enea Silvio Piccolomini, who became Pope Pius II. The subject of the context is whether the sea can be navigated in all directions. The author takes a positive view of this question and cites, in particular, arguments in favour of the navigability of the western ocean. Among the evidence he assembles is that of allegedly Indian merchants, shipwrecked, according to a twelfth-century authority, on the coast of Germany. Columbus chooses this point at which to add an observation of his own:

People have come from Cathay by heading towards the east. We have seen a good deal of evidence of this, most particularly, in Galway in Ireland, a man and a woman in two wooden boats, carried off by a storm in marvellous fashion.

If Columbus really did make this observation as early as 1477 – and we know of no other specific event with which to link it – it raises the possibility that the idea of a transnavigation of the Atlantic occurred to him at a very early date and underwent a long period of gestation. If so, the germ of the idea has to be sought in observation and practical experience rather than in book-learning and the contemplation of an erudite tradition. It would be prudent, however, to suspend judgement. What may, on first observation, have struck Columbus only as an unclassifiable oddity could have been recalled

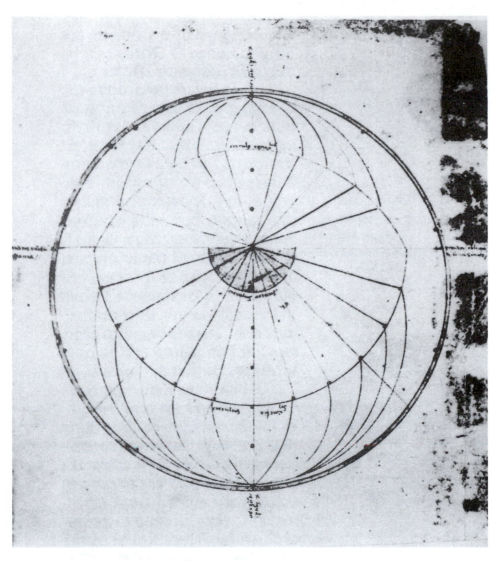

Facsimile of a planisphere drawn by Columbus in his
copy of Piccolomini's *Historia Rerum Ubique Gestarum*

Facsimile of a detail of a page of Pierre d'Ailly's *Imago Mundi*,
annotated by Columbus during his voyage to Guinea

later and re-classified as evidence of the accessibility of Asia. Most of the evidence he is said in early sources to have accumulated from observation or from seamen's reports tends to show only the possibility of undiscovered Atlantic islands, not a short route to the Orient.

Other annotations which cast light on the formation of Columbus's plan are those concerned with his trip or trips along the Portuguese gold route to West Africa. A representative example occurs early in the pages of his copy of Pierre d'Ailly's *Imago Mundi*, one of the most radically revisionist books of fifteenth-century cosmography, and the best-thumbed work in Columbus's library:

The torrid zone is not uninhabitable, for nowadays the Portuguese sail through it; indeed, it is very densely populated; and on the equinox is the fort of Mina, belonging to the Most Serene King of Portugal, which we have seen. *

In itself, this observation says no more than the recollection of the same trip – or a similar one – preserved in the fragment of the letter of 1495, which we have already considered. Columbus is again insisting on the revolutionary effects of experience on received opinions. This radical epistemology may alone have inclined Columbus to test the theory of a navigable Atlantic by hazarding a voyage. In a further marginal annotation, however, Columbus claimed that his experiences on the route to Guinea brought findings even more subversive of received cosmographical widsom; he also claimed to have made observations which, by implication, supported a project for an ocean crossing:

Note that often in sailing south from Lisbon, in Guinea, I have diligently noted the distance travelled, using the methods of sea-captains and mariners, and afterwards I have measured the altitude of the sun many times with the quadrant and other instruments, and I have found that my measurements endorse the opinion of Alfraganus: that is, that to any one degree, fifty-six and two-thirds miles correspond. Therefore, his estimate can be relied on. Therefore we may say that the perimeter of the earth at the equator is 20,400 miles, and again because the same was confirmed by the findings of Master Joseph, the physician and astrologer, and many others, sent by the Most Serene King of Portugal for this sole purpose. The same can be seen by anyone who takes the measurements from sea charts, measuring from north to

south in a straight line through the ocean beyond all the land; which he can well do, beginning in England or Ireland, south in a straight line as far as Guinea.*

This note presents difficulties of interpretation but its drift is clear enough. The problem of the distance occupied along the surface of the globe at the equator by one degree of longitude or latitude was pregnant with significance for the feasibility of an ocean crossing. The shorter the distance represented by a degree, the smaller the world. The smaller the world, the narrower the ocean. Columbus later assembled other arguments and 'evidence' in favour of his hypothesis of a narrow Atlantic. As far as we know, however, the argument from the length of a degree was his starting-point, and the first 'proof' which he claimed to have verified by empirical methods.

To understand the workings of Columbus's mind, it is important to realise that the 'proof' was fallacious and the claimed methods of verification incredible. Columbus knew of 'the opinion of Alfraganus' (the tenth-century Arab cosmographer al-Farghani) from the report of Pierre d'Ailly but failed to realise the fact that the Arab scholar's mile was much bigger than that of authorities in the Latin west: in consequence, Columbus espoused an estimate for the length of a degree, and therefore for the size of the globe, which was too small by about twenty-five per cent, and about eight per cent smaller than that of the most favourable estimate canvassed at the time.* Though the size of the globe was a matter of lively debate at the time, an underestimate as radical as that of Columbus defied any possible consensus. When he returned from his second voyage to the New World, his friend, the chronicler Andrés de Bernáldez, claimed to have told him bluntly that he could have sailed a further twelve hundred leagues without reaching Asia.*

This discrepancy concerning the value of a degree was alone enough to make nonsense of the rest of Columbus's reasoning. But even had the calculation been true, it could not have been verified in the way Columbus claims. In the first place, the 'methods of mariners' for estimating distance travelled were extremely rough-and-ready. Speed of travel was assessed by the observer's informed guesswork; more guesswork intervened when allowance was made for deflection or retardation by unseen currents. The estimated speed was then compared with the passage of time, reckoned from sand-clocks turned at half-four intervals by ship's boys; a boy's negligence or excessive zeal or eagerness to speed the change of watch could all throw the calculations seriously awry. At a typical juncture of his first ocean crossing, Columbus's pilots differed by a margin of ten per cent in their estimates of distance traversed.

Secondly, if Columbus did use a quadrant 'and other instruments' – presumably an astrolabe, perhaps a cross-staff – to read latitude, he is unlikely to have achieved an accurate result. No one, as far as we know, ever took an accurate reading with a quadrant or astrolabe on the open sea in the fifteenth century: Columbus might have taken the readings to which he refers on land, but his record as an observer of latitude in similar conditions, also allegedly with the help of instruments, in the New World, does not inspire confidence: his estimates were subject to an error commonly of about 100 per cent. His belief that São Jorge was on the equator is equally disturbing: the true reading is 5° north.

Columbus did have three means of calculating latitude at his disposal. The first two belonged to the art of 'primitive celestial navigation' (as scholars now call it), which seems to have been universally practised by western Mediterranean and Atlantic navigators in the late Middle Ages. Relative or very approximate latitude – sufficient for practical, if not for scientific, purposes – could be gauged by judging the height of the sun at noon or the Pole Star at evening with the naked eye. Experienced seamen could judge relative latitudes, at least, with uncanny accuracy in this fashion.* For the sort of exactitude demanded or affected by Columbus, the quadrant and astrolabe respectively would have to be used to supplement such observations. From the surviving records of his transatlantic voyages, Columbus can be seen to have used an astrolabe on board ship, but again with only very imperfect accuracy.

It is clear, however, that his own preferred method was to time the hours of daylight and read the corresponding latitude from a published chart, such as he copied into one of his books. There is no evidence that he did this on his way to Guinea, but for his first ocean crossing the evidence is incontrovertible: he reveals an obsession with the timing of the length of the day, and some of the inaccuracies in his pretended readings of latitude correspond to those in the table we know he had.*

Nor could Columbus's error about the value of a degree have been verified by reference to sea charts. No surviving sea charts of the period include lines of latitude, nor, as far as we know, were any of them based on attempts to take measurements, or made with allowance for magnetic drift, so that even relative latitudes appear highly misleading. Not even distance could be assessed from such maps in any but the vaguest fashion: they were intended as direction-finding devices, not guides to absolute position. A navigator using one was expected simply to take the direction indicated and keep his course until he sighted his destination. As for Columbus's appeal to the authority of Master José Vizinho, the Portuguese court cosmographer, it can best be judged by referring to the reading of latitude along the Guinea route ascribed elsewhere by Columbus to the same observer: according to this source, Vizinho's readings of latitude by astronomical means were seriously defective and may have been contrived to validate earlier traditions, including that derived from al-Farghani. Vizinho also worked on the problems of calculating latitude from the angle of the sun, as well as from the hours of daylight, and compiled tables of solar declination to which Columbus had access. It is therefore possible that his readings concurred with those Columbus claimed to have made. It seems improbable, however, that he should have endorsed Columbus's estimate of the value of a degree: he was a member of the commission of Portuguese savants that dismissed Columbus's application for royal backing.*

Why, then, did Columbus insist on assigning a verifiably false value to the length of a degree along the surface of the earth? And why did he cite all this apparently bogus evidence in its favour, not only in communications to potential patrons but also in this most private of sources, a marginal annotation, presumably addressed to himself, in a book from his own library? The inescapable conclusion is that he believed it to be true and convinced himself of the relevance of the alleged evidence, in defiance of the facts. Wishful thinking was one of Columbus's most consistent mental characteristics. He so wanted the world to be small that he genuinely believed he had seen, with the eye of experience, evidence that confirmed the image in his mind. He had entered a fantastic labyrinth of error, from which he ultimately emerged into a new world.

Historians have been bitterly divided over whether Columbus should be seen as essentially a practical mariner whose ambition of crossing the ocean was inspired by experience of the sea; a learned but mentally ill-disciplined autodidact whose project was based on book-lore; or a plagiarist who got his idea from someone else. Evidently, when he looked back in later life on the genesis of his enterprise, from the perspective of his struggle with educated court-iers and established savants, Columbus felt inclined to see himself in the first of these roles. It should be borne in mind, however, that in all the pleas for patronage that we know about, Columbus sought to justify his theories with a weighty pseudo-scientific apparatus, of which his theory of the value of a degree is only a sample. In his own mind, the practical seafaring craft came first; it inclined him 'to want to reveal the secrets of this world'. But the learning – cartographical first, as far as we know, from the time his father-in-law's papers came into his hands, and later cosmographical – always influenced the way he presented his plans.

The single-minded certainty attributed to him by most historians was a myth invented by early biographers: for Las Casas and the compiler of the *Historie*, Columbus's unshakeable conviction was a sign that 'the secrets of this world' had been divinely revealed. The myth has been sustained by scholars, who have welcomed the challenge of a mystery to solve, and by historical *vulgarisateurs*, who have relished its romance. In reality, though he could be pig-headed and obsessive, Columbus's mind had a mercurial quality which the historical tradition has overlooked. He seems, for instance, at differ-ent times, to have contemplated at least four different Atlantic projects, and to have wavered between them: first, a voyage in search of undiscovered islands, such as was frequently ventured in the fifteenth century, sometimes with success; secondly, an expedition in search of the Antipodes – a hypothetical continent of which the existence was much debated in fifteenth-century Europe and the discovery widely anticipated; thirdly, an attempt to establish a westward route to Asia; and, possibly in connection with this last venture, a voyage to Cipangu, the fabulously wealthy island, inspired by Japan, which Marco Polo had rumoured to lie in the depths of the ocean, 1,500 miles beyond the coast of China.*

By 1492 he had come to stake his claim to the patronage of Ferdinand and Isabella of Spain on the third of these possibilities, perhaps with a visit to Cipangu and the discovery of other islands on the way. Though it was to return to prominence in his mind later, the Antipodean option, which, ironically, closely matched what he was really to find, had temporarily receded and does not seem to have been actively canvassed at the time of his great voyage. The experts Ferdinand and Isabella employed to scrutinise Columbus's submis-sions seem to have rejected it by a decisive majority verdict.*

Two features were common to all the projects he put up for consideration: they all involved a voyage deep into the Atlantic, and probably, but not necessarily, a transnavigation of that intimidatingly vast sea; and they all involved the personal aggrandisement of Columbus. Though the identity of his destination seemed to be negotiable, the rewards he demanded in the event of success were not. It is hard to resist the impression that Columbus cared about where he was going less in a geographical sense than in a social one. He was at least as anxious about what he would be as where he would be when he arrived. He demanded titles of nobility, powers of government, and potentially enormous revenues in the lands he proposed to discover. His own recollection was that his suit was derided because his plans were disbelieved, but it may also have been because his pretensions seemed ridiculous. According to a creditable early tradition, it was his egregious demands that deterred the Portuguese from supporting him.*

His concern for his own status explains the form of the next document. In the version in which it has come down to us, it serves as a preface to a manuscript entitled 'The First Voyage, with the courses and route, made by the Admiral Don Cristóbal Colón when he discovered the Indies', which contains an abstract, with much quotation *in extenso*, made by Las Casas from a work of Columbus's own, in the form of a diary.* Las Casas tells us that he copied what he thought was the original 'prologue' word for word, but he was working from a copy which formed part of a huge collection of his hero's miscellaneous papers. The existing preface seems to me a pastiche, composed of three ill-fitting parts: there is no reason to doubt that each of these came originally from the hand of Columbus but it is impossible to say who was responsible for combining them in this form, or whether it was done by accident or design. The first section, which occupies the first long paragraph below, seems to me to have the flavour of a legal document, which I have emphasised by capitalising the first term in each clause, in the manner of a legal preamble. Columbus's purpose in this section seems to be to record and justify the lavish concessions which Ferdinand and Isabella granted to him when they commissioned him to make his voyage. A short section follows in which he records his departure and states his purpose and destination. Up to this point, the document could well be the sort of material Columbus might have written up from memory after his voyage and placed at the head of a journal composed for the monarchs' edification and as a reminder of what he was owed.

The third section is of a different kind, however. The copyist ran all three sections together into one continuous torrent of prose, but the distinctions between them are so marked that it seems justifiable to divide them into separate paragraphs to assist perusal. The last has the appearance of having been written at the start of a voyage; it consists of a promise to keep a daily journal, far more detailed than a conventional ship's log – such as we know Columbus did indeed keep on all his major voyages; the writer further promises to make maps as guides to the contents of Ocean Sea. It makes no sense to suppose that this section can originally have formed part of the document to which it is now appended. It might have got detached from the lost prologue; it might even have formed part of the otherwise lost journal of Columbus's second transatlantic voyage, for which his intention of mapping his route is confirmed by another source.*

Las Casas described his transcription as being only of the beginning of the preface; in a further copy of it, the extract ends with the term, 'etc.', which Las Casas usually employed to indicate the omission of something substantial.

Most Christian and very high and very excellent and very powerful Princes, our Lord and Lady, King and Queen of the Spains and of the Islands of the Sea.

WHEREAS, in this present year of 1492, after your Highnesses had concluded their war against the Moors who still reigned in Europe, and having brought that war to an end in the very great city of Granada, where, in this present year, on the second day of the month of January, I saw the royal banners of your Highnesses raised, by force of arms, on the towers of the Alhambra, which is the fortress of the said city, and saw the Moorish king come to the gates of the city and kiss the royal hands of your Highnesses and of my lord the Prince; AND WHEREAS thereafter, in that same month, in accordance with the information which I had given to your Highnesses concerning the lands of India and concerning a prince who is called the Great Khan (which in our romance means King of Kings), about how he and his predecessors had on many occasions sent to Rome to ask for teachers of our holy faith to instruct him therein, and how the Holy Father had never furnished him with them, and how so many peoples had been lost through falling into idolatry and taking to themselves religions of damnation; AND WHEREAS your Highnesses, as Catholic Christians and as princes who love the holy

Christian faith, and as augmenters thereof and foes of the sect of Muhammad and of all idolatries and heresies, thought of sending me, Christopher Columbus, to the said regions of India, to see the said princes and peoples and the lands and the disposition thereof and all, and the means that might be had to convert them to our holy faith, and your Highnesses ordered that I should not travel overland to the east, as is customary, but rather by way of the west, whither to this day, as far as we know for certain, no man has ever gone before, THEREFORE, after having expelled all the Jews from all your kingdoms and lordships, in the aforesaid month of January, your Highnesses ordered me to go with a sufficient fleet to the said regions of India; and to that end your Highnesses granted me great favours and ennobled me, so that from thenceforth I should be entitled to call myself Don and should be High Admiral of the Ocean Sea and Viceroy and Governor in perpetuity, of all the islands and mainland I might discover and gain, or that might thereafter be discovered and gained, in the Ocean Sea, and that my elder son should succeed me and his heirs thenceforth, from generation to generation, for ever and ever.

And I left the city of Granada, on the twelfth day of the month of May in that same year of 1492, one Saturday, and I came to the town of Palos, which is a sea-port, where I equipped three ships that were well suited to such an undertaking. And I sailed from the said port, well victualled and with plenty of stores and with a large complement of sea-faring men, on the third day of the month of August of the said year, one Friday, half an hour before sunrise. And I made for your Highnesses' Canary Islands, which are in the said Ocean Sea, intending from there to set my course and make sail until I should arrive in the Indies and fulfil your Highnesses' embassy to those princes and accomplish what your Highnesses had ordered me to do therein.

And therefore I thought of writing down, day by day, very exactly, throughout this voyage, everything that I should see or do or that should happen, as will be seen hereinafter. Also, my lord Princes, as well as writing down every night whatever shall have happened during the day, and by day the course and distance sailed during the night, it is my intention to make a new navigational chart, on which I shall put all the sea and lands of the ocean, in their proper places, with their wind-rose bearings; and furthermore to compile an atlas and to depict likenesses of everything in it, with their latitudes from the equator and their longitudes west. And more than anything else, the most useful thing for me is to forget sleep and concentrate on navigation, to get all these jobs done; for they will mean hard toil.

Columbus's portrait of the background to his voyage highlights his patrons' role as champions of Christendom: conquerors of the Moors, potential evangelisers of the Great Khan, and expellers of the Jews. This was calculated to match the propaganda-image which Ferdinand and Isabella projected of themselves during the Granada war, and which was endorsed at the highest level in 1492, when the Pope called them 'athletes of Christ' and bestowed upon them the title of 'Catholic Monarchs'. Accordingly, Columbus ascribes to them no material or directly self-interested motives. According to his later claims (which are, on this point, entirely credible) he represented to the monarchs at the time that the pecuniary gains he promised them would be sought not for their own sake but in order to finance the projected climax of their careers, the reconquest of Jerusalem.*

The fall of Granada helped to dispose the monarchs in Columbus's favour in at least one respect: it cut off the tributes of gold with which the Castilian economy had formerly been enriched and made the need to seek new gold-sources more urgent. What really tipped the balance of royal considerations in Columbus's favour at the time, however, was probably the creation of a party at court willing to back the project with advances of cash. The cosmographical experts had denounced Columbus: but experts rarely rule and it was on financial and political backing, not informed assent, that the launching of Columbus's enterprise depended. The monarchs were persuaded to grant him authorisation by a cogent coalition of treasury officials, Genoese financiers, Franciscan friars and members of the household of the heir to the throne. These backers had been brought together partly by his own tireless lobbying: in some respects, Columbus can be said to have bored, rather than fired, his interlocutors into submission, for there can rarely have been so loquacious a suitor for favour at court. The main catalyst, however, had been the conquest of the Canary Islands, which many of Columbus's future backers had already combined to finance and which provided a base for future Atlantic exploration.* Though the resources Columbus needed were advanced by individuals, and the traditional image of the Queen pawning her jewels must be dismissed as a romantic fable, the discovery was genuinely a public enterprise, the costs of which seem ultimately to have been charged to what could broadly be called the public sector. Luis de Santángel, for instance, treasurer of the crown of Aragon, and Francesco Pinelli, the Genoese banker of Seville, who advanced much of the initial cost, were reimbursed from the royal share of the sale of indulgences in an impoverished diocese of Extremadura.*

Columbus's reference to the expulsion of the Jews has confused some readers of this document, since the expulsion was not decreed until March or effected until August. The decision, however, may really have been taken in January. Even if not privy to it, Columbus may have taken a liberty with chronology in order to build up his intended picture of the monarchs as uncompromising Christian zealots. This is Columbus's first datable reference to Jews, though there are plenty of references to Jewish history and learning in annotations, which may have been written earlier, in the margins of his books. His attitude was not free of equivocation or ambivalence: he was inclined, at one level, to treat Jews with respect and to profess, for instance, that, like Moors and pagans, they could be accessible to the operations of the Holy Spirit. At another level, he shared prejudices common in his day, regarding Judaism as a source of heretical depravity, and was inclined to suspect his opponents of the taint of Jewish provenance.* This has helped to excite suspicions among some biographers that Columbus was of Jewish origin himself, and that his mentality was affected by awareness of it.* Rhetoric apart, and without including arguments based on forged documents, four grounds have been advanced in favour of the theory that Columbus was in some sense a Jew: it would account for his reticence about his family background; it might, if his family belonged to a community originally from Spain, explain his use of Spanish in most of his surviving writings; it would underpin the obsessive recurrence of millenarian and Messianic allusions in his writings; and it would provide a reading of some undeciphered marks in the top right-hand corners of his letters to his elder son, which, it has been claimed, are in cursive Hebrew script.

The first of these arguments is attended by all the common dangers of an argument *ex silentio*: Columbus's evasiveness about his past could be explained in any number of speculative ways and seems entirely reasonable as the self-defence of an insecure social climber. The second argument fails because no datable instance of Columbus's use of Spanish occurs before he had spent at least four and perhaps five or six years in Spain; and to the end of his life his Spanish was never free of solecisms which seem to betray the influence of the other

34

languages he can be presumed to have spoken: Genoese dialect, Portuguese, and Italian.* The third argument is entirely without merit: Messianism and millenarianism were common themes of the period in which Columbus lived and, in particular, were specific to literary traditions typical of the Franciscan world to which we know he had access.* The last argument is a highly technical one, which can only be judged by an expert: most experts have remained unimpressed by it.* The attempt to concoct a Jewish Columbus has to be understood against the background of modern Spanish historiography, which has been dominated by a school of historians intent on ascribing as much as possible of Spanish culture and achievement to Jewish and Moorish influence.* It is no mark of disrespect to the enormous value of the Jewish contribution to view with scepticism attempts to ascribe figures like Columbus, in defiance or default of evidence, to Jewish ranks.

The choice of Palos as Columbus's point of departure was determined by the availability of shipping. Two of the caravels provided in Palos were owed to the crown, by way of a collective fine for an earlier misdemeanour. Columbus's links with the port were, however, probably already well established or, at least, in course of being forged. Legend has it that he called at the nearby friary of La Rábida for the first time in 1485, begging sustenance in his poverty for his fainting son; but this is no more than the confused testimony of forgetful witnesses mixed with the stuff of romance.* He did, however, go there in the summer of 1491 to consult the guardian of the friary, Fray Juan Pérez, who then interceded for him at court. In the course of this visit, or soon after, he secured support from the most prominent seafaring family of Palos, the Pinzón. Though he was to fall out with them soon enough, the temporary friendship of the Pinzón, who had suitable shipping and a following among the seamen of Palos and nearby Moguer, was vital for the success of Columbus's plans. Two ships, the *Niña* and *Pinta*, were supplied by the family and commanded by the brothers Vicente Yañez and Martín Alonso Pinzón respectively. The third, the *Santa María*, belonged to Juan de la Cosa – probably identifiable as the future explorer of the American mainland and the man who was to make the first world map depicting the new discoveries.*

The references to India and the Great Khan prove beyond question that when Columbus executed his commission for the monarchs he was consciously heading for Asia. The terms of that commission had referred more vaguely to 'islands and mainlands in the Ocean Sea', covering all the possibilities Columbus had ever contemplated.* If his gaze was now more precisely focused on the Orient, it was because that was the only destination which would certainly yield the results the monarchs really wanted: profit – perhaps from trade but, if possible, from the direct exploitation of gold, which was thought to abound in the east. The title 'Great Khan' had not been used by a Chinese emperor since 1368; but Latin Christendom had few more recent sources of information about China.* Columbus relied on traditions derived from the work of Marco Polo, which was now two hundred years old and widely dismissed, especially by learned readers of a conventional cast of mind, as unreliable fable-mongering. Perhaps the strongest image Marco Polo communicated to his readers was of the untold wealth of the east: apart from the elusive person of the Great Khan himself, the most prominent object of Columbus's quest, in what survives of his journal of his first voyage, was the gold of Marco Polo's reputed island of Cipangu.

Columbus's emphasis on the supposed desire of the Khan to be informed about the Christian religion suggests that he knew not only about the thirteenth-century overtures exchanged between Tartary and Latin Christendom, but also the more recent story of an oriental traveller – apparently from somewhere more remote than Georgia or Armenia – who visited Eugenius IV with a reported claim 'to have been sent to the Pope to enquire about the Christians who live in the west'. This was a well attested incident, reported in a letter attributed to the celebrated Florentine scholar, Paolo dal Pozzo Toscanelli, a copy of which survives in Columbus's hand. It is therefore possible that Columbus heard of it from Toscanelli – but not certain: the historiography of the discovery of the New World has been dogged by too many rash inferences.* Other links with the cosmographical lore underlying the Toscanelli letter are Columbus's evident pride in the novelty of the proposed route to Asia by way of the west, the apparent debt to Marco Polo, and the implicit belief in a small world and hence a narrow Atlantic. If the letter is any guide, these were essential ingredients of Toscanelli's theories as well as of those of Columbus. None of this proves the influence of Toscanelli on the formation of Columbus's plan: Columbus never acknowledged the help of the Florentine in any of his surviving writings. The other learned sources to which he had access, particularly the *Imago Mundi* of Pierre d'Ailly, Ptolemy's *Geography*, and the *Historia Rerum* of

Pius II, could, in combination, have provided Columbus with broadly the same conclusions on the accessibility of Asia, while the story of the oriental traveller seems to have been a matter of common rumour. What can be said, however, unless the preface to 'The First Voyage' is itself inauthentic, is that by the time he sailed for America Columbus had devised a plan that could not have been formulated on the basis of unaided experience: he had become a geographer, albeit a not very good one, before he became an explorer.

The document as a whole is dominated by the exalted image of himself which Columbus is trying to project. He is an ambassador between great sovereigns, formally endowed with nobility, a dynast with heirs, a chief executive with unbounded responsibilities. Amid the pretensions, one can sense the insecurity. Columbus never quite believed that the monarchs would honour all the obligations for which, he claimed, they were contracted. And indeed, although they proved to be generous patrons by most standards, Columbus became bitterly disappointed and reproachful. The legal resonances of the terms with which he addressed them in this preface seem designed to remind them of the binding nature of their undertakings.

II

FRAGMENTS FROM
'THE FIRST VOYAGE'

Fragments from what appears to be Columbus's journal of his first transatlantic voyage are preserved in the manuscript 'First Voyage' or, in some cases, in Italian translation, in the biography attributed to Columbus's son, the *Historie del Ammiraglio (Histories of the Admiral)*, the earliest surviving version of which was published in Venice in 1571. In order to present as many of Columbus's own words about himself as possible, all but the very briefest or most baldly repetitive fragments have been collected in this chapter; in a few cases, passages from the paraphrases of Las Casas have been included, where the original has not survived and the passage is enormously important or markedly self-revelatory. This is particularly characteristic of the early entries, for the months of August and September 1492, from which few of Columbus's own words have been transmitted. Such passages are enclosed in square brackets so that the reader can tell easily which sections are in Columbus's words directly, and which have been mediated by Las Casas's hand.

Even by these methods, however, the reader cannot be guaranteed a clear sighting of Columbus: problems connected with the transmission of the text have left a good deal of obscuring haze. In the first place, Las Casas was working from a copy, which was in some places garbled or defective, and which he called the *Libro de la primera navegación* (or 'Book of the First Voyage', not 'diary' or 'journal' or 'log'). The *Histories of the Admiral* seems to have been compiled from the same material as Las Casas had at his disposal and the Italian in which it conveys Columbus's words represents – to judge from cases in which Las Casas reproduces the same fragments – a very free and frequently inaccurate translation of the Admiral's Spanish. Moreover, the passages Las Casas chose to transcribe word for word reflect his priorities rather than those of Columbus. He was particularly interested, for example, in any evidence of Columbus's providential mission such as might support the thesis of his own history of the Indies: that their discovery had been divinely appointed for the sake of the natives' souls. Las Casas seems to have quoted every reference Columbus made to God – even pious expletives and conventional expressions of thanks or supplication. Columbus unquestionably came to adopt the view of the discovery which Las Casas shared; but it seems to have evolved gradually in his mind and not to have begun to take shape until late in the course of the first voyage. Las Casas was, moreover, passionately committed to the vindication of the natives' rights and the accumulation of ethnographic material. Thus the direct quotations he has handed down from Columbus's journal fall mainly into two categories: pious invocations of the Deity (some of which, brief and repetitive, are omitted from our present selection); and material on the Indians, with very little else. Thus Las Casas tends to distort by selection and there is too little extra material in the *Histories* to make up a fully rounded picture.

The first brief extract captures the moment of the fleet's departure from the coast of mainland Spain:

FRIDAY, 3 AUGUST

We left on Friday, the third day of August of 1492, from the bar of Saltés, at eight o'clock. With a strong breeze veering to the west, we sailed south for sixty miles, which make fifteen leagues; then to the south-west and south by west, which was the way to the Canaries.

The bar of Saltés is a sand-bar which, at low tide, protects the harbour mouth at Palos. The route via the Canary Islands, to which Columbus also referred in the document which forms the preface to the *Book of the First Navigation*, was vital to the success of the venture. The Atlantic could only be crossed with the aid of the prevailing winds; these could be picked up in the Canaries but not much further south or north. Portuguese Atlantic explorers who set off from the Azores, for instance, tended to get blown back; Columbus himself, when he made his third crossing, got stymied in the tropics. How did he know the Canaries would be almost ideal?

It may be that he started from there fortuitously: they were the most westerly possession of the crown of Castile. But he was probably well enough acquainted with those latitudes to make the judgement for himself. It is not, for instance, necessary to postulate an 'unknown pilot' who knew the way to the New World* and divulged it to Columbus in secret. That Columbus anticipated a favourable wind can be proved from the next extract (consisting entirely in a paraphrase by Las Casas but included for its exceptional importance), which records the conversion of one of his caravels from a lateen rig, designed for tacking, to square sails, best for a following wind:

THURSDAY, 9 AUGUST

[The Admiral was unable to make Gomera until the night of the Sunday. And Martín Alonso hung back, on the coast of Gran Canaria, following orders which the Admiral issued because the ship was unseaworthy. Meanwhile, the Admiral put back to Gran Canaria and they repaired the *Pinta* very thoroughly, with a great deal of care and effort from the Admiral, Martín Alonso, and the rest, and only went to Gomera after that. They saw a great fire emerge from the summit of the island of Tenerife, which is spectacularly high. They converted the *Pinta* to square rigging, because she had lateen sails.

The Admiral returned to Gomera on 2 September with the repaired *Pinta*. The Admiral says that there were many honourable Spaniards, established residents of the island of Hierro, who had been in Gomera in the time of Doña Inés Peraza (the mother of Guillén Peraza who later became the first Count of La Gomera) who year in, year out, had spied land to the west of the Canaries, which is in the direction of the setting sun. And there were others in Gomera who were prepared to attest as much and take their oath.

The Admiral says at this point that he recalls how, when he was in Portugal in the year 1484, a man from the island of Madeira came to the King to request a caravel to make a voyage to this island which he claimed to be able to see. He swore that he saw it every year and that it always had the same appearance.

And he also says that he can recall that the same was said in the islands of the Azores, and that all these sightings were made in the same direction and all showed the same form and size.

So, having taken on board water and wood and victuals and the other stores gathered by the men he had left on Gomera when he returned to Gran Canaria to re-caulk the caravel *Pinta*, the Admiral at last hoisted sail from the said island of Gomera, with his three caravels, on Thursday, 6 September.]

A speculative reconstruction of the *Santa Maria*, one of the three caravels
in which Columbus set sail in August 1492. The original caravel
belonged to Juan de la Cosa, who is identified with
the future explorer of the American mainland

World map of Juan de la Cosa, dated c.1500:
the first world map depicting the new discoveries.
The top of the map points to the West

This paraphrase, covering the fleet's stay in the Canaries, is a good example of the editor's limitations: the compressed narrative is hard to follow; interpolated material, like the remark which I have enclosed in ordinary brackets and which must have been written after the creation of the title of Count of La Gomera in 1516, is included in the original without any indication. The flames spouting from Mount Teide, unrecorded elsewhere, must have been imagined by Columbus. Nevertheless, the passage demands to be included for three reasons.

First, it conveys the first hint of Columbus's deteriorating relations with the men of Palos. Trouble with the tiller of the *Pinta* had first occurred on 6 August, when Columbus at once attributed it to sabotage; the vessel also proved leaky; and although, at this stage, Martín Alonso Pinzón emerges honourably from Columbus's account, the Admiral gradually came to blame him for disaffection and faulty workmanship alike.

Secondly, the passage recalls alleged sightings of undiscovered islands to the west of the Canaries. This shows that Columbus was still interested in the possibility of making discoveries of that sort. The frequency of such sightings, and of unsuccessful voyages to verify them, are well documented.* They form, no doubt, part of the background of the legend of the 'unknown pilot' who has been said, at frequent intervals since the early sixteenth century, to have imparted to Columbus the secret of the New World.

Atlantic conditions are conducive to sightings of phoney islands: low clouds often present a convincing semblance of land. So many real discoveries had been made in the second half of the fifteenth century – of the remotest islands of the Azores, and of those of Cape Verde and the Gulf of Guinea – that the conviction that others lay beyond the horizon was entirely intelligible. There is no surviving depiction of the Atlantic in maps of the time that does not strew the ocean with speculative islands, some of them substantial.* Columbus's own words confirm that he consulted those like the 'man from Madeira' who claimed to have seen or sought such islands. A strong early tradition, which was repeated by several witnesses during the trial of the Columbus family's claims against the crown in the 1530s, and appears in the narrative of Las Casas and in the biography attributed to Fernando Colón, represents Columbus as influenced by the advice of Portuguese and Castilian navigators including Pedro Vasques, who had discovered the two most westerly islands of the Azores and probably reported the existence of the Sargasso Sea.* It is not therefore necessary to suppose that the story of the unknown pilot is true in order to explain how it came about.

Finally, the passage marks the beginning in earnest of the first recorded transnavigation of the Atlantic, on 6 September 1492.

Columbus kept, for his day, uniquely detailed (and astonishingly self-indulgent) shipboard records – not only of the sailing directions but also of other events and of abundant personal impressions. The commitment to literary standards and love of self-expression would alone serve to make him an interesting figure, even had his voyages yielded no concrete results. Like the letters Cortés wrote on the conquest of Mexico, Columbus's shipboard journals resist classification in any of the literary genres which existed at the time. They have to be seen as a composite work: in part, a statement of claim, addressed to the monarchs, submitted in evidence with an eye to reward; in part, a personal monument designed to perpetuate the writer's fame; in part, a ship's log; in part, a traveller's tale; in part, a personal diary.

For most of the outward journey, Las Casas is frustratingly niggardly in preserving fragments of Columbus's own account. A series of his entries from the second half of September is particularly valuable, however, either because they deal with important problems or because they interweave quotations from Columbus with the editor's paraphrases.

SUNDAY, 16 SEPTEMBER

[All that day and night they continued on their course to the westward. They must have gone thirty-eight leagues, but he (Columbus) declared openly only thirty-six. He had some cloud that day. There were showers. Here the Admiral says that on this day, and continually thereafter, they found the climate everywhere very mild, so that the scent of the morning gave real pleasure and the only thing wanting was to hear the nightingales sing, he says. And the weather was like April in Andalusia. At this point they began to see great flows of greenery, of a rich green, which – as it seemed to him – must recently have got washed away from land. Everyone thought as a result that they were close to some island, but not to a mainland, according to the Admiral,] because [he says] I place the mainland further on.

42

Las Casas's paraphrase for 16 September seems to be exceptionally close to Columbus's original words, with three assurances that Columbus is being reported in indirect speech. It refers to the double-log which Columbus began to keep on 9 or 10 September to conceal the real length of the voyage from the crew: ironically, over the voyage as a whole, Columbus's declared reckoning was much closer to the truth than the confidential record he kept for himself. The theme of the perfections of the Atlantic climate – an observation which seems to have been produced entirely by Columbus's imagination but on which he insisted emphatically thereafter – is introduced. The Sargasso Sea is entered; and the most common theme of the journey out – the recording of signs of land, almost all of which are imagined or over-optimistically interpreted – occurs.

But the most revealing feature of the entry is the rhapsodical allusion Columbus seems to have made to the song of the nightingale. His heightened appreciation of the beauties of nature on this voyage has often been noticed by readers of the journal, and scholars have been tempted to ask whether this sensitivity, generally thought to be unusual for its time, should be traced to the influence on Columbus of Franciscan values, with their peculiarly strong reverence for creation, or to Renaissance aesthetics, which are associated with interest in the realistic depiction of the natural environment. All too often, however, Columbus's attempts to evoke the beauty of nature seem crass – as here, where the nightingale is associated with the morning – or nebulous: as we shall see, his descriptions of Caribbean islands remind one of nothing so much as of Milton's Paradise: vague and undiscriminating. We should remain alert to the fact that Columbus was writing promotional literature, designed to boost the image of his discoveries and attract further investment and royal favour to his enterprise. He had an interest in stressing a salubrious environment, because it would help to make his route exploitable. Nor, in any case, was he much of a judge of climate. At one point he claimed to have found the Gold Coast 'very temperate'.*

By 19 September, Columbus seems to have felt that he had made enough headway to hope for an Asiatic landfall without finding an island staging-post on the way. Perhaps because this resolve isolated him from his companions, he began from the following day to record frequent 'murmuring' – the traditional term for dissent in a religious community – among his men. The entries for 22 and 23 September contain only very brief fragments of Columbus's own words – but highly characteristic ones, in which he revels in his role as lone manipulator and dramatises his plight with a comparison from sacred history.

WEDNESDAY, 19 SEPTEMBER

[He continued on his course and by day and night together, because they were becalmed, he might have covered twenty-five leagues. He entered twenty-two in the log. At ten o'clock that day a heron* came to the ship, and another in the afternoon. These birds do not usually fly more than twenty leagues from land. There came some showers, without a wind, which is a sure sign of land. The Admiral did not want to take up time beating to windward to see whether there was any land, though he took it as certain that to north and south there lay some islands – as was indeed true – and that he was sailing between them. For his intention was to make straight for the Indies] and the wind is favourable; for, God willing, we shall be able to see all the rest on the way back. [These are his own words. At this point the pilots declared their calculations: the *Niña*'s pilot thought they were 440 leagues beyond the Canaries; the *Pinta*'s 420; and the pilot of the Admiral's ship thought exactly 400.]

SATURDAY, 22 SEPTEMBER

[He sailed on in a more or less north-westerly direction, tacking from side to side. They must have travelled thirty leagues. They hardly saw any weed. They saw some petrels and another bird.

The Admiral now says:] This adverse wind was very much what I needed, because my crew were in a highly nervous state, for they thought that no fair wind for a return to Spain would ever blow in those waters. [For a spell that day no weed was seen but it later appeared, very thick.]

SUNDAY, 23 SEPTEMBER

[He sailed north-west and at times north-west by north and at times by his chosen course, which was to the west; and he must have gone about twenty-two leagues. They sighted a dove, a heron, and another little river-bird and some other white birds. There was a great deal of seaweed and they found crabs in it. As the sea was smooth and unruffled, the men murmured and said that as there was never a high sea there would never be a fair wind for a return to Spain. But after that the sea rose a lot, but without any wind, which astonished them greatly. That is why the Admiral says at this point,] So I badly needed this high sea, which was never seen before except in the time of the Jews when they fled from Egypt behind Moses, who led them out of bondage.

By 24 September, to judge from the narratives of Las Casas and the *Historie*, Columbus was becoming apprehensive of a possible plot among the crew to murder him by pitching him overboard one night. The story they allegedly would have concocted – that Columbus had fallen while trying to measure the height of the North Star with a quadrant – brilliantly evokes the figure of the outlandish foreigner practising his new-fangled ideas of astronomical navigation, and struggling on a rolling deck with an unwieldy instrument. According to the *Historie*, Columbus suspected Martín Alonso of backing the mutineers, but no hint of this is conveyed by the surviving fragments of the journal. Instead, the entry for 25 September concentrates on the co-operation the two captains practised in attempting to interpret a navigational chart.

TUESDAY, 25 SEPTEMBER

[On this day there was a long calm and afterwards the wind blew and they went on their way westwards until nightfall. The Admiral was talking to Martín Alonso Pinzón, captain of the second caravel *Pinta*, about a map which he had sent to him aboard the caravel three days earlier, on which, it seems, the Admiral had certain islands depicted in that sea. And Martín Alonso said that they were in that area and the Admiral replied that it seemed so to him, too, but that, as they had not encountered any islands, they must have been affected by currents which had continually pushed the ships to the north-east, so that they had not covered as much distance as the pilots said. And in the course of discussion the Admiral said that the map should be sent back to him and when it had been sent over on a cable the Admiral settled down to plot their voyage on it with his pilot and mariners.

When the sun set, Martín Alonso went up on the poop of his ship and called out to the Admiral in great joy, asking for a reward for having sighted land. And when he heard this confidently asserted, the

Admiral says that he flung himself to his knees to give thanks. And Martín Alonso said the *Gloria in Excelsis Deo* with his crew. The men on the Admiral's ship and the *Niña* did the same.

They all climbed the mast and rigging and all affirmed that it was land. And the Admiral thought that it was so, about twenty-five leagues away. They all went on affirming that it was land until nightfall.

The Admiral ordered that his westward course should be changed and that they should all sail to the south-west, where the land had been sighted. They must have made four and a half leagues to westward that day and another seventeen leagues to the south-west during the night, which make twenty-one, although he told his crew thirteen leagues. For he also pretended to the crew that they were making little headway, so that it should not seem too far to them. In this way, he kept two logs of that voyage: the false one showed the shorter distances and the true one the longer.

The sea was very calm, so that a lot of sailors jumped in for a swim. They saw a lot of dory and other fish.]

What was this chart? Las Casas himself assumed that it was one of the most intriguing lost documents of the fifteenth century: a map reputedly made in 1474 by the Florentine physician and cosmographer, Paolo dal Pozzo Toscanelli, to illustrate the navigability of a western route to Asia. A copy of such a map was among Columbus's papers handled by Las Casas: it is over-cautious to doubt Las Casas's word on this, as a letter from Toscanelli, which refers to the map as an enclosure, exists in a copy made by Columbus's own hand;* a further letter, which survives only in versions transmitted by Las Casas and the *Historie*, dates Toscanelli's presumed correspondence with Columbus to the period of the latter's residence in Portugal.* Columbus submitted a map or globe to Ferdinand and Isabella as part of his project and this must have had some elements, at least, in common with the Toscanelli map.

Columbus's entry in the journal for 25 September refers only to a map depicting 'certain islands' in the mid-Atlantic. This could apply to almost any Atlantic nautical chart of the period: several survive and all show speculative islands in the Ocean. Yet, since Columbus clearly possessed a map which purported to show the whole of a western route to Asia – whether the Toscanelli map, or a work of Columbus's own, made with reference to that of the Florentine – it seems incredible that he should have failed to take it, or a copy of it, with him.

In the rest of the entry, the growing rift with Martín Alonso can be discerned. The latter argued consistently for a more south-westerly course, which Columbus resisted: resentment at the disappointment caused by his colleague's false sighting seems apparent in Columbus's treatment of the episode.

The entry for 30 September shows Columbus the celestial navigator at work and gives, in his own words, an account of a type of observation he made frequently on this and other voyages: that is, his attempt to calculate the length of the hours of darkness and daylight on a given day by measuring the movement of the Little Bear around the Pole Star. Every twenty-four hours, the Guards – the index-stars of the constellation – describe a complete circle around the Pole Star; navigators in Columbus's day dissected the circle into eight equal divisions. These were normally named after parts of the body so that the north-east division was called 'the right shoulder' or 'above the right arm', the east division, 'the right arm', the south-east 'below the right arm', and so on. By observing the movement across three of these divisions, Columbus established his figure of nine hours for the duration of the night and, by inference, a figure of fifteen hours of daylight. The purpose of the calculation was to arrive at an assessment of latitude.*

Columbus's interest in latitude placed him in what might be called the cosmographical avant-garde. The idea of mapping on a grid of lines of latitude and longitude had been made familiar by Ptolemy; but techniques of measurement, particularly of longitude, were still in their infancy and the practical application of Ptolemy's system was only beginning to be broached. Two leading figures in the field were José Vizinho, who translated tables of latitude based on the angle of declination of the sun, a copy of which Columbus himself possessed, and Toscanelli, who made a map on a grid system.* In boasting to his patrons that he would compose an atlas recording the longitude and latitude of places in the Ocean Sea, Columbus was thus paying tribute to two of his most admired contemporary cosmographers. He was also fantasising, as usual: his efforts with latitude were erratic. He did not even attempt any calculations of longitude, as far as we know, until he was ashore after his second transatlantic voyage, and then with bizarre results.*

SUNDAY, 30 SEPTEMBER

[He continued on his westward course. That whole day and night he made fourteen leagues because of the calms; he declared a count of eleven. Four rush-tails were sighted, which is a powerful sign of land, for when birds of the same species are seen together it is proof that they are not wandering aimless and lost. On two occasions they saw four heron and a lot of weed.]

Note that at nightfall the stars known as the Guards appear in relation to the North Star on its western side and that by morning they appear below the north-east dividing line, so that it looks as if they only move through three divisions, equivalent to nine hours, every night. [This is what the Admiral says.] Also, at nightfall the compass needles vary to the west by one division of the compass-rose and by morning they are exactly aligned with the North Star. This suggests that the North Star moves, like the other stars, while the compass needles always point in the same direction.

The last two sentences constitute one of a series of records made by Columbus of his observation of magnetic variation: the difference, that is, between the direction shown by the compass needle (magnetic north) and the 'true north' indicated by the position of the Pole Star. In the eastern hemisphere, variation to the east was a familiar phenomenon. Columbus's are the first known recorded observations of variation to the west. On 13 September, he recorded slight variation in both directions, perhaps because he was passing between zones. From 17 September onwards he noted strong and increasing variation to the west. The question arises, 'Did he recognise this phenomenon for what it was?' The same question has been asked, in a larger context, of his discovery of America, and it is useful to see Columbus's mind grappling with the problems – conceptual and classificatory – of fitting a new observation into the framework of existing knowledge.

His first response seems to have been entirely practical: he had to guarantee his crews' confidence in the reliability of the compasses and therefore sought to minimise the problem by taking readings at the most favourable time of day, when the Pole Star was apparently in its most westerly position. This, together with his sustained interest in making readings and noting the results, suggests that he at least considered the possibility that the apparent fluctuations of the

48

compass were genuine. By 30 September however, if the last two sentences of our fragment are genuinely Columbus's words rather than an interpolation or paraphrase, he seems to have resolved the problem in his own mind by explaining it as the apparent result of the instability of the North Star: to judge from the language of the passage, this was an explanation in which he believed, not a mere deception concocted for the benefit of his crew.*

The first ten days of October were dominated by increasing tension and anxiety over the non-appearance of land; by 3 October Columbus privately reckoned that they had covered over 2,000 miles of open water; on the 6th, Martín Alonso demanded a change of course to the south-west 'for the island of Cipangu', presumably because that was where it was marked on the chart. Columbus refused, on the grounds that 'it was better to go first to the mainland'. He may have persevered in his insistence on an almost unmodified due-westerly course because new discoveries on the latitude of the Canaries belonged, by treaty with Portugal, to the crown of Castile. His avowed reason, however, suggests that he simply felt a straight course was likely to be quickest: Las Casas's paraphrase, which is all we have, could mean either 'The Admiral saw that if they missed Cipangu they would not be able to make land so quickly' or 'The Admiral saw that if they departed from their course they would not be able to make land so quickly'.

In any event, Columbus's resistance was short-lived. On 7 October, apparently attracted by the direction of the flight of flocks of birds, but perhaps persuaded by an outbreak of mutinous behaviour, he altered course for the south-west.* By 10 October, to judge from the paraphrases, the men 'could endure no more', but the following day sightings of flotsam multiplied and as night fell everyone seems to have been excitedly anticipating land. During the night there were a number of claims to have spotted lights from on shore, the earliest of which Columbus ascribed to himself. At two minutes past midnight land appeared two leagues off. They stood off and went ashore on Friday morning.

An enormous amount of time and effort has been wasted on attempts to identify the island where Columbus made his first landfall.* The toponymy of the island he visited on this first voyage has changed too much, and his surviving descriptions, except of Cuba and Hispaniola, are too vague, inaccurate, and mutually contradictory, to reconstruct his route around them with any confidence. The first island, supposedly called Guanahaní by the natives and named San Salvador by Columbus, was small, flat, fertile and dotted with pools. It was largely protected by a reef, with what Columbus calls a lagoon in the middle, and a small spit or peninsula at one point on the eastern side: this formed an exploitable natural harbour. Apart from the 'lagoon', the meaning of which is unclear, none of these is a potentially distinguishing feature. As he was approaching from the latitude of Gomera and heading south-west, Columbus could have arrived at almost any of the islands of the Bahamas and Turks and Caicos, which screen Cuba and Jamaica from such an approach.

Before noticing anything about the island, Columbus – if Las Casas's paraphrase can be trusted – recorded Europeans' first sight of the natives, whom he calls 'naked people'. This was not just a description, but a classification. A late fifteenth-century reader would have understood that Columbus was confronting 'natural men', who could not be considered civilised and were unlikely to possess legitimate political institutions, but who might none the less be naturally good – dwelling in the sort of silvan innocence which humanists associated with the 'age of gold', or in the state of dependence on God which for Franciscans was symbolised by nakedness.* Columbus's observation therefore prepared the way for what came next: the formal taking possession of the island in the names of Ferdinand and Isabella, recorded by the ship's scribe.

Las Casas then provides us with the first long extract in Columbus's own words. Characteristically, the subject is the nature of the indigenous people. Five themes can be detected, underlying Columbus's treatment. First, he constantly compares them, implicitly or explicitly, with Canary Islanders, Blacks, and the monstrous humanoid races which were popularly supposed to inhabit unexplored parts of the earth. The purpose of these comparisons is not so much to convey an idea of what the islanders were really like as to establish doctrinal points: the people were comparable with others who inhabited similar latitudes, in conformity with a doctrine of Aristotle's. They were physically normal, not monstrous, and therefore – according to a commonplace of late medieval psychology – fully human and rational. This qualified them as suitable potential converts to Christianity, which it was a professed objective of the voyage to find.

Secondly, Columbus seems anxious to establish their natural goodness: he portrays them as innocent, unwarlike creatures, uncorrupted by material greed – indeed, improved by poverty – and with an inkling of natural religion undiverted into what were considered 'unnatural' channels such as idolatry. By implication, they are a moral example to Christians. This picture is strongly reminiscent of a long tradition of late medieval treatment of pagan primitives, especially from Franciscan and humanist writers.

Thirdly, Columbus is on the look-out for evidence that the natives are commercially exploitable. At first sight, this seems at variance with his praise for their own moral qualifications; but many of his observations cut two ways. The natives' ignorance of warfare establishes their innocent credentials but also means they will be easy to conquer. Their nakedness evokes a silvan idyll or an ideal of dependence on God, but also suggests savagery and similarity to beasts; their commercial inexpertise shows that they are both morally uncorrupted and easily duped; their rational faculties make them identifiable as humans and exploitable as slaves. Columbus's attitude was not necessarily duplicitous, only ambiguous; he was genuinely torn between conflicting ways of perceiving the natives.

Fourthly, in his description of the Indians, as of everything else he found in the New World, Columbus seems to have been influenced by his desire to provide his patrons with what he thought they wanted. Hence the emphasis on the non-African, and therefore possibly Asiatic nature of the natives; hence, too, the emphasis on easy conquests and the speculations about the powerful mainland race nearby. This may also be the reason for the prominence Columbus gives to the inhabitants' prospects of conversion to Christianity; nevertheless, it must be acknowledged that Columbus shows an early and earnest interest in a programme of evangelisation. Apart from their nakedness, included in paraphrase before the fragment of Columbus's own words begins, his first point concerns their prospects of conversion; and he suggests, true to the missionary traditions of his mendicant friends, that it can best be accomplished by loving and peaceful means. At the end of the day's entry, he returns to the theme, expressing confidence in the ease with which they can be introduced to Christianity, and linking his seizure of potential interpreters to the plan for a mission, though he does not attempt to conceal that there were also other, more pressing reasons why interpreters were needed.

Finally, Columbus beheld the natives with eyes accustomed to images from another late medieval literary tradition: *mirabilia*, or travellers' tales. He singles out whatever strikes him as bizarre, funny, quaint, or picturesque. Throughout his journeys to the New World he remained undecided between these rival perceptions of the people – as potential Christians, as types of pagan virtue, as exploitable chattels, as figures of fun.

It is noticeable that in none of his initial impressions of the New World – neither in the land nor its people – does Columbus appear to detect any evidence that he is in Asia: the terms in which he apprehends his discovery seem rather to be indebted to the experience he had had of the African gold coast: he calls canoes, for instance, *almadías* and spears *asagayas* – both Portuguese West African terms.* The search for gold, however, and for Cipangu, began on the day after his arrival. The first fragment is headed 'Thursday, 11 October' because it is included under that day's entry in the *Book of the First Navigation*. The events related, however, took place on Friday, the 12th.

THURSDAY, 11 OCTOBER, 'San Salvador'*

[What follow are the Admiral's exact words, in his *Book of his First Navigation and Discovery of these Indies*.] In order [he says] that they should feel great friendship for us, because I realised that they were people who were more likely to be delivered and converted to our holy faith by love than by force, I gave them some red bonnets and some glass beads which they hung around their necks, and many other things of little intrinsic value, with which they were highly delighted. And they ended up so much obliged to us that it was a wonder. Afterwards, they came swimming to the ships' boats where we were waiting, and they brought us parrots and cotton thread in little balls and spears and many other things, and traded them for other things which we gave them, such as small glass beads and hawks' bells.

In fine, they took and gave to us of all that they had with good will, but it seemed to me that they were altogether impoverished folk. They all go as naked as their mothers bore them, and the women too, though I saw only one, who was extremely young. And all the men whom I saw were young, for I saw none who was more than thirty years old, very well formed, with very handsome bodies and very good faces, hair that is thick, rather like the strands of a horse's tail, and short. They wear their hair down to their eyebrows, save for a few locks at the back which they wear long and never cut. Some of them paint themselves black – and their natural colour is that of the

Canarians, neither black nor white – and some paint themselves white and some red and others with whatever pigment they find. And some paint their faces, and some the whole body, and some just their eyes, and some just the nose. They carry no weapons, nor are they aware of them; for I showed them swords, and they picked them up by the blade and cut themselves through ignorance. They know no iron. Their spears are rods without any iron and some of them have a fish's tooth at the end, and others are tipped with other things.

All of them without exception are of goodly stature and fair of face and well proportioned. I saw some who had the marks of wounds on their bodies and I made signs to ask what those were, and they showed me how men from other islands, which lay nearby, came there and tried to capture them and they defended themselves. And I thought and do believe that men come here from the mainland to take them as slaves. They must make good servants, of ready grasp, for I see that they very smartly repeat whatever is said to them. And I believe that they will easily be made Christians, for it seemed to me that they belonged to no religion. If it please our Lord, at the time of my departure, I shall take six of them to your Highnesses so that they can learn to talk. I saw no beast of any sort save parrots in this island. [All are the Admiral's words.]

SATURDAY, 13 OCTOBER, 'San Salvador'

After sunrise, there came many of these men to the beach, all young men, as I have said, and all of good stature, very handsome folk; their hair is not curly, but lank and coarse like horsehair; and their foreheads and heads are very wide, more so than any other race I have seen to this day; and their eyes are very fair and not small; and none of them is black, but of the colour of the Canary Islanders, nor ought one to expect otherwise, since the island is on a straight line from east to west with the island of Hierro in the Canaries. They have very straight legs, without exception; none is obese, but rather very well proportioned. They came to the ship in little oared craft, made from the trunk of a single tree, resembling a longboat built all in one piece, and marvellously fashioned considering the nature of the place, for forty or forty-five men could fit into some of them; and others were smaller, until there were some which carried a single man. They rowed with an oar that resembled a baker's long-handled spatula. The craft go fast and if one capsizes they all jump out to swim and right it and bail it out with calabashes which they carry with this in mind. They brought little balls of spun cotton and parrots and spears and other little things which it would be tedious to record, and they handed it all over in exchange for whatever they were given.

And I was keeping my eyes open and trying to find out if there was any gold, and I saw that some of them wore small pieces of it hanging from a hole pierced in the nose. I was able to learn by sign language that, if one went south or rounded the island to the south, there was a king who had great jars of it and owned a very great deal. I tried hard to get them to go there, and then I saw that they would not agree to make the journey. I decided to wait until late the following day and then to make sail to the south-west. For to judge from what a lot of them gave me to understand, they said that there were lands to the south and to the south-west and north-west; and that from those to the north-west men often came to make war on them. And so to depart: to go south-west to look for the gold and precious stones.

This island is fairly big and very flat, with very green trees and plenty of fresh water, and a huge lagoon in the middle, with no mountains, and it is all very green, which is a pleasure to behold. And the people are entirely docile; and in their anxiety to have some of our goods, and in fear lest they be given nothing without offering something in exchange which they do not have, they take whatever they can carry and then dive in to swim to us with it. But whatever they have they trade for anything that is given to them. They even trade for bits of broken plates and glassware. I even saw sixteen balls of cotton thread given for three *ceutis* of Portugal, which are worth one Castilian *blanca*, and there must have been about one *arroba* of spun cotton in them.* I should have forbidden this exchange and would not have allowed anyone to make it, save that I ordered it all to be taken for your Highnesses if there were a large amount available. The cotton originates here in this island, but through shortage of time I could not absolutely verify this for certain. And the gold they wear in their noses also originates here, but, so as not to lose time, I want to go and see if I can come across the island of Cipangu.

Now, as it was night, they all went back to the land in their dug-outs.

54

SUNDAY, 14 OCTOBER, 'San Salvador'

At dawn I ordered the boats to be made ready from the round ship and the caravels and went along the coast of the island to the north-north-east [sic] to see the other side, which was the eastern side, and also in order to see the settlements. And there I saw two or three, and the people who all came to the beach calling to us and giving thanks to God. Some brought us water, others brought other things to eat. Others, when they saw I had no wish to come ashore, dived into the sea and came swimming, and our understanding was that they were asking us whether we had come from heaven. And one old man came aboard my boat, and others called to everyone in loud voices, 'Come and see the men who have come from heaven! Bring them food and drink!' Many came, including many women, each bringing something, giving thanks to God and flinging themselves on the ground, and they raised their hands to heaven and then called loudly to us to come ashore.

Meanwhile I had to inspect a great reef of rocks which circles the entire island, and within it there is a deep bottom and a harbour big enough for all the shipping in Christendom and the entrance to it is very narrow. It is true that inside this barrier there are some shallows but the water is as still as a well. And it was in order to see all this that I set out this morning so that I should be able to give your Highnesses an account of everything, including where to build a fortress. And I saw a spit of land which is almost an island, but not quite, on which there were six buildings and which could be dug out to turn it into an island, although this does not appear necessary to me, as these people are very unpractised in warfare, as your Highnesses will see from seven [sic] of them whom I ordered to be seized to take them off and learn our language and then return them. But your Highnesses, when you so order, can take the whole population off to Castile, or keep them as captives on the island itself, because with a garrison of fifty men they could all be held in subjection and could be made to do whatever was required. What is more, next to the said little peninsula are orchards of trees, the loveliest I ever saw, and as green as any, and with their leaves like those of Castile in the month of April or May, and there is plenty of water.

I saw the whole of that harbour and then I returned to my ship and made sail, and I saw so many islands that I could not make up my mind which to go to first. And the men I had taken told me by signs that there were lots and lots, more than you could count, and they named more than a hundred by name. Therefore I looked for the biggest and determined to go to it, and that is what I am doing now. It must be about five leagues from this island of San Salvador. Some of the others are farther, some nearer. All are very flat, without mountains, and very fertile and all are inhabited. And they make war on one another, although these men are very innocent and of fine build.

Columbus spent the period from 15 to 23 October reconnoitring three small islands which he called Santa María de la Concepción, Fernandina, and Isabela. He had thus honoured our Lord, our Lady and the King and Queen of Spain, in that order. Again it is difficult, if not impossible, to identify them with any certainty. Many of the sailing directions in the manuscript make little or no sense: leagues are confused with miles and terms for 'south-east' and 'south-west', 'north-east' and 'north-west', are muddled. Distances are treated in a cavalier fashion that seems to have been typical of Columbus: his cartographer's expertise may have equipped him with a keen sense of relative distance, but he had no gift for expressing measurements of distance in absolute terms. The modern Crooked Island – given its size and position – is likely to have been one of them, and the modern Long Island perhaps another.

A reading of the following fragments in Columbus's own words shows that he felt – or wished to give the impression – that he was making progress as he sailed among them. The natives, though all apparently much the same as one another, gradually became, in Columbus's eyes, more civilised or more astute. In one place they knew how to drive a bargain; in another the women wore a sketchy form of dress; in another the houses were well and cleanly kept. Through sign language, or interpreted from utterances of the natives, indications multiplied of mature polities, headed by kings. Though we cannot know where to place these islands on a map of the Caribbean, they occupy an important position on the map inside Columbus's mind: serially aligned, leading onwards towards the 'imagined land which must be profitable'. In the Admiral's imagination, the first big piece of gold reported to him, on 17 October, became an example of the coinage of some great prince.

Columbus's perceptions of the natural world are affected by the same tension of mounting expectations. He claims to see hybrid plants which cannot have existed; he notes the abundance of mastic where none grew, dangling false prospects of a lucrative trade; he speculates about dyes, drugs, and spices, which, he admits, he cannot identify. The fragment headed 15 October includes, however, the first record of one genuinely valuable product: tobacco.

MONDAY, 15 OCTOBER, 'Fernandina'

I had stood off and on during the night, afraid of drawing close enough to anchor before morning, because I did not know whether the coast was free of shoals; and I intended at dawn to take in sail. And because the island was more than five leagues away – indeed, nearer seven – and I was held back by the tide, it must have been midday by the time I got back to the island; and I found that the coast which was on the side towards San Salvador runs for five leagues from north to south, while the coast I was on ran from east to west and extended for more than ten leagues. As I could see from that island another larger one to the west, I took in sail and thus made way all that day until nightfall, for I should have been unable in any case to reach the most westerly cape before then. I gave it the name of the Island of Santa María de la Concepción.

And when it was nearly sunset I anchored close to the said cape to see if there was gold there because the men I had captured on the island of San Salvador told me that big gold chains are worn there on the legs and arms. I could well imagine that everything they said was a trick to give themselves a chance of escape. My intention withal was to pass no island by without taking possession, although, one having been taken, the ceremony could be said to have applied to the others. I hove to and remained until today, Tuesday, when at daybreak, I landed with the armed boats and disembarked.

And the natives, who were numerous, and of the same condition as those of the other island of San Salvador, allowed us to go over the island and gave us what I asked for. And because the wind was freshening from the south-east across my bows, I did not want to wait and I set off for my ship. And a big dug-out was alongside the caravel *Niña*, and one of the men from the island of San Salvador, who was on board, leaped into the sea and climbed in (and the previous night another had escaped overboard) and we went after the dug-out which sped off so fast that no ship's boat could ever have caught it. Because we pressed it hard, however, they beached and left it. And some of my own ship's company went ashore after them and they all fled like chickens; and we took the dug-out they abandoned on board the caravel *Niña*, to where, from the other end of the island, another small dug-out now arrived with a man who had come to trade a ball of cotton. And some sailors dived into the sea and seized him, because he was unwilling to come aboard the caravel. And I, who saw it all because I was on the bridge of my ship, sent over for him and gave him a red bonnet and some green glass beads, small ones, which I wound round his arm, and two hawks' bells, which I fitted to his ears, and I told him to return to his dug-out, which he had with him on board, and I sent him back to his home.

Afterwards I made sail for the next big island I could see to the west. I had ordered the other dug-out, which the *Niña* was carrying abaft, to be set adrift, and later I saw it on shore, about the time the other one arrived — the one to whom I had given the things I mentioned. And I had not wanted to take the cotton from him, although he wanted to give it to me. And all the other natives came up to him and he thought it was a great marvel and could well believe that we were good men and that the other native who had fled must have done us some harm and that was why we were carrying him off. And it was with this purpose in mind that I had ordered him to be released, and I gave him the goods I mentioned so that he should esteem us well; thus another time when your Highnesses send someone here, they should not encounter a bad reception. And everything I gave him was worth less than four *maravedis* all told.

And so I departed at what would have been about ten o'clock, with a south-east wind veering south, to cross to this other island, which is very big and where there is much gold, according to the sign language of all the men I am bringing from San Salvador. They say that the inhabitants wear it in chains on their arms and legs and ears and noses and breasts. And from the island of Santa María to this one there were nine leagues due west. And all this coast of the island runs from north-west to south-east. And it seems there could well be more than twenty-eight leagues of coastline along this face of the island. And it is very level, without any mountains, just like those of San Salvador and Santa María. And all the beaches are clear of rocks, except that they all have a few rocks close to shore below the surface of the water, so that it is essential to keep one's eyes open, if one wants to anchor, and not to anchor too close inshore, although the waters are always very clear and the bottom visible. And, if a ship

58

stands off two lombard shots from the shore, there is so much draught off all these islands that the bottom cannot be found.

The islands are very green and fertile and the air is very healthy. They could have a lot of commodities which I cannot learn about, because I have no wish to raise sail, but want rather to go on to seek and explore plenty of islands in order to find gold. And as these men of mine keep saying by signs that people wear it on their arms and legs – and it is indeed gold because I showed them some pieces of what I have with me – with our Lord's help I shall not fail to find where it originates.

When I was midway between these two islands – that is, Santa María and this big one, which I named Fernandina – I found a man alone in a dug-out travelling from the island of Santa María to that of Fernandina, and he was carrying a little of the sort of bread they have – say, about a fistful – and a calabash full of water and a bit of red earth, powdered and mixed to a paste, and some dried leaves which must be held in great esteem among the people here, for some had already been brought to me as a gift on San Salvador; and he carried a basket of the sort they have here in which he had a string of glass beads and two *blancas*, by which I knew that he came from the island of San Salvador and had been to Santa María and was crossing to Fernandina. He came aboard my ship. I bade him board, and he for his part requested it; and I made him stow his dug-out on board and keep everything he was carrying and I ordered that he be given bread and honey and drink. And so I shall carry him to Fernandina and I shall give him all his belongings, so that he shall give good tidings about us. And so, if it please our Lord, when your Highnesses send another mission here, those who come will be received with honour and the people shall give us whatever we need.

TUESDAY, 16 OCTOBER, 'Fernandina'

I left the islands [*sic*] of Santa María de Concepción at what must have been about midday, bound for the island of Fernandina, which reveals itself as being very large at its western end. And I sailed the whole of that day in a calm. I was unable to arrive early enough to see the bottom and find a clear spot to anchor in, for it is important to take great care over this so as not to lose anchors. And so I lay to for the whole of this night until daylight, when I came to a settlement – the one to which the man whom I found yesterday in that dug-out in the middle of the sea was coming – and there I anchored. He had given such good reports of us that all through the night there was no lack of dug-outs coming alongside the ship, bringing us water and whatever else they had.

And I ordered that something be given to every one of them, such as a few beads – ten or twelve, of glass, in a string – or some of those tin bangles that cost a *maravedi* each in Castile, and some tunic tags, all of which they held in great esteem; and I also ordered them to be given something to eat whenever they came on board, and some sugar syrup. And later, at about the hour of terce, I sent my ship's longboat ashore for water. And with a very good grace they showed my men where the water was and they brought the full barrels to the boat themselves and took great delight in pleasing us.

This island is very big and I have decided to sail round it, because, if I understand aright, in it or near it there is a gold mine. This island is almost eight leagues away from that of Santa María sailing due west, and reckoning from this cape I had reached. The whole of this coast runs north-north-west to south-south-west [*sic*]; and I saw a good twenty leagues of it, but it did not stop there.

Now, while I have been writing this, I have made sail with the south wind to proceed to circle the whole island and try to reach Samaet [*sic*], which is the island or city where the gold is, for so say all those who visited the ship here, and the men of the islands of San Salvador and Santa María told us so, too.

The people here are similar to those of the islands previously mentioned, with the same language and customs, except that these here seem to me to be somewhat more civilised, more commercially-minded and cleverer, for I have noticed that whenever they have brought cotton or some other little thing to my ship, they are better at settling the price than the others. And on the last island I even saw cotton cloth woven into wraps, and better-mannered folk, and the women wear a little slip of cotton in front of their bodies which scantily covers their private parts.

The island is very green and level and very fertile, and I have no doubt that they sow and reap grain all year, and all other manner of produce. And I saw many trees that are different from ours. Many of them have branches of different sorts growing from a single trunk, and one branch is of a different sort from the next, and all so diverse that it is the greatest wonder in the world how much variety there is from one to the other. For example, one branch had leaves like sugar cane, another like mastic, and so on, with five or six different types in a single tree and all as different from each other. Nor are they grafted – for people might claim that this was done by grafting – for these trees grow in the natural woodland and are not cultivated by the natives.

I do not recognise any known religion here and I think the people will turn Christian very readily, for they are of a good understanding.

The fish here are so different from ours that it is a wonder. There are some that look like John Dory, of the finest colours in the world – blue, yellow, red, and every sort of colour – and some are streaked with a thousand tints, and the colours are so fine that there can be no man who would not marvel at it and feel refreshed by the sight. There are whales, too. I saw no beast ashore of any sort save parrots and lizards. One boy told me he saw a big serpent. I saw no sheep nor goats nor any other beast, but I have of course spent little time here – in fact, only half a day; but if there were any, I could not have failed to see them.

I shall write about the circumnavigation of this island after I have circled it.

WEDNESDAY, 17 OCTOBER
off the south-east point of 'Fernandina'

At midday I left the settlement where I was anchored and where I took on water to sail around this island of Fernandina. And the wind was in the south-west and south. Although it was my intention to follow the coast round to the south-west, and so back to where I was, because the whole coastline runs from the north-north-west round to the south-south-west, and although I wanted to head in a southerly and south-westerly direction because all the Indians I have with me (and another who made signs at me) inform me that it is on this route to the south that the island called Samoet lies, where the gold is, yet when Martín Alonso Pinzón, captain of the caravel *Pinta*, on which I had ordered three of the Indians to be carried, came to me and told me that one of them had very emphatically given him to understand that the island would be much more rapidly circumnavigated by the north-north-west, I realised that the wind would give me no help in the direction in which I wanted to go and that it was favourable in the other direction.

I made sail to the north-north-west, and when I was close to the furthest point of the island, two leagues away from it, I found a most marvellous harbour with a way in, or two ways in, one might say, for there is an island in the middle, and both are very narrow and inside it seemed big enough for a hundred ships, provided it was clear and deep at the entrance. It seemed to me worthwhile to examine it thoroughly and take soundings and so I anchored outside and went in with all the ships' boats and we saw that it had no bottom. And because I thought when I saw it that it was the mouth of some river, I had ordered casks to be carried to take on water. And on shore I found about eight or ten men who then approached us and showed us their settlement nearby; I sent my men there for water, some with arms, others with casks; and so they obtained it. And because it was a fair distance away, I was delayed for two hours. I spent the time walking amid the trees there, which was as beautiful a sight as any ever beheld, for I saw as much verdure as in the month of May in Andalusia. And all the trees were as different from ours as night is from day, and so were the fruits and the grasses and the stones and everything. It is true that there were some trees of the same types as are found in Castile, yet even these display considerable differences, and the trees of other types were so numerous that no man could count them nor compare them with those in Castile.

The people were the same as the others previously described, of the same condition, and similarly naked and of the same build; and they exchanged whatever they had for anything they were given. And here I saw some of the ships' boys exchange a few bits of broken plates and glassware for some spears. And the men who had been for the water told me how they had been inside the houses and that within they were well swept and clean and that their beds and the furnishings where they keep their things are made of what appears to be cotton netting. The houses all have the shape of campaign tents and are very tall with good fireplaces, but in all the settlements I saw there appeared to be none of more than twelve or, at most, fifteen houses. At this one they found that the married women wear cotton loincloths, but not the younger women, except for a few who were already about eighteen years old. And there were dogs – mastiffs and pointers.

And there they found one man who wore in his nose a piece of gold which must have been about half the size of a ducat, on which they saw letters incised. I upbraided them for not having traded it and given whatever the owner asked, so that we could see what it was and whose was the coinage; and they told me that the man would not dare ever to barter for it.

After taking on the water I returned to my ship and set sail and made to the north-west, until I had covered the whole of that side of the island as far as the point where the coastline trends from east to west. And after that all the Indians on board again began to say that this island was smaller than the island of Samoet and that it would be as well to turn back so as to arrive at the latter more quickly. The wind fell calm at that point and began to blow west-north-west, which was opposite to the direction we had followed on our approach; and so I turned about and sailed all last night heading east-south-east, and at times due east and at times south-east; and this was to distance myself from the land for it was clouding over heavily and the weather was very threatening. There was little wind and I could not get inshore to drop anchor. And so during the past night it rained very heavily from after midnight until nearly daylight and there are still rain clouds above.

And we are off the extreme point of the island to the south-east, where I hope to lie at anchor until the weather clears before seeing the other islands that I have to go to. And so it happens that every day, since I have been here in the Indies, it has rained a little or a lot. Your Highnesses can rest assured that this is the best and most fertile and most temperate and most level land there could be in the world.

THURSDAY, 18 OCTOBER, 'Fernandina'

Once the weather had cleared I sailed with the wind and rounded the island as far as I could. And I dropped anchor when the weather became unsuitable for sailing but did not go ashore. And at daybreak I set sail.

FRIDAY, 19 OCTOBER, 'Isabela'

At daybreak I weighed anchor and sent the caravel *Pinta* east-south-east and the caravel *Niña* to the south-south-east and with my own ship I made to the south-east, after giving orders that they should keep their course until midday, then change course and rejoin me. And then, before we had made three hours' sail, we saw an island to the east, whereupon we fired a signal shot. And all three vessels reached it before midday, at its northernmost point, where there is an islet, with one rocky reef beyond it to the north and another between the islet and the main island. The men I brought from San Salvador called this island Saomete [*sic*]. I gave it the name of Isabela [MS

Yslabela]. The wind was in the north. And the islet I mentioned was on a bearing due east of Fernandina island, from where I had set out.

From the islet the coast of the main island ran west for twelve leagues as far as a cape which I named Cape Hermoso, which is on the western side. And it is indeed beautiful, of rounded shape, set in very deep water without off-lying shoals and the promontory is low and rocky and beyond it is a sandy beach, as on most of this coast.

And so I lay at anchor last night, Friday, until morning. The whole of this coast and all the island as far as I can see is almost all like a sandy beach. And the island is the most beautiful thing I have seen, for if the other islands are lovely, this is more so. It has many trees, very big ones and very green; and the land here is higher than on the other islands I have found and there is a little hill or two, which could not be called mountains, but which add beauty to the whole. And there seems to be plenty of fresh water.

From this side towards the north-east there is a huge inlet right into the middle of the island, as far as some very dense and extensive woodlands. I wanted to anchor inside it to go ashore and see such great beauty, but the bottom was shallow and I could not drop anchor except at some distance from the shore, and the wind was very good to bring me to this cape, where I am at anchor at the moment, to which I have given the name Cape Hermoso because it is so beautiful. And that was why I did not anchor in that inlet, and also because I could see this cape from there, green and lovely as it was, and as are all the contents and lands of these islands, so that I do not know where to go first, nor do my eyes tire of seeing such beautiful greenery, so different from our own. And I believe that these islands must contain many herbs and woods which are valued in Spain for dyes and for drugs and spices, but I cannot recognise them, much to my regret. And when I arrived at this cape there came to me so good and sweet a smell from the flowers or trees that it was the sweetest thing in the world. In the morning before I leave I shall go ashore to find out what it is.

Here at the cape there are no settlements, only further inland, where the men I have with me say the king is; and they add that he has plenty of gold. And in the morning I want to go so far ahead as to find the settlement and see or speak to this king, who, according to the signs these folk give me, is lord of all these islands around about: he also wears clothes and wears much gold on his person, although I do not have much faith in what they tell me, both because I do not

64

understand them well and also because I know that they are so poor in gold themselves that however little this king has would seem to them a lot.

This place which I call Cape Hermoso may, I think, be an island separate from Samoete and there may even be another little one between them. I am not going to trouble to see everything in such great detail, which I should not be able to do in fifty years, because I want to see and discover as much as possible before returning to your Highnesses, if it please our Lord, in April. Of course, if I find gold or spicery in quantity, I shall wait until I have gathered as much of it as possible, and that is why I am doing nothing but travelling to see if I can come across it.

SATURDAY, 20 OCTOBER, 'Isabela'

Today, just after sunrise, I weighed anchor from where I was, with my ship at anchor off this island of Samoete at the south-west extremity, to which I gave the name Cape La Laguna. The island I called 'Isabela'. My purpose was to sail north-east and by east from the southern and south-westerly side, to where – as I understand the men I have with me – the main settlement and the king of the island are located. And I found that the bottom was everywhere so shallow that I could not approach the settlement under sail. And I saw that if I set my course to the south-west it would be a very long way round. And therefore I determined to go back along the north-north-easterly route I had taken from the western side and circle the island that way.

And I had so little wind that I could make no way at all along the coast until nightfall. And because it is dangerous to anchor in these islands (except by daylight when you can see where to drop anchor with the naked eye), because the seabed is very uneven, clear in places and not in others, I resolved to lay to under sail all this night of Saturday to Sunday. The caravel did drop anchor because they got inshore early enough, and they supposed that, in response to their usual signals, I would drop anchor too, but I was unwilling.

SUNDAY, 21 OCTOBER, 'Isabela'

At ten o'clock I arrived here at this cape with the islet and dropped anchor, as did the caravels. And after a meal I went ashore, to a place close at hand where there was no settlement except for one dwelling, in which I found nobody: I believe they had fled in fear, because I found all their household goods inside.

And I ordered that nothing be touched, but I went out with my captains and men to see the island, and if the others we have seen already are very beautiful and green and fertile, this one is much more so, with woodlands which are big and very green. There are some big lakes here and around them is woodland in abundance, and here and all over the island the trees are all green and the grass is like that in April in Andalusia, as is the singing of the birds. And so it seems unlikely that a man would ever want to leave this island, and the flocks of parrots that darken the sun, and the birds large and small and so many divers kinds and so different from our own that it is a wonder. And what is more there are trees of a thousand kinds and all give fruit after their kind, and the smell from all of them is a wonder, so that I am the saddest man in the world at being unable to recognise them for I am sure enough that they must all have useful properties, and I am bringing samples of them back – as also of the herbs. As I went on foot in search of one of the lakes, I saw a serpent, which we killed, and I am bringing the skin back for your Highnesses. When it saw us, the creature dived into the lake and we followed it in because it was not very deep, until we killed it with lances. It is seven palms long. I believe there are many like it in these lakes.

I recognised some aloe wood here and I have decided to have ten *quintals* of it brought to the ship tomorrow, because they tell me it is very valuable.

Also, as we were going on foot in search of very good water, we went to a settlement nearby, half a league from where I have dropped anchor. And when they became aware of us, the inhabitants all took flight and left their houses and hid their textiles and everything they had in the woods. I allowed nothing to be taken, not even to the value of a pin. Afterwards, some of their men approached us, and one came right up to whom I gave some hawks' bells and beads of glass, and he became very contented and very happy. And to cement the friendship further, and for the sake of asking something in return, I ordered that he should be asked for water, and after I had returned to my ship they came to the beach with their calabashes full and took great pleasure in giving us some. And I ordered that they should be given another string of glass beads and they said that they would return here in the morning.

I should like to fill up all the ships' casks with water here. Then, if weather permits, I shall leave to circle the island until I can speak with the king and see if I can get hold of some of the gold that I hear he wears: then on to another very large island which I think must be Cipangu, to judge from the sign language used by the Indians I am taking with me, and in which they say there are many big ships and mariners; and from that island to another which they call Bofío [Bohío] which they also say is very big. And the others which are in between I shall see as I pass, and according to whether I find rumours of gold or spices, I shall decide what to do. Further still, I am determined to go to the mainland, to the city of Qui[n]say and give your Highnesses' letters to the Great Khan and ask for a reply and return with it.

MONDAY, 22 OCTOBER, 'Isabela'

All last night and today I have been waiting here to see if the king of this place or any other people would bring gold or anything else of any value. And plenty of these folk have come, similar to those on the other islands, similarly naked and painted, some in white, some in red, others in black and so on in lots of different ways. They brought spears and some balls of cotton to trade, which they traded here with some of the seamen for bits of glass from broken drinking vessels and for bits of earthenware plates. Some of them wore pieces of gold hanging from the nose, which they very willingly exchanged for a hawk's bell of the sort we tie to a falcon's foot, and for little beads of glass, but there is so little of it that it is virtually nothing, which is true of all the little things we give them. They too thought our coming was a great marvel and believed that we had come from heaven. We took on water for the ships at a lake which is near here, near the Cape of the Islet, as I called it. And in this lake Martín Alonso Pinzón, captain of the *Pinta*, killed another serpent, like the one yesterday, seven palms long. And in the same place I had my men load as much aloe wood as could be found.

TUESDAY, 23 OCTOBER, 'Isabela'

Today I should like to leave for the island of Cuba, which I think must be Cipangu, to judge from the signs these people give me of its size and wealth. And I shall wait here no longer, nor shall I sail around this island in an attempt to go to the main settlement, as I had formerly decided, with the aim of speaking with the king or lord. My intention is to lose no more time, for I can see that there is no gold mine here, and to make a circuit of one of these islands requires frequent changes of wind, and the wind does not blow as men might wish.

And since the right course is to go where great commerce is, one should not tarry, say I, but carry on and discover plenty of lands until one encounters a land that is truly profitable; though it is my belief that this one could be very rich in spices, except that I cannot recognise them. This gives me the greatest sorrow imaginable, for I see a thousand kinds of trees, each of which bears fruit after its kind and is now as green as those in Spain in the months of May and June, and a thousand kinds of herbs and the same of flowers. And of all of them I recognised none save the aloe wood, a great deal of which I ordered to be brought to the ship today to take it to your Highnesses. And I have not set sail for Cuba, nor am I doing so yet, for there is no wind, only a dead calm, and it is raining a good deal and it rained yesterday without being at all cold; rather, the days are warm and the nights mild, as in May in Spain, in Andalusia.

Columbus's conviction that he was drawing close to Japan and perhaps to China presumably reflects the sense of the neighbourhood of great lands conveyed by his native informants. Cuba, Jamaica, and Hispaniola were indeed vast territories by comparison with the islands of the Bahamas. The Indians' information was received by a mind over-alert for evidence of the Orient. The reference Columbus made on 21 October to royal letters for the Great Khan, for instance, shows how thoroughly he and his patrons were committed to the search for Asia at the time the fleet set sail.

For the letters really existed. They were addressed vaguely to 'The Most Serene Prince our dearest Friend' and might have served as a document of credence to any potentate Columbus encountered. The Admiral clearly regarded them, however, as intended particularly for the ruler of China. That the same notion was in his patrons' mind is suggested by specific references to a destination in the Indies in a letter patent carried by Columbus as a sort of passport, and by the general climate of expectation in which he set out.*

The letters of credence to the unnamed prince, moreover, justify Columbus's prospective embassy on the grounds that Ferdinand and Isabella have heard 'with how much affection in your heart you desire to be informed of our affairs'. This may be a reference to the long tradition of contacts between Latin Christendom and the Mongol courts; for all the Spaniards knew, the Mongols were still ruling in China; and the last effective contact with a Mongol ruler had indeed been with a Castilian king: the embassy of Rodrigo de Clavijo to Timur Leng, or Tamburlaine, early in the century.* In the letter to the monarchs in which his departure was recorded, and which became part of the preface of 'The First Voyage', Columbus had linked his embassy to China with the tradition that the Mongol Khans were keen for information about Christendom.

Columbus therefore approached Cuba in a mood of heightened expectation that he was approaching his goal. He was to spend most of what remained of his time in the Caribbean exploring that profitless place in an increasingly desperate search for some sign that it was, at least, in the neighbourhood of Cipangu or Cathay. The fragment headed 24 October includes a reference to Cipangu cartographically depicted; on balance, this perhaps tends to reinforce the presumption* that Columbus had such a map on board. As Toscanelli's letter featured Cipangu very prominently, it is likely that his lost map would have done so, too. The globe made in 1492 in Nuremberg by Martin Behaim, which reflects a picture of the world in some respects very close to Toscanelli's, places a large Cipangu athwart the Atlantic, though somewhat displaced to the north and east from the position in which Columbus found himself, on and overlapping the parallels of the Canaries. Of surviving maps of the period, the depiction of Cipangu in a position most nearly corresponding to that of Cuba occurs in a world map ascribed to a shadowy figure known as Henricus Martellus Germanus, dated 1489 but, apparently, with modifications made later.* As a matter of common sense, Columbus can be presumed to have treated the cartographical evidence of the whereabouts of Cipangu with a generous licence.

WEDNESDAY, 24 OCTOBER
at sea between 'Isabela' and Cuba

Last night at midnight I weighed anchor where I lay off the island of Isabela, at the Cape of the Islet, which is on the north coast; and I set sail for the island of Cuba, which, I have heard from people here, is very big and has extensive trade, gold, spices, great shipping, and merchants, and they have told me that I can get there by sailing west-south-west. And I am sure they are right, because, if the island is as indicated by the sign-language of the Indians of these islands and of those I have in my ships – for I do not understand their spoken language – I believe it is the island of Cipangu, of which marvellous things are told. And in the globes and painted planispheres I have seen, it is located in this area.

And so I sailed till daybreak to the west-south-west. And at first light the wind fell and it rained, and so it continued for what was left of the night. And I remained thus, with little wind, until after midday. And then the wind turned very friendly and filled all the sails of my ship – the mainsail and two bonnets, the foresail and spritsail, the mizzen and topsail, and the sail of the ship's brig hoisted abaft. And so I made sail, on course, until nightfall, when I could see to the north-west the green promontory of Fernandina island, which is on the southern part of the western coast, about seven leagues away.

And because the wind was now blowing strongly, and I did not know how much farther I should have to make to reach Cuba, I decided to avoid making my landfall by night, for the water is so very deep around all these islands that there is no bottom to be found anywhere within two lombard shots of the shore, and there the sea-bed is all uneven, in some spots with rocks and in others with shoals, and for this reason it is impossible to anchor safely except by sight. I therefore decided to take in all sail except the foresail and run with the wind. And after a little while the wind increased and blew us on a course I was not sure of, and the sky clouded over and it rained a lot. I ordered the foresail to be turned and that night we did not make two leagues . . .

The fragments of Columbus's account which cover the period from 28 October to 5 December were written in Cuba. Having named one island after each of the Catholic Monarchs, Columbus called this new discovery Isla Juana, after their heir, Prince Juan. The experience he had of Cuba was subtly different from what he had previously encountered, and led him to modify his perception of his discoveries – or, at least, the way he chose to present them. This was an incomparably bigger island than those he had found so far. Indeed, Columbus could hardly bring himself to believe that it was only an island and eventually, on his second voyage, discarded the natives' assurances altogether in favour of his own conviction that it must be part of a continent. He seems to have realised almost at once that

Cuba was not Cipangu, as he had hoped during his approach: certainly references to Cipangu cease, and those to Cathay multiply. The revelation faced him with a dilemma: to continue the search for Cipangu offshore, or to seek the court of the Great Khan in the interior of Cuba. For a long time he inclined to the second course, at one time even despatching an embassy with his 'Chaldaean-speaking' official interpreter to enquire inland. The entry for November, when he was convinced he was off the Chinese mainland, employs Marco Polo's names for the Chinese ports of Hung-chou and Chang-chou. Although Columbus bought a copy of *The Book of Marco Polo* only in 1497, he seems to have been familiar with much of its contents by the time of his first Atlantic crossing.

Gradually, however, over the period of his stay, he stressed increasingly the peculiar merits of Cuba and professed to appreciate it for its own sake. The themes of praise of the local environment and enjoyment of its beauty, which had been broached earlier in his narrative, now became dominant. He was preparing for the monarchs – and, perhaps, persuading himself of – a case for the colonisation and direct exploitation of his discoveries for their own products, quite apart from any value they might have as entrepôts for the imagined benefits of oriental trade.

Cuba emerges from his stilted descriptions not as a real place, but as a literary *locus amoenus*, where nothing is described in detail but everything is of the sweetest and fairest, and man is at one with the harmonies of nature. It is a superlative land which excels the powers of tongue to relate or pen to record. Generally Columbus confesses his inability to be specific about the produce of the soil – but when he thinks he recognises mastic, he is wrong; he assumes, however, that all the prolific vegetation must contain much that is marketable.

His treatment of the natives, too, undergoes a change, or at least the sharpening of one of his accustomed themes at the expense of the others. As the prospects of exploiting them for profit recede, Columbus's hopes of their evangelisation expand. His injunctions to the monarchs to expedite their conversion are never separated from cruder incentives – the monarchs' realms will be expanded and enriched in the course of the work; yet a strong sense that the conversion will be worthwhile for its own sake seems to emerge from these fragments. In the entries for the 6 and 27 November, for instance, Columbus adumbrates a vision of a purified model Catholic Church constructed in the monarchs' dominions, partly with the unspoiled raw material with which God has presented them in the Indies, which would be kept unsullied from contaminating influences. This project for an ideal apostolic community in the New World captured the imagination of some Spanish Franciscans and was a powerful spur to the missionary efforts of the next century.* In Columbus's mind it enlarged, during the remainder of his life, until it came to form, perhaps, the dominant element in his perception of his discoveries and to inform his sense of his own special dignity and role as the executant of a divine mission, the agent of a providential purpose.

In the entries for 12 and 27 November, it is worth noticing the references to the sea and river 'of Mars'. On three successive days during his exploration of Cuba he invented place-names derived from the celestial bodies which governed those days: the sun for Sunday, moon for Monday, and Mars for Tuesday. This is the first indication of Columbus's interest in astrology, which was to play an increasingly prominent role in his mental world and eventually helped to shape his belief in himself as a man of destiny.

THURSDAY, 1 NOVEMBER

This people [says the Admiral] are like in kind and customs to the others who have been found. They belong to no sect that I recognise. For to this day I have not seen those I have aboard with me offer any prayer of their own. Rather, they say the *Salve* and the *Ave Maria* with their hands raised to heaven as they are shown to do, and they make the sign of the cross. Also, the language they all speak is one and the same and they are all friendly with each other and so, I believe, are all these islands. And I believe that they are at war with the Great Khan, whom they call Caniba, and his land, which they call Bafan. They too go naked just like the others. [This is what the Admiral says. He says the river is very deep and that at the mouth the ships can come alongside as far as the shore. The fresh water reaches to just less than a league beyond the mouth, and it is very sweet.] It is certain [says the Admiral] that this is the mainland and that I am [he says] before Zaytun and Quinsay, little more or less than one hundred leagues the one from the other. And this is well shown by the sea which here takes on a different character from that which it has shown so far. Yesterday, when I was going north-west, I found that the weather was cold.

SUNDAY, 4 NOVEMBER
Cuba, in the mouth of the 'River of Mars' probably at Gibara*

[The Admiral further says:] These folk are very docile and very timid, naked as I have said, knowing neither weapons nor law. These lands are very fertile. They have filled them with yams, which are like carrots that taste of chestnuts, and they have beans and pulses very different from our own, and much cotton. They do not plant it and it grows wild in the woods on big trees and I believe that they have it to pick all year round, because I saw the buds open and others which were opening and others in flower, all on the same tree, and a thousand more sorts of fruit which it is impossible for me to write down and it must all be exploitable produce. [All this the Admiral says.]

TUESDAY, 6 NOVEMBER

They are people [the Admiral says] very much without malice and are unwarlike, all naked, men and women, as their mothers bore them. It is true that the women wear something of cotton, only big enough to cover their private parts and no more. And they are very good-looking and not very dark-skinned, rather less than Canarian women.

I take it as read, Most Serene Princes [the Admiral says here], that if some devout members of religious orders were to learn the language, all these people would then become Christians. And so I hope in our Lord that your Highnesses with all diligence will resolve to turn such numerous peoples to the Church, and will convert them, just as your Highnesses have destroyed those who refuse to acknowledge the Father, Son and Holy Spirit. And your Highnesses, when their days are accomplished – for all of us are mortal – shall leave your kingdoms in a very peaceful condition and free of heresy and malice, and shall be well received in the presence of the eternal Creator. May it please Him to give your Highnesses long life and great increase of enlarged kingdoms and lordships, and the will and inclination to extend the holy Christian religion, as your Highnesses have done in the past. Amen.

Today I shall release the ship from its housing and I am hurrying to leave on Thursday in God's name to sail to the south-east to look for gold and spiceries and to discover land. [These are all the Admiral's words.]

Fragments from 'The First Voyage'   73

MONDAY, 12 NOVEMBER
in the mouth of the 'River Sun', possibly Sanía Bay*

[He said that the day before, Sunday, 11 November, he had the idea of taking some of the people of that valley to the king and queen to learn our language, in order for us to get to know what there was in the country and because when they returned they would be interpreters for the Christians and adopt our customs and the contents of our faith.] For from what I could see and tell [the Admiral says] this people has no recognisable religion nor are they idolaters. But they are very meek and do not know what it is to wreak evil or murder or enslave others; and they are without weapons of war and are so timid that a hundred of them will flee from one of our men, however good-humoured his approach. And they are very open to persuasion and they are aware that there is a God above us and convinced that we have come down from heaven. And they are very quick to copy any prayer we recite for them and they can make the sign of the Cross.

Therefore your Highnesses should resolve to make Christians of them, for I believe that once a start is made, a great multitude of peoples will have been converted to our Holy Faith in a short time; and your Highnesses and all your peoples in Spain will acquire great new lordships and riches thereby. For there is no doubt that there is a very great quantity of gold in these lands. And it is not without reason that these Indians I have with me claim that there are places in these islands where they dig up gold, and wear it from the neck and in the ears and on the arms and legs; and their bracelets are very thick. And there are gems besides and precious pearls and any amount of spices.

And along this river of Mars, from where I set sail this night, there is without doubt an enormous amount of mastic; and there could be more, if more were required, because the trees take very readily when planted. There are many of them and all very big; and they have leaves and fruit like those of our mastic, only bigger than Pliny describes,* and bigger than any I have seen in the island of Chios in the archipelago. And I ordered many of these trees to be cupped to see if they would yield resin which we could take away; and because it has rained all the time I have been in this river I could hardly get any of it, except a little which I am bringing to your Highnesses. It could also be that this is not the right season for cupping, for I believe that this occurs at the time when the trees begin to emerge from winter

74

Discovery of the Bahamas: 'these lands are good and fertile over so great a territory . . . that no man could describe it and none believe it without seeing it for himself'

An Indian dug-out: 'a dug-out with six young men
aboard came alongside the ship and five of them
came on board'

Detail of a stern of a ship

and are seeking to put out buds, whereas here the fruit is already almost ripe.

And there could also be a huge amount of cotton here and I think it could be sold very profitably, not taking it to Spain but rather to the cities of the Great Khan, which we shall doubtless discover, and to many other cities of other lords who will be only too pleased to co-operate with your Highnesses. And there we shall offer them other commodities from Spain and from the lands of the Orient, since the latter lie to the west of us.

And there is also any amount of aloe wood here, though it is not the sort of product from which fortunes can be made. The mastic, on the other hand, ought to be looked into carefully, for it is not to be had anywhere else save on the island of Chios, and I believe they get a good 50,000 ducats' worth from there annually, if I remember aright.

And here in the mouth of the said river is the best harbour I have seen to this day, clear and spacious and deep; and the position and site are good for building a town and fort so that ships of every sort would be able to berth right up against the walls. And the land is healthy and high and well watered.

And so to yesterday's events, when a dug-out with six young men aboard came alongside the ship and five of them came on board. I ordered these to be detained and am bringing them back with me. After that, I sent a raiding party to a dwelling which stands on the western side of the river and they brought back six head of females, all told, women and girls, and three boys. I did this because males will fare better in Spain if they have females of their own land with them. For it often happened in the past that when men from Guinea were carried off to Portugal to learn the language, and were then brought back, and people expected that they would be helpful in their homelands after the good fellowship they had received and the gifts which had been given them, the result was that once ashore they never appeared again, and did not behave as expected. And so, if they have their females with them, they will be more inclined to carry out the business assigned to them. Also, these women will do a lot to teach our people their language, which is the same throughout these islands of India; and they all understand one another and travel everywhere with their dug-outs, which is not the case in Guinea, where there are a thousand different varieties of mutually unintelligible tongues.

This night there came alongside in a dug-out the husband of one of these women, father of three of the children – one boy and two girls – and asked us to let him come with them. I was very willing and all of them now seem much happier with him, for they must all be related. And he is a man of forty-five years. [All these are the exact words of the Admiral.]

TUESDAY, 27 NOVEMBER, 'Puerto Santo' or Baracoa*

When I went with the boats southward from the entrance to the harbour, I found a river that a galley could easily have entered. So hidden was its mouth that it could only be discerned from close by. The beauty of the river induced me to go upstream, even as far as a boat could take me. I found its depth was five to eight fathoms. I proceeded a considerable way upriver, for I was enchanted by the beauty and luxuriant vegetation of this river and by its crystal-clear water, through which even the sandy bottom could be seen. I was also taken with the numerous palm trees of many varieties, which were taller and fairer than any I had yet seen, and by innumerable trees of other kinds, all big and very green. The little birds, the green of the fields – all made one want to stay there forever.

This land, Most Serene Princes, is of such marvellous beauty that it surpasses all others as the day excels the night. That is why I have often told my men, despite my best efforts to give your Highnesses a perfect account of it, that my tongue cannot recite the whole truth of it, nor my pen describe it. Truly, I was so awestruck at the sight of all that beauty that I do not know how to express myself. For, in telling of other lands, I wrote all that could be said of their trees and fruits, their plants and harbours and all else that they displayed. And my men all agreed that no more beautiful country could ever be found. But now I am speechless. I only wish that others will come and show how much better they can describe this most excellent land than I.

[The Admiral says these further words here:]* How great the benefit will be that can be got from this place, it is not for me to write. What is certain, Sovereign Princes, is that where there are lands like these there must also be innumerable exploitable commodities. But I am not lingering in any port, because I should like to see all the lands I can in order to give an account of them to your Highnesses. And also, I do not know the language, and the people of these lands do not understand me, nor can I nor any of the men I have with me

76

understand them; and as for the Indians I have aboard, it often happens that I mistake what they are trying to say for its very opposite. Nor do I have much faith in them, for they have tried to escape many times.

But now, if our Lord pleases, I shall see as much as may be, and little by little I shall come to understand more and recognise more and I shall make members of my household learn this tongue, for I can see that there is only one language here so far. And then the benefits will be revealed and the labour of converting all these people to Christianity will be done, for it will be easy to do, because they have no known religion and are not idolatrous. And your Highnesses will order a city and fortress to be built in these regions and the lands will be converted.

And I can assure your Highnesses that nowhere under the sun could any lands be superior in fertility, in temperance between extremes of heat and cold, in abundance of good pure water – and not like the rivers of Guinea, which are all pestilence – for, our Lord be praised, to this day, of my entire company, not one has had a headache nor been in bed through sickness, except one old man, with pain from a stone from which he has suffered all his life, and even he felt better after two days. What I am saying is true of all three ships.

And so it shall please God that your Highnesses shall send here, or hither shall come, learned men, and then they shall see the truth of it all. And it is clear that what I said before – about the position of the town and fort in the sea of Mars, because of the good harbour and the nature of the country – is all true. But there is no comparison between that place and this, nor with the Mar de Nuestra Señora, because in this place there must be great towns inland and innumerable people and produce of great value. For both here and in all the other places, those already discovered and those I hope to discover before I return to Castile, it is my opinion that there will be plenty of business for the whole of Christendom, and all the more for Spain, to whom all these lands must be subject.

And it is my opinion that your Highnesses should not permit any foreigner to trade or set foot here, except Catholic Christians, for such was the beginning and end of this enterprise, that it should be to the growth and glory of the Christian religion, nor should anyone be allowed to come to these lands who is not a good Christian. [All these are his words.]

As November drew on Columbus's satisfaction with Cuba seems gradually to have diminished. On the 12th he made the first of several attempts to leave for a reputedly wealthy island which the natives called Babeque. He was confined to Cuba, however, by a combination of adverse winds and enticing distractions. An encounter with Indians on one of these excursions, on 3 December, is described in a fragment of Columbus's own writing. Unable to sail away because of the weather, he decided to explore 'a very beautiful cape'. At first, the obvious poverty of the inhabitants made contact seem unprofitable, but they gathered in large numbers on the beach, where the Spaniards became alarmed by a display of signs of fear and hostility:

MONDAY, 3 DECEMBER

I went right up to them and gave them some morsels of biscuit and asked them for their spears. And I paid some of them with a hawk's bell, others with a little tin token, others with some small beads, as a result of which they all calmed down and all came to the boats and traded all they had for whatever they were given. The sailors had killed a turtle and its carcase was on board in bits, and the ship's boys gave them what seemed to be its claw, and the Indians gave them a handful of assegais in return.

These people are like the others I have found [says the Admiral] and share the same beliefs; and they believed that we came from heaven, and they give of whatever they possess in exchange for any truck — which is little enough, of course. And I think they would do the same with spices and gold, if they had any. I saw a fine house, not very big, with two doors, for they are all like that, and I went inside there and saw a marvellous piece of handiwork, like compartments fashioned in a way I could not describe, and set into the ceiling were shells and other things. I thought it must be a temple and I called them and asked by signs whether they offered prayer there. They said no. And one of them went aloft and offered me everything that was there, of which I accepted something.

This description of the supposed temple is one of Columbus's most distinctive passages on the material culture of the native people and is all the more striking in a context where he had dismissed the locals as too poor to be of interest. The nature of the building Columbus saw

78

on this occasion is impossible to establish and the decoration he reports is hard to classify. Not even in his own estimation does it seem to have constituted evidence that he was approaching sophisticated civilisations like those of the Far East. Nevertheless, as he explored the central Antilles, Columbus was among Arawak peoples – the Taino and Ciguayo, especially – who produced artefacts and moulded an environment potentially capable of impressing a European onlooker of the time. In the four or five centuries before the coming of the Portuguese, they evolved elaborate stonework and woodwork in ceremonial spaces reminiscent of meso-American ball-courts, some of which were probably used for playing *batey*. Stone collars and pendants, stylised human forms in stone, and richly carved wooden stools known as *duhos* are the typical and distinctive products of the culture. Anthropomorphic or zoomorphic symbols, called *cemis*, decorated personal ornaments, especially, in Hispaniola, of gold.*

What is remarkable is how little Columbus saw – or, at least, noticed – of all this. Apart from stools and the gold, he reports nothing, despite his active interest in detecting signs of superior material life in his discoveries. On the other hand, his sense of passing through a series of levels of development may reflect a growing awareness of the achievements of native societies. He was now about to reach Hispaniola, where, by European standards, material civilisation was more advanced than in any other island of the Caribbean.

On 20 November, Martín Alonso Pinzón had sailed off without leave. This seems to indicate either satiety with the beauties of Cuba or frustration with its poverty. Columbus saw no more of him until 6 January and filled parts of the journal which Las Casas reduced to paraphrase with indignation at this 'treachery'. The deserter seems to have spent the time in island-hopping and in gathering rumours and samples of gold as well as tall stories of fabulous islands. After this breaking of ranks, neither Columbus nor his remaining men were likely to endure Cuba for long, baited by fears that their erstwhile companion might be growing rich in their absence. Believing that Martín Alonso was heading for Babeque, Columbus resolved on 23 November to seek the other place which had impressed him in the Cuban natives' reports, the island they called Bohío. Adverse conditions detained him until 4 December, and made him revert to the plan of going to Babeque. It was only a last-minute change of wind that sent him to Hispaniola, the most important discovery of this first voyage and the only gold-yielding island he was to offer his patrons.

From Columbus's first five days in Hispaniola, Las Casas gives us no fragments of the explorer's own words; the paraphrases, however, suggest that Columbus was mainly interested in representing the island as a potential colony: in particular, he develops a theme which was only faintly hinted before: the island's alleged similarity to Castile. This was a serious delusion, as it helped to give the impression that colonists could be easily acclimatised, which, as later events proved, was far from the case. The very name Columbus gave the island, Isla Española, suggests a comparison with mainland Spain. Columbus may have wished to convey the impression of a diminutive in coining this name – in which case it would mean 'little Spain'; it seems more likely, however, that *española* should be understood in its common sense as an adjective and that the name was therefore intended to mean 'Spanish Island'. Of the names Columbus coined after members of the Spanish royal family, the first, Fernandina, was given an obviously adjectival ending; and the third, Juana, was given a feminine ending, to agree with the word for 'island', as if it were an adjective. The other name, Isabela, was unmodified, perhaps because it was a feminine term already.

The first surviving fragment written on Hispaniola is included under the date 11 December. It is of particular interest for Columbus's treatment of the rumours of cannibals. Here, and in most other references in the surviving text (which, it must be remembered, has passed through the hands of Las Casas and at least one other copyist), the indigenous term *cariba* is transliterated as *caniba*. Applying a rather crude kind of etymology, Columbus supposes that the term must be related to the oriental title 'Khan', which he renders in the form 'Can'. At this early stage, he professes scepticism about the anthropophagous habits of the cannibals, partly, no doubt, because he is anxious to interpret the rumours as evidence of the proximity of China, but partly too, perhaps, because he recognises this story as a commonplace of medieval imaginative travel literature. After a few more weeks in the New World, he was to show more receptivity to such tales; he apparently accepted, for instance, stories perhaps originated by Martín Alonso Pinzón, of islands populated respectively by Amazon women and bald men.

This suggests that Columbus's notion of reality and grasp of the limits of the possible were deeply affected by the experience of the New World. The way the environment defied his understanding –

presenting him, for example, with all that bafflingly unclassifiable vegetation, trouncing the expectations aroused by his sea-chart, and surrounding him with the unintelligible babble and gestures of his captive guides – helps to explain this effect.

So does the isolation he endured: in part, what emerges from his account is the sense of collective isolation shared by the whole expedition, whose members doubted whether they would ever get back to Spain; Columbus, however, also had a sense of personal isolation which verged on paranoia. He suffered the loneliness of command; he was a member of none of the almost ethnic cliques of which his crews were composed – the Basques, for instance, who rioted together, or the men of Palos and Moguer, who were the friends and employees of Pinzón. He suffered the unremitting fear of mutiny or perfidy.

The entry for 11 December also raises the problem of how, and how effectively, Columbus communicated with the natives. Up to this point almost all the information he culled had been the sort that could be transmitted by gesture: sailing directions and descriptions of the size of places, the location of gold, and the behaviour of people. The conspicuous exception is the phrase frequently put by Columbus into native mouths, 'Come and see the men from heaven!' – or words to that effect. This occurs in the *ipsissima verba* fragments (above, p. 67) and at intervals in the paraphrases. Presumably, this was a construction Columbus himself put on the natives' manner and gestures, by means which Las Casas summarised as 'guesswork' (*discreçion*). While purporting to be a reflection of the natives' perceptions of the Spaniards, the phrase quoted therefore really tells us more about the newcomers' perception of themselves: god-like creatures accomplishing marvellous deeds, or perhaps divinely commissioned voyagers. Versions of the same sentence continue to occur at later stages of Columbus's account of his encounters with the natives, when some verbal communication with his interpreters must be presumed to have begun; it is easy to believe that the interpreters would have been willing to endorse an assumption which Columbus had already made independently.

TUESDAY, 11 DECEMBER, at Puerto de la Concepción

And so I say again what I have often times said [says he], that Caniba is none other than the people of the Great Khan, who must be very close by here. And they must have ships and come to carry the natives off and because they do not come back, they think they must have been eaten.

Day by day we understand these Indians better, and they us, for many times they have mistaken what we have said to them [says the Admiral].

The paraphrases which cover the next few days insist strongly on the comparability of Hispaniola with Castile and attempt to convey an impression of a land of sedentary folk who till the soil assiduously. Columbus seems therefore to have been well prepared mentally to identify a chief, whom he first encountered on 16 December, as a 'king', whose domains include solid buildings and whose people evince intelligence and, Las Casas reports, 'are white-skinned enough'. The entry for 16 December includes two fairly widely-spaced passages of Columbus's exact words, which are given here with a linking passage of para phrase, both because of its exceptional intrinsic interest and because it seems particularly close to the terms of the original, with frequent assurances from Las Casas that he is reporting the text very closely.

WEDNESDAY, 12 DECEMBER, at Puerto de la Concepción

A cross was placed at the entrance to the harbour on the western side as a sign [he says] that your Highnesses hold the land for your own and chiefly as the sign of our Lord Jesus Christ and for the honour of Christendom. After setting it up, three seamen went into the woods to see the trees and grasses and they heard a great crowd of people, all naked, like those before, whom they called and pursued, but the Indians took to flight. And in the end they caught one woman, for they could not catch any others, because I [he says] had told them to capture some of the natives, so that they could be honourably treated and made to lose their fear and so that we could find out whether the land contained any exploitable produce, for it seemed it could not be otherwise, given the beauty of the land. And so they brought the woman, who was very young and handsome, to the ship, and she talked with the Indians aboard, for all were of the same tongue.

SUNDAY 16 DECEMBER
off a village 'twelve miles' west of Trois Rivières

[And he says] because they are the best folk in the world, and the most docile, and above all because I have great hope in our Lord that your Highnesses will make Christians of them all, and that they will all be yours, I treat them as if they were already your subjects. [He saw, too, that the said king was on the beach, and that all men made obeisance to him. The Admiral sent him a present, which, he says, was received with impressive protocol; and he was a young man who must have been no more than twenty-one years old, and he had an elderly tutor and other counsellors who advised him and spoke for him, and he uttered few words. One of the Indians whom the Admiral had with him spoke to him and told him how the Christians came from heaven, and that the Admiral was travelling in search of gold and that he wanted to go to the island of Babeque. And the other replied that it was good, and that in the said island there was much gold. To the Admiral's constable, who brought the present, he showed the route they had to take, and he said that they could get there in two days; and that if they needed anything from his own land he would give it to them with a very good will.

This king and everybody else went naked as their mothers bore them, and the women did so without any shame. And they were the fairest men and women they had found up to that time, so pale-skinned that, if they wore clothes and protected themselves from the sun and air, they would be as white as people are in Spain, because this country is cold enough, and the best that tongue can describe. It is a very high land; yet oxen could plough over even the highest hills. And it is all moulded into dales and downland. In all Castile there is no country to compare with it for beauty or fertility. The whole of this island and that of Tortuga are as well cultivated as the farmland around Cordoba. They have it sown with cassava, which is a little plant they cultivate, and at its foot grow roots like carrots, which can be made into bread, and they grate them and mash them and make bread from them. And then they replace the same plant in another spot, and it again yields four or five of those roots, which are very tasty: the flavour is that of chestnuts. Here they are the biggest and best that he had seen in any land, because he also says that they had them in Guinea: those in this place were as broad as your leg.

And he says that all the people there were stout and strong and not weak like the others he had encountered previously; their customs were gentle and they belonged to no recognisable religion. And he says that the trees thereabouts were so richly nourished that the green of their leaves was so deep it was more like black. It was a thing to marvel at to see those valleys and the rivers and sweet waters and lands for wheat, and for livestock of all sorts – of which the people there have none – and for horticulture and for all the things of this world that a man could want.

Later in the afternoon the king came to the ship. The Admiral paid him the honour which was due and had it explained to him that he had been sent by the King and Queen of Castile, who were the greatest princes in the world. But the Indians the Admiral had with him, who served as interpreters, would not believe it, and nor would the king. They believed only that they came from heaven and that the realms of the King and Queen of Castile were in the sky. They laid before the king a meal of Castilian food and he ate a mouthful and then gave it all to his counsellors and to the tutor and to the others whom he had seated with him.]

Your Highnesses can rest assured that these lands are good and fertile over so great a territory, and especially those of this island of Hispaniola, that no man could describe it and none believe it without seeing it for himself. And your Highnesses can rest assured that this island and all the others are as much yours as is Castile, for nothing is wanting here save to establish a foothold and command them to do whatever your Highnesses shall wish. For I with the men I have with me, who are not many, could travel all these islands unchallenged. I have already seen just three of my seamen go ashore where there was a multitude of Indians and all of them fled, though no one intended to do them harm. They have no weapons of war and are all naked and without skill in fighting and very timid, so that a thousand of them could not hold up three. And so they are good to be told what to do and made to sow seed and do whatever else may be needful and build towns and be taught to go about in clothes and generally as we do.

On 18 December, Columbus had a further personal encounter with the 'king', whom he now called 'King of the island of Hispaniola', in whom he claimed to recognise majesty of a European order. The events described are sufficiently like those of 16 December to raise the suspicion that they have been duplicated by error. The circumstantial details, however, are sufficiently different in each case to warrant inclusion of both:

TUESDAY, 18 DECEMBER, the same anchorage

[And the Admiral says to the King and Queen:] No doubt it would seem well to your Highnesses that all hold him in such estate and deference, although he goes about naked like the rest. When he came aboard the ship, he found that I was eating at my table under the stern-castle and hastened to sit down beside me and he would not give me a chance to come to greet him nor rise from the table, but insisted that I should continue eating. I thought he would be well inclined to try some of our food; so I ordered things to be brought to him for him to eat. And when he entered under the stern-castle he made signs with his hand that all his people were to wait outside, and they complied with all the speed and deference in the world and they all sat down on the deck, except for two men of mature years, whom I took for his counsellor and tutor, and who came and sat at his feet. And of the dishes I set before him, he took enough to display his confidence, and then he sent the rest to his people and they all ate of it. And he did the same in drinking, just raising it to his lips, and then similarly giving it to the others, and all with wonderful dignity and few words. And the words he did utter, as far as I could gather, were very acceptable and prudent, and the other two beheld his lips and spoke for him and with him with deep respect.

After the meal, a squire brought a belt, made like those of Castile, only decorated differently, which he took and gave to me, and two pieces of wrought gold, which were very fine, which made me think that they do not get much of it here, though I believe they are very close to where it comes from and is plentiful. I saw that he liked a counterpane which I had on my bed. And I gave it to him, with some very good amber beads which I wore on my breast and some red shoes and a flask of orange-blossom water, with which he seemed so pleased that it was a wonder.

And he and his tutors and counsellors feel profound sorrow at our inability to understand each other. In spite of all this, I was aware that he was saying that if I needed anything from here, the whole island was at my disposal. I sent for a rope of beads of mine, on which, as a token, I have a gold ducat on which your Highnesses are depicted and I showed it to him, and I told him again, as on the day before, that your Highnesses were rulers and lords of all that was best in the world, and that there were no princes so great. And I showed him the royal banners and the other depicting the Cross, with which he was well impressed. And 'What great lords must your Highnesses be!' he said, for his counsellors' benefit, 'since they have sent you thus far from heaven and from so far away without any fear!' And they said many other things to one another which I could not understand, though I could see that they thought everything was very marvellous.

It is worth noticing that in a brief passage of reminiscence in the entry for 21 December, in which Columbus tries to validate his obviously exaggerated appraisals of the harbours of the Caribbean by citing his practical experience as a mariner, he does not claim even to have been as far north as England, let alone Iceland (cf. p. 21 above).

FRIDAY, 21 DECEMBER
Acul Bay, or 'Puerto de la Mar de Santo Tomás'

[And he says further thus:] I have been voyaging for twenty-three years upon the sea, without being out of it for any length of time worth counting, and I have seen all the east and the west, and I have been on the route to the north, which leads to England, and I have travelled to Guinea, but in all these parts you will find no harbours so perfect as these, of which each new one is better than the rest. For I have contemplated what I have written for a long time, and I say again that what I wrote was right, and yet this harbour here is the best of all and in it all the shipping of the world would fit, and it is so sheltered that, with a chain in place, the oldest ship in the world could hold it secure.

And let it not be said that they gave freely only because their gifts were of little value [says the Admiral] for those who gave pieces of gold did so in the same way and as freely as those who gave a gourd of water. And it is an easy thing to see when something is given with a heart full of the joy of giving. [These are his words.]

These people have no rods nor spears nor other weapons of war, nor do any of the other people of the island, and I am sure it is very big. They are as naked as their mothers bore them, men and women alike; for in the other lands, on Juana and those of the other islands, the women wore some slips of cotton in front which concealed their natures, somewhat like a pair of men's drawers, especially when they were more than twelve years old; but here neither the young nor the old have them. And in the other places all the men made their womenfolk hide from the Christians, because they were jealous of them, but not here; and there are women with very handsome bodies, some of whom were among the first to come to give thanks to heaven

86

and bring whatever they had, especially things to eat, like bread made from cassava and tiger nut meal and five or six kinds of fruit.

The remaining events of Christmas Eve and Christmas Day 1492 are important because during the night between them, at about midnight, Columbus's own ship, the *Santa María*, was lost when she ran on to a reef. Infuriatingly, Las Casas omits Columbus's own account of the grounding of the ship, substituting a summary of his own. The missing text, however, is given in Italian translation in the *Historie di Cristoforo Colombo*. This text has to be used with caution, because it might be a pastiche reconstructed from the Las Casas paraphrase; and, if it is original, the translator may have introduced just as many distortions as the summariser. This episode is so interesting, however, that it seems worthwhile to include the fragment from the *Historie*:

MONDAY, 24 DECEMBER, at sea off Acul Bay

[Here the Admiral addresses these words to the King and Queen:] Your Highnesses can rest assured that in all the world there can be no better people nor more docile. Your Highnesses should feel great joy because you will go on to make them Christians and will have instructed them in the good customs of your kingdoms, for there can be no better people nor land. And of people and land there is so much that I do not know how to describe it, for I have written with the highest praise of the people and land of Juana, which they call Cuba; but there is as much difference between the people and land there and those here as between night and day. Nor do I believe that anyone who shall have seen it would do otherwise or say less of it than I have said. And I declare it for a fact that it is marvellous what things there are here, and how big are the villages of this island of Hispaniola, as I named it or, Bohío as they call it [*sic*]. And the people are all of a very singular loving disposition and sweet of speech, unlike the natives of the other islands who appear menacing when they talk, and all the men and women are of good stature and not too dark in colour. It is true that they all paint themselves, some black and some other colours, and most red. I have learned that they do so because of the sun, so that it should do them less harm. And the produce and places are so beautiful, and there is proper government everywhere, with the equivalent of a judge or lord, and the way they obey him is wonderful. And all these lords are of few words and very fine manners and their orders are signified by motions of the hand, which are then understood, which is a marvel. [All are the Admiral's words.]

MONDAY, 24 DECEMBER,* off Acul Bay

[I go on with the Admiral's own account. He tells of how it was very calm on Monday, 24 December, with only light breezes that blew him from the Mar de Santo Tomás about one league beyond Punta Santa. At the end of the first watch, about eleven o'clock, he retired to his cabin, for he had gone two days and one night without sleep. Because of the calm, the seaman who worked the tiller handed it over to a ship's boy,] which [says the Admiral] I had forbidden throughout the voyage, commanding that with or without a wind they must never let boys have charge of the tiller. But in truth, I was feeling quite secure from rocks or shallows, for my boats, when I had sent them to the king on Sunday, had gone three and a half leagues east beyond Punta Santa and the sailors had inspected the entire coast, with the shoals that lie some three leagues to the south-east of the point. And they had seen the course we had to follow; a reconnaissance like this had not been made before in all our voyage.

TUESDAY 25 DECEMBER
ashore near the mouth of Grande Rivière

At midnight, while I lay in bed, and we were in a dead calm, as still as water in a saucer, and when everyone went to take his rest, leaving the tiller in the hands of a boy, it pleased our Lord that a rising sea should gradually drive the ship on to one of the rocks, on which waves were crashing so that they could be heard a good league away. At once the boy, feeling the scrape of the rudder and hearing the noise, began to cry aloud. I felt it too, and rose up at once, for no one else had yet realised that we were grounded on that spot. Soon enough, the master of the ship, whose watch it was, came out. I told him and the other seamen to take the boat that was attached to the outside of the ship and cast an anchor astern. Because he and a lot of others got aboard the boat, I supposed that they were going to do what I had said. Instead, however, they rowed off, fleeing with the boat towards the caravel, which was half a league away. Seeing them make off with the boat, while the water ebbed and the ship was in peril, I

88

hurriedly ordered the mast to be chopped down to lighten the ship as much as possible; but because the waters ebbed further, the ship would not move and began to list. The seams gave way and water flowed in. Meanwhile the boat from the caravel had come to my help. The crew of the *Niña*, realising that the men in our boat were taking flight, declined to receive it. And for this reason they were obliged to return to our ship.

When it was apparent that there was no further possible way of saving my ship, I abandoned her to save my men's lives and went with them to the *Niña*. As the wind was blowing from on shore, and a good part of the night was already past, and we had no means of finding our way through the shallows, I lay to with the caravel until first light, when I at once headed through the shoals towards the ship. I had already sent a boat ashore under Diego de Arana, from Cordoba, the constable of the fleet, and Pedro Gutiérrez, steward of your Highnesses' household, to inform the king of what had occurred, namely that on my way to visit him in response to his invitation of the previous Sunday, I had lost my ship on a rock a league and a half from his village. The king wept when he heard of our misadventure and at once sent all his people and many big canoes to the ship.

So, with their help, we began to unload and thanks to the king's willing help in this matter we had soon removed the lot. Then in person, with his brothers and other kin, he kept vigilant watch on board and on shore to ensure that all was fittingly done. And at intervals he sent one of his folk to comfort me and tell me not to repine, since all he had was at my disposal. Let me assure your Highnesses that in all Castile no better care could have been taken of our supplies, for not one bit of string was lost. He had all our goods collected near his house and they stayed there while two buildings he offered as warehouses were emptied. He put two guards to watch over the stores by night and day. And he and all his people wept as if our misfortune were their own.

For the next fragment we revert to 'The First Voyage'. There is also a version in the *Historie*, which shows how free the latter's Italian translation is. The last line, for instance, is rendered as 'how curious they are to enquire after the cause and effect of everything', which conveys an impression of sophisticated ratiocination much beyond the level evoked by Columbus's original:

TUESDAY, 25 DECEMBER, Christmas Day, same location

[The Admiral says:] They are loving folk, free of covetousness, and adaptable to every purpose, for I assure your Highnesses that in all the world I believe there can be no better people nor better land. They love their neighbours as themselves and have a way of speaking that is the sweetest in the world and soft and always offered with a smile. They go naked, men and women, as their mother bore them, but your Highnesses can rest assured that they preserve good customs amongst themselves and that the king is of very wonderful estate, in a formal style, so orderly that it is a pleasure to behold it all. And what memories they have! And they want to examine everything and ask what it is and what it is for. [All this the Admiral says.]

Misfortunes always tended to turn Columbus's thoughts to religious sources of solace. He fitted the disaster of the loss of his ship into his providential scheme of things by characterising it as a miracle intended to provide him with the means of building a fort.

WEDNESDAY, 26 DECEMBER
off the same coast, aboard the *Niña*

And for this purpose [he says] there were so many things to hand that in truth it had not been a great disaster but a great stroke of luck, for it is certain [he says] that if I had not gone aground I would have lain off without anchoring in this place, for it is located here inside a great bay and in it are two or more banks of shoals. Nor would I have left men here on this voyage nor, even if I had wished to leave them, could I have given them such good preparation, or equipment, or victuals, or materials for the fort. And it is indeed true that many of the company who are on the voyage with me have asked me or have made representations to me to be pleased to grant them leave to remain.

Now I have ordered a tower and fort to be made, all very well, and a big storehouse – not that I think it necessary for the natives here, because I am taking it for granted that with the men I have with me I could conquer the whole island, which I think is bigger than Portugal with double the number of inhabitants – only they are naked and without weapons of war and very unwarlike beyond all help. But it is right that this fort should be built, and in due form, because it is so far from your Highnesses, and because the natives must be made to realise the skill of your Highnesses' people and what they are capable of, so that they will obey them out of fear and love.

And so the men will be left with planks with which to build the fort, and stocks of bread and wine for more than a year, and seed to sow, and the ship's boat, and a caulker, a gunner, a carpenter and a cooper. And many of them are men who are anxious, for your Highnesses' service and to comply with my pleasure, to find the mine where the gold is gathered. Thus everything has turned out very conveniently for a good start to be made, and above all, when the ship went aground, she did so so smoothly that it was hardly noticeable, without either a ripple or a wind.

[All this the Admiral says. And to show that it was a great blessing, and the express purpose of God that his ship should run aground there in order that he should leave some of his men, he further adds that the ship would have been saved but for the treachery of the ship's master and the crew, who were almost all from the same area as the master; for they refused to cast the anchor astern to draw off the ship as the Admiral ordered them. And had that happened they would not have learned about the land, he says, as they came to do during the days he spent there, and as those he decided to leave behind would do thereafter. For he always went with the intention of making discoveries, and not tarrying in any place for more than one day, except for want of a wind; for he says that the ship was very heavy and not suited to the job of exploration. And he says that the ship was taken because of the men of Palos, who failed to fulfil what they promised to the King and Queen – to provide ships suited to the expedition; and they did not do it.

The Admiral ends by saying that of everything that was in the ship not a strap nor a plank nor a nail was lost, for she was as sound as when they set out except for some cutting and breaking to get out the casks and all the truck. And they put it all ashore, under heavy guard, it is said. And he says that he hopes in God that on his return, which he hopes to make from Castile, he will find a barrel of gold, traded for by those he is going to leave behind; and that they will have found the gold mine and the spicery in such quantities that within three years the King and Queen could undertake to prepare to conquer the Holy House:] for thus [he said] did I insist to your Highnesses that all the profit from this enterprise of mine should be spent, in the conquest of Jerusalem. And your Highnesses laughed and said that it would please them, and that it was their desire even without this. [These are the Admiral's words.]

This reference to a project for the conquest of Jerusalem must be reliable, since it could easily be verified by the monarchs, to whom it is addressed. The suggestion Columbus claims to have made belongs in the context of a long tradition particularly lively at the Aragonese court, which linked millenarianism with an ambition to rule over Jerusalem. Aragonese kings had never been active crusaders to the Holy Land, but they had often talked about the possibility. In the late thirteenth and early fourteenth centuries the prophetic writings of Arnau de Vilanova had specified an eschatological role for Aragonese kings, including the renovation of the church, the conquest of Jerusalem, and the creation of a united world-wide empire.* This programme was borrowed from the late twelfth-century biblical divinations of Abbot Joachim of Fiore, who was one of the most influential sources of late medieval chiliastic traditions.

Joachimism was widely affected by Franciscans of a type who constituted some of Columbus's closest friends, and may have inspired some of his most deeply held convictions. In later writings Columbus cites Joachim, albeit not from direct knowledge, and seems to show some awareness of Arnau's ideas. In the entourage of Ferdinand the Catholic, a revival of these millenarian traditions seems to have been under way when Columbus joined the court. The King was seen by some admirers as a potential 'Last World Emperor' who would fulfil some of Joachim's pre-conditions, including the conquest of Jerusalem, for the end of the world.*

For most advocates of this vision it was, perhaps, merely a propaganda device; but propaganda has to be credible to be effective. During his time at court Columbus may have been exposed to enough propaganda of this sort to convince him at least that the monarchs were serious about their chances of conquering Zion. He would have heard musical settings of the prophecy that Ferdinand and Isabella would conquer Jerusalem, and a song of the distinguished poet, Juan de Anchieta, which attributed to 'Scripture and to Saints' the vision of the monarchs crowned by the Pope before the Holy Sepulchre.* There is some reason to suppose that material of this sort may have wrought a deep conviction within Columbus, and that in advocating an expedition to Jerusalem he was not merely collaborating in a propaganda exercise but foreshadowing a 'grand design'.*

The evidence is contained in the marginal annotations he made in his copy of the collected works of Pierre d'Ailly, in which, as well as highlighting the cosmographical data and *mirabilia* which we should expect, he displays a strong interest in prophecy of various kinds and, in particular, in astrological and chiliastic divination. His annotations draw attention to d'Ailly's discussions of the celestial signs of great mutations, calculations of the age of the earth, and estimates of its life-expectancy. He had certainly begun his perusal of the works of d'Ailly by 1488: although it is impossible – except in two cases, datable to 1488 and 1491 respectively – to know when he made particular notes, it is at least possible that a chiliastic vision, embracing the recovery of Jerusalem and the end of the world, was already in his mind before his departure across the Atlantic.*

The loss of the *Santa María* turned Columbus's thoughts homewards; he claimed to want to explore further, but his delay was perhaps caused by a preoccupation prominent in the paraphrases: his desire to accumulate a large sample of gold. Columbus had gathered small amounts from 12 December onwards, but until his meeting with the 'king', he was disinclined to believe they originated on the island. Numerous presents of gold artefacts in the last fortnight of December, however, seem to have convinced him that the source of the gold was close at hand, and in the early days of January the evidence mounted encouragingly. On 6 January, Martín Alonso Pinzón rejoined the expedition, bearing a further large quantity of gold which he claimed to have obtained by trading. He presented excuses for his conduct, which Columbus privately dismissed as lies designed to cloak avarice and pride. To judge from the paraphrases, Columbus implicitly accused him of keeping the royal share of the treasure for himself and his men, but refrained from an outright denunciation, 'so as to give no leeway to the evil works of Satan, who desired as much as ever to impede that voyage'. The consolation Columbus derived from this evidence of the proximity of gold outweighed even his indignation with Martín Alonso:

SUNDAY, 6 JANUARY, off Monte Christi

[The Admiral adds, addressing the King and Queen:] And so, Lordly Princes, I acknowledge that it was by a miracle that our Lord ordained that this ship should come to rest in that place, for it is the best place in the whole island to establish a foothold, and the closest to the mines of gold.

WEDNESDAY, 9 JANUARY
off Punta Roja or Punta Cabo Isabela

[He says that this night he will depart on his voyage in the name of our Lord, without delaying for anything, since he has found what he was looking for and because he wants no further unpleasantness with Martín Alonso until their Highnesses hear the news of his journey and of what he has done.] And after that [says he] I shall no longer have to endure the behaviour of wicked men of scant virtue, such as have the presumption to try to carry out their own wishes, in defiance of him who gave them their position of honour and without deferring as they should.

THURSDAY, 10 JANUARY
at Rio de Gracia or Puerto Blanco

[And when it was time to set sail from there, he carried off four Indian men and two boys by force. The Admiral ordered them to be well dressed and returned to shore so that they could go back to their homes.] This [he says] is for your Highnesses' service, for all the men and women here belong to your Highnesses, especially here in this island, as well as in all the others. But here, where your Highnesses already have an establishment set up, there is a particular reason for showing honour and favour to the inhabitants, since in this island there is so much gold and good land and spicery.

MONDAY, 14 JANUARY, Samaná Bay

[The Admiral says further that the caravels were shipping water badly at the keel, and he complains bitterly of the caulkers, saying that in Palos they do very bad caulking and that they fled when they saw that the Admiral was aware of their bad workmanship and wanted to make them put it right. But despite the large amounts of water shipped by the caravels, he trusts in our Lord who brought him here, that He will return him, out of His pity and mercy. For His High Majesty well knew how much controversy he underwent before he was able to launch his expedition from Castile, for there was none other in favour of it but Him, who knew his heart, and, after God, their Highnesses. And everyone else had been against him without any good reason. And he says further:] And they have been the cause of losses to the royal crown of your Highnesses of a hundred millions

94

of revenue beyond what you have received since I came to serve your Highnesses, which is seven years ago on 20 January, this very month, plus the increase that would have accumulated by now. But God Almighty will make all things well. [These are his words.]

After delays during his passage along the coast, Columbus encountered a fair wind for Spain on the night of 15 January and lost sight of Hispaniola on the following day. Though disappointed in his expectations of finding more islands on the way back, he enjoyed fair weather, punctuated by occasional calms, for nearly a month of sailing. To judge from the paraphrases of Las Casas, the journal for that period contained only sailing directions, though interesting entries for 7 and 10 February suggest that Columbus had located the favourable wind-belt in the latitudes of the Azores by accident: he thought he was well to the south of what was probably his true position and heading towards the African coast, roughly on the parallel of Madeira or a little to the north of it. The point is an important one, since it tends to undermine the notion that Columbus was 'animated by certainty', based on foreknowledge of the way to the New World and back.

On 14 February, he ran into a terrible storm which provoked the first of a long series of increasingly febrile religious experiences. For the first time in his writings, Columbus here expresses a sense of divine election so intense that it would nowadays be regarded as evidence of suspect sanity. The passage was only summarised by Las Casas, but again, the *Historie* quotes directly, albeit in translation. So important is this moment for an understanding of Columbus's self-perception that it is useful to have both Las Casas's version and that of the *Historie* to compare. Despite suspicions over the fidelity of the *Historie* to Columbus's original text, the juxtaposition shows how much immediacy is sacrificed in Las Casas's paraphrase.

THURSDAY, 14 FEBRUARY
in the vicinity of the Azores

[Here the Admiral writes of the reasons that made him fear that our Lord might desire that he should perish, and of others that gave him hope that God would bring him to safety in order that such news as he was bringing to the King and Queen might not be lost. It seemed that the great desire he felt to be the bearer of such great tidings, and to demonstrate that he had been proved truthful in what he had said and promised, filled him with a very great fear that he would be unable to accomplish it. For a single mosquito, he says, could upset and impede him. This fear he ascribes to his want of faith and lack of trust in God's providence. He was comforted, on the other hand, by the mercies God had shown him in granting him so great an achievement: the discovery of all he had discovered and God's fulfilment of all his wishes, after the many trials and adversities he had suffered during his efforts in Castile. And since he had formerly dedicated his purpose and directed all his work to God, and He had heard him and given him all that he had asked, it was therefore natural for him to believe that He would yet grant him the accomplishment of what he had begun and would bring him to safety – not least because He had delivered him from danger on the outward voyage, when he had had more cause to be afraid of trouble with the seamen and the company he had with him, all of whom with one voice were determined to turn back and rose up against him, uttering imprecations. And the eternal God had given him strength and courage against all of them.

And there were many other things of great wonder which God had performed in him and through him in the course of that voyage, besides those which their Highnesses knew from members of their household. Therefore he says that he ought not to fear the said storm but his weakness and anguish] did not let me quieten my soul. [He says further that the thought of the two sons he had left studying in Cordoba, whom he would be leaving orphaned without father and mother,* in a strange land, also caused him great distress; for then the King and Queen would not know the service he had done them on that voyage or the advantageous news he was bringing to them, which might move them to help the boys.]

Fragment extracted from the Historie*

I could have endured this raging sea with less anguish if my person alone had been in danger, for I knew that my life was at the disposal of Him Who made me; and I have been near death so often and so close that it seemed that the best step I could take was the one that separated me from it. What made it so unbearably painful this time was the thought that after our Lord had been pleased to enflame me with faith and trust in this enterprise, and had crowned it with victory, so that my foes would be humbled and your Highnesses served by me to the honour and increase of your high estate, His Divine Majesty should now choose to jeopardise everything with my death. I could have succumbed happily but for the danger to the lives of the men I had taken with me on the promise of a prosperous outcome. In their terrible affliction they cursed their coming and regretted that they had let me cajole or coerce them into sailing on, when they had so often wished to turn back.

Then my anguish was redoubled, for I seemed to see before my eyes the remembered vision of my two boys at school in Cordoba, abandoned without help in a foreign land, before I had accomplished for your Highnesses the service that might dispose you to remember them with favour – or, at any rate, before I had made you aware of it. And I tried to console myself with the thought that our Lord would not allow such an enterprise to remain unfinished which was so much for the exaltation of His Church, and which I had brought to pass with so much travail in the face of such hostility; nor would He want to break me. Yet I realised that He might choose to humble me for my sins, to deprive me of the glory of this world.

Then, amid the confusion of these thoughts, it occurred to me that your Highnesses' stake in the venture was at risk; and I wondered how I could get news to you of what had happened, even if I was dead and the fleet destroyed. Then the victory I had achieved would not be lost. Therefore I wrote on parchment – hurriedly, as was inevitable in the circumstances – of how I had discovered those lands, as I had promised, and what was the length of the voyage and the route thither, and how fair the country was and what its people were like, and how I had left your Highnesses' vassals in possession of all I had discovered. I addressed this paper to your Highnesses, rolled up and sealed, and enclosed a promise in writing that whoever delivered it to your Highnesses with the seal unbroken would be rewarded with 1,000 ducats. I did this lest it fall into the hands of foreigners, who would be restrained by the thought of the reward from betraying the contents to others. At once I ordered a barrel to be brought and, after wrapping the paper in a waxed cloth and placing it inside a tablet of wax, I dropped it into the barrel, which I had bound tightly with hoops. And I cast it into the sea. All the crew believed this was some votive offering. I was still afraid that the barrel would never come to a safe resting-place but as the ships drew ever closer to Castile I stowed another barrel with the same message at the highest point of the sterncastle, so that if the ship sank, the barrel would be buoyed up on the waves and carried away on the high sea.

The conviction that he had a special place in the providential scheme of things grew from this point on almost without interruption, until, by the late 1490s or early 1500s, Columbus seems to have come to regard himself as an almost Messianic figure, a chosen instrument of God to expedite the pace of history and the approaching end of the world. The project for the conquest of Jerusalem may have been proposed to the monarchs against a background of reading in prophetic literature on which he had already embarked.

Three aspects of his character seem to have drawn him towards this rather egotistical cosmology: his habit of turning to God in adversity; a mental condition approaching paranoia; and a tendency to crack under strain. Most of the evidence from Las Casas's paraphrases shows not that Columbus cast himself in a providential role from the start of his voyage, but only that he was conventionally devout and piously fatalistic. The long and lonely struggle, however, against his suspicions of the Pinzón brothers, as well as the intense dangers, heavy responsibilities and bewildering new experiences which beset him throughout the voyage, seem to have driven him to an ever closer and more fervid relationship with God. On 6 January, according to Las Casas's paraphrase, he had identified Martín Alonso Pinzón as an instrument of Satan, part of a diabolic plan to waylay the voyage: this conveys, by implication, the first hint of the formation of a sense of being on a providential mission, which crystallised in the storm of 14 February and helped to induce the apparition.

In the course of the storm, Columbus was again separated from Martín Alonso Pinzón. In a sense, a race was now on to be the first to report back to the monarchs. Had Ferdinand and Isabella heard Pinzón's version first, or been made aware of the grounds of his quarrels with his commander, they might not have been inclined to trust Columbus further. In the event, Columbus not only won the race, but was the sole survivor. Though Pinzón managed to get back to Spain, through the storm, in his leaky vessel, he died on arrival, apparently exhausted by the hardships of the voyage and without making a report.

A fragment quoted only in the *Historie* records Columbus's safe arrival in the Azores. This was not the end of his troubles, for he first encountered hostility from the Portuguese officials, who attempted to prevent him from returning to Castile, then faced further stormy weather. This prompted reflections, reported by Las Casas under the date 21 February, that the mid-Atlantic climate was much milder than that nearer home. Columbus seems already to have associated this supposed feature of Atlantic weather with the presumed proximity of the earthly Paradise: 'The Admiral says that those sacred theologians and learned philosophers spoke well when they said that the earthly Paradise is at the extreme point of the Orient, for it is a most temperate place. And so those lands which he has now discovered are, says he, the extreme point of the Orient.' Columbus was to keep this reflection in mind and develop it later in his career.

Fragment extracted from the Historie*

[Thus says the Admiral in his journal:] In the evening of Saturday, 16 February, I reached one of those islands [*of the Azores*] but the storm made it impossible for me to know which one it was. I had a little rest that night, such as I had not had since the previous Wednesday. Ever since, I have suffered pain in the legs from exposure throughout that time to cold and wet and from having taken too little nourishment. After dropping anchor on Monday morning I learned from the inhabitants that the island was Santa María of the Azores. They all marvelled that I had emerged from so terrible a tempest, which had raged through those seas for fifteen days.

On 4 March Columbus took refuge in Lisbon – apparently driven by a storm, though he had three interviews with the King of Portugal before leaving on 13 March. He seems to have intended to make for Seville but on the 15th found himself off Palos with the tide in his favour for crossing the bar.

FRIDAY, 15 MARCH, Palos

[For certainly, what he already knew and believed firmly, strongly and without reservation] that His Divine Majesty has made all things well and that all things are good except sin and that nothing can avail or be conceived without His permission has, I acknowledge [says the Admiral] been shown miraculously by this voyage, as can well be seen from this account, by the many remarkable miracles wrought on the voyage. And I acknowledge that He has done as much for me, who was so long in your Highnesses' court, facing opposition and contrary opinions from all the principal members of your household, all of whom were against me and made fun of me, that I hope in our Lord this achievement shall be the greatest ornament of Christendom ever to have been so lightly accomplished. [These are the concluding words of the Admiral Don Cristóbal Colón concerning his first voyage to the Indies and the discovery thereof.]

Detail from the Piri Reis Map of Turkish origin, 1513:
'The fish here are so different from ours that it is a wonder . . .
There are whales too'

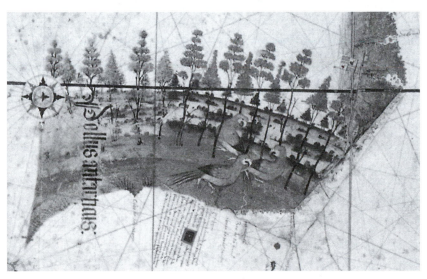

Detail from the Cantino Map of Portuguese origin, 1502:
'I saw no beast ashore of any sort save parrots and lizards'

The young Ferdinand and Isabella, 'the Catholic Monarchs':
portraits from a contemporary document

III

THE LETTER TO
LUIS DE SANTÁNGEL

As well as the fragments from 'The First Voyage', a synoptic account of the voyage survives in the form of a letter purportedly from Columbus, addressed to Luis de Santángel, treasurer of the crown of Aragon, who had been instrumental in putting together the consortium that advanced the money for the enterprise. In a closely similar variant, the addressee is Santángel's colleague, Gabriel Sánchez. On the face of it, this is either the letter which Columbus reported writing aboard ship in the entry (above, p. 97) of 14 February, or another similar letter written at the same time. To judge from the fragments from 'The First Voyage', it was kept in a barrel on board. Thus it could have been forwarded to the royal court at Barcelona, with the appended postscript (below, p. 109–10) when Columbus was safely in Lisbon.

Three significant scruples, however – among many which are less impressive – have made historians suspicious of the status of this letter. First, it is datelined 'above' or 'towards' or 'off' the Canary Islands, whereas on the date ascribed to it Columbus was off the Azores; secondly, the postscript is dated '14 March' and includes a claim that Columbus had just arrived in Lisbon, whereas he had certainly been there by that time for ten days. Thirdly, though the work was widely printed and translated, and became something of a best-seller in its day, no copy in Columbus's hand has survived. The earliest versions appear to be an edition rushed through the press with extraordinary haste in Barcelona, in advance of Columbus's arrival in the city to make his report to the monarchs, and a manuscript version in the royal archives, which, because the errors of transcription closely match misprints in the first edition, appears to be a copy made either for or from the press.* It could also be said that, though the letter is consistent in style and content with what Columbus wrote in the fragment of 'The First Voyage', it does have features which suggest that it was consciously addressed to a popular readership and was therefore perhaps intended for the press. *Mirabilia* are given prominence, particularly those which seem to suggest a topsy-turvy, looking-glass world of the sort favoured by imaginary travellers: women who do men's work, men who have hair like women's, islands of bald men, tailed men, cannibals, and Amazons.

Two attractive theories have been put forward to explain the textual problems. The first is that Columbus wrote the letter to conceal the treasonable negotiations he might have had in Lisbon with the King of Portugal, tampering with the datelines accordingly and staking a claim through the press to a discovery which royal anger, or the envy of the Pinzón family, might deny him.* The second is that the letter is a pastiche concocted at court from Columbus's papers and printed hurriedly to establish the priority of the claims of the Castilian crown to the lands discovered.* This involves the supposition that the manuscript version is the original of the pastiche and the copy from which the printers of the first edition worked; it has, perhaps, the merit of explaining errors of fact and of transcription which Columbus is unlikely to have committed.

Explanations of this kind, however, whatever their merits, are more elaborate than the problems require. The vague dateline of the main text seems consistent with Columbus's avowed uncertainty of his whereabouts on the way home (above, p. 95), and with the fact that he admitted, in a surviving fragment, that until he landed at the island of Santa María, he did not know where he was during the storm of 14 to 16 February. The date of the postscript could be a printer's or copyist's error. Another such error occurs in the first sentence of the text, which represents the outward voyage as twenty days long. A further curious example occurs in the description of Hispaniola, the coast of which is said to be as long as that of Spain 'from Corunna to Fuenterrabía'. From other references it is clear that Columbus believed the coastline of Hispaniola to be longer than the whole of that of Spain, and therefore 'Collioure' (now in French Catalonia) has been suggested as a possible true reading for 'Corunna'.* Columbus's handwriting was so poor that such a mistake is easy to credit. In writing this letter – or, if it is a pastiche, in supplying the materials for it – Columbus may well have been seeking to indemnify himself against possible accusations of disloyalty; he and his correspondents at court may well have been anxious to establish the status of the monarchs' title to sovereignty over the discoveries. It is proper to read the document with those considerations in mind. There is no reason, however, to see it as other than wholly or substantially Columbus's work.

A curious remark about the slave trade, almost at the end of the letter, demands attention. In a list of the islands' potentially exportable products, slaves are listed with the qualification 'and these will be taken from among the idolaters'. So far, the letter has insisted that there are no idolaters in the Indies, and Columbus made repeated observations to the same effect in the course of the first voyage. Tender consciences in Castile were well aware that slavery was an unnatural condition, not lightly to be imposed, except on those who deserved it. Idolatry, which was generally considered to be an offence against natural law, could be regarded as a clear qualification for slavery, whereas the sort of natural religion which Columbus appeared to ascribe to the Indians might be thought to exempt them from any lawful depredations by slavers. Except in this one remark, Columbus shows no awareness of the need for any such scruples. It is apparent that he would cheerfully have enslaved any or all of the natives, if given the chance, and although he seems to have realised that this practice was objectionable to the monarchs and to some Castilian jurists, he does not, from his other references, appear to understand why.* The conclusion seems inescapable that either this remark in the letter to Santángel was made by Columbus in a moment of exceptional sagacity, or it was interpolated by an alert editor at court prior to publication.

Letter to Luis de Santángel, 15 February 1493

My lord, because I know that you will take pleasure in the great victory which our Lord has granted me on this voyage, I write you this letter, by which you will learn how in twenty [*sic*] days, with the fleet which our most illustrious lord King and lady Queen gave me, I crossed to the Indies, where I found many islands populated with innumerable inhabitants; and I have taken possession of all of them for their Highnesses, with proclamation made and banner unfurled, and no man gainsaid me.

To the first that I found I gave the name of San Salvador, in recollection of His Divine Majesty who marvellously has granted all this. The Indians called it Guanahaní. To the second I gave the name of the island of Santa María de la Concepción; to the third Fernandina; to the fourth Isabela Island, to the fifth Juana Island; and so on, a new name to each one.

When I reached Juana I followed its coast towards the west and found it so big that I thought it must be a mainland, the land of Cathay. And as I could find none of the towns and localities one might expect on the coast, only little villages, with the inhabitants of which I was unable to have any talk, because they all ran away immediately, I sailed further on the same course, thinking that I could not fail to find great cities or towns. And after many leagues, since nothing new had turned up, and the coastline was carrying me northwards, whereas I would have preferred to go in a different direction – because winter was already putting on flesh and my intention was to spend it in the south, and the wind continued to carry me onwards – I decided to wait no longer, and went back on my course until I came to a remarkable harbour. And from there I sent two men inland to find out whether there were a king or any large cities. They travelled for three days and found innumerable small settlements and population beyond number, but no evidence of overall government. Therefore they returned.

I fully understood from other Indians, whom I had already captured, that this land was one perfect island, and so I followed the coast of it eastwards for a hundred and seven leagues, where it came to an end. From the cape at that point I could see another island to the east, eight or ten leagues away. To it I subsequently gave the name of Hispaniola. And I went there and I followed the northern coastline for fully 178 [*sic*] leagues, counting from Juana in a straight line, in an easterly direction.

It is very defensible, as are all the other islands, to an exceptional degree, and this one extremely so. It has many harbours on its coasts, beyond comparison with any I know in Christendom, and plenty of rivers, wonderfully good and big. Its lands are lofty and there are many ranges and high mountains – incomparably more than on Tenerife – all most beautiful and of a thousand forms, all scalable, and furnished with trees of a thousand kinds, so tall that they seem to reach the sky. And I take it as apparent that they never lose their leaves, as far as I could tell, for I saw them as green and fair as in Spain in May. And some were in flower and some in fruit and others at other stages according to their kind. And the nightingale sang, and a thousand other sorts of birds in the month of November, which is when I was there. There are six or seven different types of palm tree, which it is a wonder to see for the eye-catching diversity between them, though it is just as great among the other trees and fruits and grasses. There are marvellous pine groves and vast downlands and there is honey, and many sorts of birds, and a great variety of fruits. Inland there are many mines, yielding metals, and there are people too numerous to count.

Hispaniola is a marvel: the hills and mountains and prairies and downlands and soils are fair and rich for planting and sowing, for raising livestock of every sort, for building towns and settlements. As for the harbours, no one could believe them without seeing them; and the same is true of the rivers, large, plentiful, sweet-watered, most of which carry gold. In the trees and fruits and grasses there are great differences from those of Juana: on this island there are many spice-growing areas and great mines of gold and other metals.

The people of this island, and of all the others I have found and possessed or heard of, all go naked, men and women, as their mothers bore them, although some of the women cover themselves up in just one place with a leaf of grass or a slip of cotton which they make for the purpose. They have no iron or steel or weapons of war, nor any aptitude for it, not because they are not well built folk of fine stature but because they are incredibly timid. They carry no arms except for staves cut from canes that have gone to seed, on which they fix a sharp point at the tip – and those they do not dare to use, for many times I happen to have sent two or three men to some village to have a talk, and a countless horde of inhabitants has come out to them and, seeing them, have run immediately away, the fathers not even tarrying for their sons. And this is not because any harm might have come to them. On the contrary, wherever I have stopped and been able to talk with them, I have given to them whatever I had, both cloth and many other things, without accepting anything in return; but they are irremediably timid.

It is a fact that once they gain confidence and lose their fear, they are so ingenuous and so free with what they possess that no one would believe it without seeing it. Whatever they have, if you ask for it, they never say no, but rather offer it with a full heart, and show so much good will that they would yield their souls. And whether it be some item of value or a thing of little worth, they are happy with any little thing of any sort whatsoever which might be given to them for it.

I forbade that they should be given things as cheap as broken platters and bits of broken glass or fasteners, though when they could get hold of such things, they thought they had the greatest jewel in the world. One sailor claimed that for a tag he got gold of two and a half ducats' weight, and others that they got a lot more for much less. Again, for shiny new *blancas* they gave all they had, even if it were two or three ducats in gold or a bushel or two of spun cotton. They even accepted bits of broken barrel-hoops and gave what they had like beasts. So it seemed ill to me and I forbade it. And I gave willingly a thousand goodly things which I had with me so that they should feel friendship for us; and, looking ahead, they will become Christians, for they will incline to the love and service of their Highnesses and of the whole Castilian nation, and will try to join together to provide us with all the things which they have in abundance and which are needful to us. And they know no organised religion nor idolatry, save that they all believe that all strength and goodness comes from heaven; and they firmly believe that I and my ships and men came from heaven and once they had lost their fear received me with corresponding deference wherever I stopped. This does not happen because they are ignorant – rather they are men of very ingenious mind, and can sail all the seas in that part of the world, and it is a marvel how good an account they can give of everything – but because they have never seen men in clothes or ships like ours before.

And as soon as I reached the Indies, on the first island I found I took by force a number of them so that they could be taught to give me information of what there was in those regions. And thus it was that they later came to understand us and we them, whether by words or signs. And they have been of great use. I have them with me today and they are still of the opinion that I must come from heaven, despite all the talk they have had with me. And these were the first to say it wherever I landed, and the others went running from house to house and to neighbouring villages, loudly crying, 'Come! Come to see the people from heaven!' Thus did they all come to us, men and women alike, once they were sure of us at heart, so that neither old nor young were left behind, and they all brought something to eat and drink, which they gave with marvellous friendliness.

In all the islands they have many canoes, rather like oared barges, some big, some small, and many a one bigger than a lighter with eighteen crew. They are not so broad, because they are wrought of a single piece of timber, but one of our lighters could not compete with

them for speed, for the way they move is unbelievable. And in these they sail all those islands, which are without number, and transport their merchandise. I have seen some of these canoes with seventy or eighty men in them, each with an oar.

In all the islands I did not observe much diversity in the way the people go about their business, either in customs or speech. Rather, they all understand one another, which is a very singular thing and makes me hope that their Highnesses will be resolved on the conversion of the people to our Holy Faith, to which they are very well disposed.

I have already said that I had travelled 107 leagues along the coast of Juana Island in a straight line from west to east. Therefore, on the basis of that journey, I can say that this island is bigger than England and Scotland combined, because beyond those 107 leagues remain two more provinces on the western side, which I have not been to. One of them is called Auan, where men with tails come from. These provinces cannot be more than fifty or sixty leagues across, from what I can understand from the Indians I have with me, who know all the islands. This other island of Hispaniola has a perimeter longer than the coast of Spain all the way from Corunna [*sic*, perhaps for Collioure] to Fuenterrabía in Biscay, for on one side I covered 188 full leagues in a straight line from west to east. It is an island to desire and, once seen, never to be left.

Although I have taken possession of all of these islands for their Highnesses, and although all are better provided than I have the skill and knowledge to express (and I hold them so securely for their Highnesses that they can dispose of them as well and as fully as of their kingdoms of Castile), yet of all of them, it was in this Hispaniola that I took possession of a great town to which I gave the name of Villa de Navidad. There I have built a stronghold and fortress, which by about the present time will have been completely finished. It is a most suitable place – the best for gold mines, and for trade both with the mainland here and that over there belonging to the Great Khan where great trade and profit can be had. And in it I have left men sufficient for a feat of this sort, with arms and artillery and victuals for more than a year, and one lighter, and a master-shipwright qualified in all departments, to build more, all of them in great friendship with the king of that land in such degree that he prided himself on calling me brother and treating me as such. And though his attitude might change if the garrison should give offence, neither the

king nor his men know even what weapons are, and they go naked as I have said. They are the most timid folk in the world, so that just the men that have been left there are enough to destroy the whole of that land and the island harbours no threat to their persons if they behave sensibly.

In all these islands, it seems to me, all the men are content with one wife, and to their elder or king they allow up to twenty. The women, it seems to me, do more work than the men. I have not been able to determine whether they have personal property, for it seemed to me that all shared in whatever any had, especially in things to eat.

So far in these islands I have found no monstrous beings, such as many people expected, but rather all the people are of very handsome appearance. Nor are they Blacks, like in Guinea, but rather have long, lank hair; nor do they breed where there is too much scorching from the rays of the sun. It is true that the sun has great force there, for it is twenty-six degrees away from the equator. In these islands, where there are high mountains the cold is severe in winter, as at present, but they endure it both by habit and with the help of the foodstuffs they eat, being excessively piquant and with many spices.

So I have found no report even of any monsters, except for one island, which is 'Carib', the second as one enters the Indies, which is inhabited by a people who in all the islands are accounted very fierce and who eat human flesh. They have many canoes with which they travel over all the islands of India. They rob, and take what they want. They are no more ill formed than the others, except that they have it as their custom to wear their hair long like women, and they use bows and arrows, made all alike from staves with a little pointed stick at the end for want of iron, which they do not possess. They are ferocious by the standards of the other peoples here, who are cowardly to an excessive degree, but I do not reckon them any more highly than the others. It is these men who have intercourse with the women of Matrimonyo [sic for Matinino], which is the first island encountered in the Indies if one approaches from Spain, and which has no men at all. The inhabitants do not practise womanly ways, rather preferring bows and arrows, made, like those mentioned before, from staves, and for their armour and covering they use sheets of amber, of which they have an abundance.

They assure me there is another island, bigger than Hispaniola, where the people have no hair. On Hispaniola there is an incalculable quantity of gold and from it and from other islands I am bringing Indians to bear witness.

In conclusion, to speak only of what has been achieved on this voyage, which was just a sort of quick tour, their Highnesses can tell that I shall give them all the gold they have need of, with a very little help which their Highnesses shall give me presently; and of spices and cotton as much as they shall order to be laden; and of mastic all they shall order to be laden – which hitherto has not been found anywhere except in Greece, on the island of Chios, where the lords ask for it whatever price they fancy; and of aloe wood all they shall order to be laden; and of slaves all they shall order to be laden, and these will be taken from among the idolaters. And I believe I have found rhubarb and cinnamon, and a thousand other things of value shall swiftly be discovered by the men I have left there. For I tarried at no point, as long as there was wind to sail by, except at Villa de Navidad in order to leave it secured and well placed. And, truth to tell, I should have accomplished much more if the ships had served me as it was proper to expect.

This is enough and [*now praise be to*] our Lord God everlasting, Who gives to those who walk in His way the conquest of what appears impossible. And this, conspicuously, was just such a conquest, for although these lands may have been inferred and written about, it has all been speculative up to now, without confirmation by sight, without full understanding – so much so that most of those who heard about them listened and adjudged them more likely to be legendary than anything else. And so it is that our Redeemer has granted to our most illustrious King and Queen, and to their famous kingdoms, the achievement of so lofty a matter, at which all Christendom must rejoice and celebrate great festivities and give solemn thanks to the Holy Trinity, with many solemn prayers, for the exaltation that shall be derived from the conversion of so many peoples to our holy faith, and, secondly, for the material benefits which will bring refreshment and profit not only to Spain but to all Christian people. Thus far, to the present day, and thus briefly.

Dated aboard my caravel, above the Canary Islands, on 15 February 1493.

Your obedient servant, the Admiral

After writing this, when I was in Castilian waters, a south and south-east wind arose against me, which made me lighten the ships, but today I ran into the port of Lisbon here – which was the greatest marvel in the world – where I decided to write to their Highnesses.

The letter to Luis de Santángel   109

Throughout the Indies I found winds like those of May. I went there in thirty-three days and returned in twenty-eight, except that these storms kept me running on this sea for thirteen days. All the seafaring men here are saying that there never was a worse winter nor so many lost ships.

Dated on the fourteenth [*sic*] day of March.

IV

THE TORRES
MEMORANDUM

Even in Columbus's moment of triumph, when he paraded his exotic curiosities before the eyes of his monarchs in Barcelona, few observers were prepared to believe that he had got to Asia. He had, it was thought, probably stumbled on an outlying part of the Canary archipelago, or on some unknown islands or on the long-suspected Antipodes. Incontestably, however, he had brought back samples of gold, and for the time being his enemies were effectively silenced. He had no difficulty in obtaining a commission to return to his discoveries to establish a colony, initiate trade and extend exploration. He was further commanded to produce a map that could be used for negotiations with Portugal on the division of the spoils of exploration.* He also needed to complete a job of his own, by proving that his new lands were genuinely Asiatic in character. This was not just a matter of *amour propre*, keen though he was to vindicate his own view in the teeth of learned opposition; he was bound to deliver his own part of his bargain with the monarchs in order to be sure of his claim to their favour in return.

In some ways, this second voyage marked the climax of his career. Some 1,300 men strong, it was the largest expedition he ever commanded in his life; it sailed on the rising tide of his reputation, which did not begin to ebb until he arrived in the New World to be confronted by disaster and disillusionment. The crossing was completed swiftly and dextrously, in twenty-nine days. Unluckily, however, no account of Columbus's own survives, unless reflected darkly in the versions of Las Casas and the *Historie*. Nor has Columbus left any substantial fragment from his own hand from the entire time he spent out of Castile on this expedition – with the exception of the document which follows, which is commonly known as the Torres Memorandum. It was written in Hispaniola for Antonio de Torres, Columbus's messenger to his monarchs, and dated 30 January 1494.*

Although it is not strictly autobiographical and by no means as intimate as many of Columbus's outpourings, the face of his sufferings can be glimpsed through the mask of official prose.

The Memorandum was written at a time when Columbus was wracked by anxieties and disappointment. His arduous further explorations, especially of Cuba, seem only to have isolated him among his men in the conviction that his discoveries were close to, or part of, Asia. His return to Hispaniola had belied almost all his hopes. The Indians, whom he had extolled as peaceful and labelled as biddable, had risen up and massacred the garrison he had left behind. The climate he praised had reduced almost his entire force to sickness. The site he had earmarked for a settlement proved indefensible and unhealthy. The gold he anticipated was hard to extract and slow to emerge. Of the commercial products he had hoped to export, only slaves were readily available. His new world was threatened with ruin almost before it had begun.*

The Torres Memorandum was therefore an attempt to salvage his reputation from the wreck of his hopes. The structure of the document is revealing. It opens with a cascade of reassurance and praise of Hispaniola's potential: this is Columbus's attempt to bolster or restore royal confidence in his judgement. A series of damning admissions follow, wrung from the writer with obvious pain. One by one, Columbus's earlier false predictions – about the gold, the climate, the Indians – are stripped away and the horrible reality of life on a savage frontier is exposed. Columbus deals deftly with these difficult passages, interweaving excuses with the admissions and reporting some disasters only obliquely. He turns quickly to his vision of the island's future, to which he devotes a great deal of space and detail. Though expressed with enthusiasm and urgency, as a future gage for present failures, the vision is in many ways a bleak one. The islands are to be transformed into ersatz versions of the old world, planted with wheat, vines and sugar, and grazed by Castilian livestock. The natives are to be subjugated and evangelised, wrenched into a European way of life or exported as slaves. An intruded settler population will engage in petty industry or commerce or the military occupation of the territory; but they will have to consist of more tractable types than those Columbus found among his own men: he stresses heavily the need for family men to come out, who will have a long-term stake in the success of the colony. It was a plea often repeated in the history of the colonisation of the Hispanic New

World, but rarely fulfilled. Finally, Columbus shows his abiding preoccupation with his own share of the profits to be yielded by his discoveries.

A brief guide to the individuals mentioned in the Memorandum is necessary. Torres himself was a loyal confidant of Columbus; he had joined the outward voyage and had been appointed by the monarchs to bring the returning fleet home. His sister was the royal heir's nurse – a permanent position in the princely household – to her Columbus later directed an appeal intended to influence the monarchs in his favour. Torres may have become implicated in Columbus's fall from grace; he never attained the leading position in the affairs of the Indies for which he supplicated, and ended life as Governor of Gran Canaria. He was drowned in a shipwreck in 1503.

Fray Bernardo Buil was a monk of Montserrat who had joined the Friars Minim; his earlier record was in diplomacy and administration, and, though apparently attracted to the Franciscan tradition, he seems to have had little vocation for evangelism. For reasons which remain obscure, he fell out with Columbus, who seems, however, still to have been satisfied with him at the time he was writing the Memorandum. Columbus seems to have been unable to sustain in the New World the sort of good relations he established with clerics in the Old.

Ginés de Gorbalán and Alonso de Hojeda were deputed by Columbus to explore parts of the hinterland of Hispaniola. The former returned to Spain in 1494 and seems to have played no further part in the history of the Indies. Hojeda, however, became a figure of major importance. Characteristically, the praise Columbus lavished on him at first acquaintance turned to rancour and bitterness when they fell out. The Admiral felt betrayed by Alonso's self-transformation into an explorer on his own account, particularly in 1499 when he made a voyage with Vespucci (another friend who betrayed Columbus's trust) and Juan de la Cosa, to the pearl fisheries near the mouth of the Orinoco, which Columbus claimed to have discovered. The Duke of Medina Celi, who was something of a *bourgeois gentilhomme* – a great entrepreneur with extensive commercial interests – had been approached by Columbus as a possible patron and claimed to have been instrumental in drawing royal attention to the enterprise of the Indies. When Columbus returned from his first voyage, having apparently made an exploitable discovery, the duke was quick to demand a share in the proceeds, and the appointment of Hojeda may have been due to him.

Pedro Margarit was another young man of whom Columbus had high hopes which were to be dashed by bitter experience. He was put in command of the garrison Columbus left on Hispaniola during the exploration of Cuba, to maintain a presence in the gold-bearing region of Cibao. Because of the guerrilla warfare waged by Caonabó, the most indomitable of the chiefs of the island, Margarit needed what was, in the circumstances, a huge force of some 500 men. The resulting problems of forage were a severe strain. Columbus's instructions were riven with contradictions and practical difficulties. He enjoined, for instance, that above all the Indians were to be well treated, and yet their misdemeanours were to be punished with the utmost severity, including mutilation for theft. No goods were to be extorted from them, other than by way of trade, and yet the supplies needed by the garrison were too great to be wholly acquired by barter. Columbus delegated all his judicial role to Margarit, and yet was to resent his exercise of it. From some points of view, Margarit's part was well played; he made military measures his priority, successfully devoting himself, in accordance with stress clearly laid in Columbus's instructions, to the capture of Caonabó. But Columbus found his men undisciplined and relations with the Indians exacerbated as a result of their excesses. Margarit joined Fray Buil in withdrawing to Spain and filing complaints against the Admiral.

Juan Aguado was an important figure in Columbus's world. He was a household servant of the Queen's, who, after eliciting this testimonial from Columbus, returned to Spain with Buil and Margarit. This suggests that he sided with Columbus's critics. The fact that their criticisms were heeded at court is shown by Aguado's return in 1495 with supervisory powers. Outraged at first, Columbus seems, surprisingly, to have established some sort of working relationship with Aguado, whom he later came to see as exemplary in comparison with other royal servants whose powers were more extensive and whose interference less deferential.

Dr Diego Alvarez Chanca, official physician to Columbus's expedition, is known mainly through his remarkable account of his experiences – particularly of encounters with cannibals and of his struggle against the ill health which dogged the Spaniards. Like Columbus, Chanca was inclined to blame the anaemic local diet for much of the trouble, and to call for wine and beef from Spain to remedy it. It was clear from his report, however, that Columbus's claims for the healthy environment of his discoveries were cruelly deceptive.

Pedro Hernández Coronel was one of the few companions with whom Columbus never seems to have fallen out. He accompanied Columbus on his return to Spain and was entrusted with command of a supply flotilla shortly afterwards. He seems to have obtained the office Columbus solicited for him. Gil García, 'Gaspar' and 'Beltrán' are not known from other sources. Juan de Soria, however, is mentioned in further correspondence between the monarchs and Columbus. 'Our will', the monarchs wrote in August 1493, 'is that he and the others should serve and honour you as is just.'* The rebuke may have been precipitated by the incident Columbus complains of in the Memorandum. Soria's background in the household of the heir to the throne, with other associates of Columbus such as Antonio and Juana de Torres, suggests that he was chosen for a role in preparing Columbus's expedition because of his links with the circle of Columbus's friends at court. Finally, Pedro de Villacorta was, according to Las Casas, the treasurer of the expedition. He retained the confidence of the monarchs after the Admiral's fall and, after a period back in Spain, returned to the Indies in his former capacity in 1502.

Memorandum to Antonio de Torres, Isabela, 30 January 1494

This is what you, Antonio de Torres, captain of the ship *Marigalante* and magistrate of the city of Isabela, shall say and beseech on my behalf in the presence of our lord King and lady Queen, as follows.

First, having presented the credentials which you are to bear from me for their Highnesses, you shall kiss their royal hands and feet on my behalf and shall commend me to their Highnesses as to my King and Queen and natural lords, in whose service I hope to end my days, as you will be able to say at greater length to their Highnesses, according to what you have seen and known of me.

Item: although, by means of the letters which I am writing to their Highnesses, and also those of Father Fray Buil and the treasurer, their Highnesses will be able to learn – and fully, too, in detail and at length – of everything that has been done here since our arrival, nevertheless, you shall say to their Highnesses on my behalf that God has been pleased to grant me such favour in their service that up to the present I have found and continue to find nothing less in any respect than what I wrote and said and affirmed to their Highnesses in days gone by. Indeed, I hope by God's grace that it will in fact appear even more brilliant, and very soon too. For in the matter of spices, on the seashore alone, without going further inland, so great are the signs and beginnings of them that are to be found that there is cause to hope for very much better results. And the same is true of the gold mines, for of only two parties sent to discover them, without staying out there because they were few in number, both have found such great rivers, so full of gold, that any man of those who saw it and gathered it, albeit only with their bare hands for a sample, has returned so joyful and singing such hearty praises of its abundance that I feel at a loss for words in writing of it to their Highnesses. But as Gorvalán, who was one of the discoverers, is going back there, he will be able to tell of what he saw, though another, who is called Hojeda, is staying here. He is one of the Duke of Medina Celi's men, a very circumspect young man, and of great prudence, who, beyond doubt and indeed beyond comparison, has made much greater discoveries as appears from the list of rivers he has brought; and he says that in every one of them there is an incredible amount of gold, for which their Highnesses can give thanks to God, for that He has been disposed so favourably in all things.

Item: you shall say to their Highnesses, that despite what may already have been written to them, I should greatly have desired to be in a position to send them, in the present fleet, a quantity of gold exceeding our expectations of what can be gathered here, had it not been that, of the men who are available here, the greater part fell suddenly sick. But this fleet could no longer be detained here, both on account of the great expense it entails, and because the weather is now favourable for the voyage out – and for the return journey by the men whose responsibility it will be to bring back all the things which are in short supply here, for if they were to delay their departure those who must return would not be able to start back in time for May. And what is more, I should like to take the healthy men who are to be found here, both aboard ship and on land in the settlement, on an expedition to the mines or rivers at once; but it would be very difficult or even dangerous. At a distance of twenty-three or twenty-four leagues from here, there are mountain passes and rivers to cross, and for so long a journey we should have to take plenty of provisions which could not be carried up the mountainsides. There are no beasts of burden in this country to do the job, nor are the roads and passes adequately made, though a start has been made at surfacing them to make them manageable. And further, it would be very ill-advised to leave the sick men here in an open place and in huts, and to leave the supplies and victuals which are ashore, for, although these Indians have shown themselves to the discoverers and daily confirm themselves to be simple people devoid of malice, yet it seems withal, since they come here among us every day, that it would not be prudent to put at risk and expose to loss the men and supplies here. As they come and go all the time, by day and night, a single Indian could do the job with a firebrand, setting light to the huts, and because of them we keep guard over the camp while the settlement remains open and unwalled.

Further, as we saw that most of those who went inland to explore fell sick on their return, or even had to turn back on the way, this was a reason to fear that the same might befall those healthy men who might make such an expedition now. And two perils might threaten them there in consequence. First, if they were to fall sick out there in the course of the work, where there is no house nor refuge of any sort from the chief they call Caonabó (who by all accounts is a very bad man and – even more – a very bold one), he, seeing us there enfeebled and ill, would be able to undertake that which he would not dare if we were in normal health. And along with this there would be a second difficulty: how to get back here with the gold we would be carrying, because we should either have to carry a little and go back and forth every day, increasing the risk of sickness, or send the gold with only a part of our force and equally run the risk of losing it.

And so you shall report to their Highnesses that these are the reasons why the fleet has not been delayed for the present nor more gold sent, apart from the samples. But with trust in the mercy of God Who in all and through all has guided us thus far, the men will soon get better, as they are beginning to do already, for the country only causes them a few days of sickness and then they get up again. And it is a fact that if they had some fresh meat to get better with they would all be on their feet soon enough with God's help, and most of them would indeed be better already. With the few fit men who remain here we are endeavouring day by day to enclose the settlement and put it into some sort of state of defence with our supplies secured. This should be completed within a few days, because earth walls are all that is needed. For, unless they were to catch us asleep, the Indians are not the men to make any sort of attempt on us even were they to think of it, as they did with the other lot of men who remained here [*after my first voyage*] who invited attack by their failure to take precautions. For the Indians would never have dared to attempt to harm those men – few as they were and however often they gave the Indians a chance of doing what they did – had they seen that they were on the alert.

When the fortifications are complete, then the problem of going to the said rivers shall be undertaken, either by following the road from here and making the best way we can, or by going round the island by sea as far as the part of the coast from which, it is said, there can be no more than six or seven leagues to the said rivers. In such a manner the gold can be gathered in safety, and stored in the protection of some fort or tower which could be built there to house it after it has been gathered, until the time when the two caravels return here. It would then be sent on afterwards under strong guard as soon as the weather is favourable for an ocean crossing.

Item: you shall tell their Highnesses, as has been said, that the causes for so widespread a sickness among all the men is the change of water and air, for we can see that though it affects all our muster it imperils few lives. In consequence, the best means under God of conserving their health is to have these men provided with the diet they are used to in Spain, for their Highnesses will not be able to be served, either by these or others who come after them, unless they are fit. And these provisions will have to be supplied until the groundwork has been laid here for the planting and sowing which we intend – that is, of wheat, barley, and vines. Little has been done this year because a start could not be made until we had established a settlement, and once we had established one, the few farming men we had with us fell sick. Even had they been fit, they had few animals to work with, and those were so stringy and feeble that they could not do much with them. Even so, they have done a little planting, but only enough to test the soil, which seems wonderfully good, so that we can hope to obtain some relief from it for our needs. We feel fully assured, because it has been proven in practice, that wheat and vines will grow very well in this land, but we have to await the harvest. If it turns out as well as appears from the readiness with which the seed corn has taken and certain other few seeds which have been sown, it is certain that neither an Andalusia nor a Sicily will be wanting here. The same is true of sugar canes, to judge from the way a few that have been planted have taken. For it is a fact that the beauty of the land in these islands – as well in woodlands, mountains and waters as in grasslands where there are abundant rivers — is so fair to the sight that no other land under the sun could be better to behold or more appealing.

Item: you shall say that because much of the wine which the fleet was bringing was spilt on this voyage, and this, according to most opinions, was because of bad workmanship by the coopers in Seville, the most serious shortage we now have here, or expect to have, is of wine. And although we have both wheat and biscuit for a longer period, it really is necessary to send us some reasonable quantity, for the way is long and there is not enough for a daily ration; and similarly some meats, that is, bacon and some other preserved meat which should be of better quality than what we brought with us. Some live beef cattle too, and, even more, some lambs, male and female, with more females than males, and some small calves and heifers — these should be sent every time a caravel is sent here — and some asses, male and female, and hacks for working and sowing, for here there is not a single animal from which a man can get use or service. And because I fear that their Highnesses will not be in Seville, and that their officials or servants, without express instructions, will be unwilling to supply what it is necessary to have sent here right away on the first sailing; and because by the time the request has been made and reply received, the season will have passed for the ships to set off from them (for it is essential that they should be here by the beginning of May), you will say to their Highnesses, as I have confided and ordered you, that you have entrusted all the gold you have taken with you to a merchant in Seville, that the merchant may advance against it the sum required to load two caravels with wine and wheat and the other things which appear on your list. Then he shall take or send the said gold to their Highnesses, who shall see and receive him and order him to be paid for what he shall have advanced for the loading and despatch of the said two caravels. And to relieve and succour the men who remain here, it is necessary for the ship to be ready in good time to be able to get here by the beginning of May, so that the people here all see the goods and get some benefit from them, before the start of the summer.

You will take particular care to despatch sick rations, of which we are experiencing severe want here, such as raisins, sugar, almonds, honey and rice, of which a lot ought to have come and there came but little. That which did come is largely consumed and exhausted, even the greater part of the medical supplies which were brought from over there, because of the large numbers of sick. And of all these things aforesaid you are carrying lists, signed by my hand, of rations for fit and sick alike, which you will meet in full if there are sufficient funds, or at least procure what is most needed at present so that it can then be brought in the said two ships. And you shall arrange with their Highnesses that whatever remains will be sent in other ships as soon as possible.

Item: you shall say to their Highnesses that because there is no interpreter here through whom the native people can be given an understanding of our Holy Faith, no matter how hard we try, as their Highnesses desire – and so do those of us who are here – we are now sending with the present sailing some men, women, boys, and girls, all belonging to the cannibal people. These their Highnesses can order to be placed in the charge of persons with whom they can best learn our language and who can give practice in useful employment and who, little by little, can order them to be nurtured with more care than other slaves, in such a way that they learn in isolation from one another, without speaking to each other or seeing each other until some time has passed; they will learn more perfectly over there than here, and will be much better interpreters (though we shall not cease to do all we can here).

It is true that as the people of one island here have little to do with those of the others there are certain differences between them in their languages, according to how close to or far from each other they are. But by comparison with the other islands those of the cannibals are many, large and thoroughly well populated, and it seemed to us here that it could only be a good thing to take some people from them, both male and female, and send them over there to Castile, for they shall be inclined to abandon forever that inhuman custom which they have of eating people. And there in Castile, once they understand the language, they shall more readily receive baptism and do their souls good; and even among the peoples here who are not given to those customs, great credit will be gained for us when they see that we take and make captive some of those from whom they are accustomed to receive harm, and whom they fear so much that they flee from their very name.

Inform their Highnesses that here in this land the arrival and sight of this fleet, well and handsomely arrayed as it is, has very greatly strengthened the authority with which this conversion is being undertaken, and very greatly improved future prospects, that all the people of this island, which is so big, and of the others, shall readily come to obedience, when they see the good treatment that shall be meted out to the good and the chastisement of the wicked. And their Highnesses shall be able to command them as vassals, although already, wherever a man of them is found, not only do they set about everything they do willingly, but also apply themselves on their own initiative to anything they believe might please us. And their Highnesses can also feel sure that over there, among Christian people, no less than here, the coming of this fleet will have given them great prestige in many connections of present and future importance alike, which their Highnesses will better be able to imagine and understand than I to write.

Item: you shall say to their Highnesses that the good of the souls of the said cannibals, and even of those who remain here, raises the presumption that the more we send over there the better. And their Highnesses can be served therein in this manner: seeing how badly cattle and working animals are needed here for the sustenance of the men who have to be stationed here, and for the good of all the islands, their Highnesses will be able to grant a licence and permits for a sufficient number of caravels to come here every year and bring the said cattle and other provisions and the things needed to settle the country and exploit the soil – and to do so at reasonable prices and at the carrier's expense. The goods could be paid for with slaves, drawn from among the cannibals, who are folk so wild and naturally so well equipped, well formed and of good understanding, that once freed of their inhumanity we believe they would make better slaves than any other people. And they will lose that inhumanity once they are away from their land. And we shall be able to take them in large numbers with the oared frigates we are intending to build, provided always that on each of the caravels which comes from their Highnesses a reliable person is placed, who shall prevent the said caravels from landing at any place or island save here, where all merchandise must be loaded and unloaded, including any slaves they may carry away. Their Highnesses could receive their dues over there. And bring back or send a reply to this proposal, so that the necessary equipment can be made here with greater confidence, if it seems well to their Highnesses.

Item: you shall also say to their Highnesses that it is more remunerative and less expensive to commission ships the way merchants do for the Flanders trade – by tonnage, rather than any other criterion. For this reason I gave you orders to commission two caravels, which you are to send on arrival, in this matter. And the same can be done with all the others which their Highnesses may send, if they think it meet for their service. But I do not mean this to apply to the ships that have to come under licence to ship the slaves.

Item: you shall tell their Highnesses that, to prevent greater expense, I ventured the caravels shown on the list you are carrying, with the aim of retaining them here with the two round ships we have, namely the *Gallega*, and this other one, which is the flagship. And of the latter I likewise ventured three-eighths of the cost at the valuation which appears in the copies of the account which you are carrying, signed by my hand. These ships will not only provide support and security for the men who have to remain inland, living with the Indians, in order to extract the gold, but will also be useful in the event of any other danger which might be caused by outsiders. Also the caravels are needed for the discovery of the mainland and of other islands which lie between here and there. And you shall beseech their Highnesses that payment be made at the promised time of the monies owed for these ships, for without doubt they will be well worth their cost as I hope from God's mercy.

Item: you shall say to their Highnesses, and beseech them very humbly on my behalf, that they should be well pleased to look at what can be seen at greater length in my letters and other writings, touching the peace and quiet and mutual harmony of the men who are over here; and that, for the sake of what concerns their Highnesses' service, they should appoint such persons as shall not be objects of mistrust but shall consider the purposes for which they are sent here rather than their personal interests. And in this matter, since you saw and knew all that happened, you shall talk to their Highnesses and tell them the truth of it all, as you have understood it. And let any ruling which their Highnesses may make in this connection come with the first sailing, if possible, so that no scandal may arise here in a matter which so closely concerns their Highnesses' service.

Item: you shall tell their Highnesses of the foundation of this city and the beauty of the country around it, as you saw and understood it; and of how I made you a magistrate of the city, using the powers granted me for this purpose by their Highnesses, whom I humbly beseech that in partial recompense of your services they may endorse my said appointment, as I hope they will.

Item: because Pedro Margarit, gentleman, their Highnesses' servant, has served well, and I hope that he will do so henceforth in such matters as shall be entrusted to him, I have been pleased that he should remain here; and also that Gaspar and Beltrán should be placed in positions of responsibility because they are known as servants of their Highnesses. You shall beseech their Highnesses to grant to the said Master Pedro in particular, who is married and has children, an income from the territories of the Order of Santiago, of which he is a member, so that his wife and children shall have the means of life. Similarly you shall give an account of Juan Aguado, their Highnesses' servant, how well and diligently he has served in whatever has been commanded of him; and say that I beseech their Highnesses to treat him and those aforesaid as coming before them with the highest recommendation.

Item: you shall tell their Highnesses of the work Dr Chanca has had to do in the face of so many sick men and also the shortage of provisions; and throughout it all he has applied himself with great diligence and charity in everything which pertains to his role. And as their Highnesses sent me the salary which had to be given to him here – for while he is here it is clear that he does not take nor can he charge any fee from anybody, nor can he profit from his work as he did or could in Castile where he could be at his ease and live in a very different manner from that in which he lives here; and although he affirms that what he was earning over there is much more than the salary which their Highnesses give him – I am unwilling to offer him more than 50,000 *maravedis* a year for the work he does, for the time he remains here. I beseech their Highnesses to authorise payment of this sum with the salary due to him as a member of the expedition. And in the same connection, whereas he states and affirms that physicians who go on royal business of this sort have a customary right to one day's pay in a full year from all the members of the expedition, yet I have been informed withal and am told that, be that as it may, the custom is to give the physicians a certain fixed rate, at their Highnesses' pleasure and orders, in commutation of that day's pay. Therefore you shall beseech their Highnesses to make a ruling about it – both about the salary and about this custom – in such a manner as to give the said doctor reason to be content.

Item: you shall tell their Highnesses concerning Coronel how he is a man fit to serve their Highnesses in many things, and how he has served them up to now in all that is most needful, and how we feel the want of him now that he is so ill. And that since he has served in such a fashion it is right that he should enjoy the fruit of his service, not only with grants of favour later, but also in the manner of his salary now, in such a way that he and those who are here should feel that their services are rewarded; because to judge from the work we have had here to collect the gold, people who display so much diligence are not to be reckoned of little value. And since by virtue of his ability he was appointed here by me to the office of chief constable of these Indies, and in his letter of appointment the amount of the salary is left blank, you shall say that I beseech their Highnesses to have it set as high as may be for their service, taking his duty done into account, at the same time confirming the appointment made here in his favour and making it permanent.

Similarly, you shall tell their Highnesses how the Bachelor of Arts Gil García came here as chief justice and no salary for him has been either paid or fixed; and he is a person of good antecedents, well educated and diligent and his presence here is very much needed. I beseech their Highnesses to order that his salary be fixed and sent so that he can maintain himself, and that it be paid to him with his wage as a member of the expedition.

Item: you shall tell their Highnesses how the horsemen who joined me from Granada mounted a display in Seville where they showed some good horses; then later, at embarkation time, I did not see what they were doing because I was rather unwell. And the horses they embarked were such that the best of them does not look to be worth more than two thousand *maravedis*, for they had sold the others and bought this lot. And something of the same sort was done with a good many of the men whom I had seen and thought very well of in the labour market in Seville. It seems that after Juan de Soria had been given their pay, for motives of his own he substituted other men for those I was expecting to find, and obtained men I had never seen before. There has been much wickedness in all this of such a sort that I do not know whether he is the only one I ought to complain of. This being so, let them know how the expenses of these horsemen, apart from their wages, have been paid up to now, and those of their horses too, and are still being paid; and these are the sort of men who, when they are ill or when they take offence, refuse to allow their horses to work with anyone else, and, similarly, will not admit that they are bound to serve except on mounted duty, which is not very much required at present. And since it seems that it would be better to buy their horses from them, as they are worth so little, and not to have these daily disputes with them, let their Highnesses decide how best they would be served in this matter.

Item: you shall tell their Highnesses that more than two hundred unsalaried men have come here, and some of them are doing good service while the rest are at least being ordered to do the same. And it would be a great benefit for the first three years we are here to get a thousand men established on the island, and to put the rivers of gold in a state of defence. And if a hundred of the men were horsemen nothing would be lost, but rather some such provision seems necessary, and although their Highnesses could defer a decision about the cavalry until they receive gold, they should let us know whether these two hundred persons are to be paid a salary like the rest who are working satisfactorily, for they are certainly necessary, as I have said, to make a start here.

Item: because the expense of maintaining the people here could be reduced by putting them to work in ways practised in other countries – where the outlay could be more easily justified than here – it would seem well to order any ships that may come here to bring, in addition to the other things that are needed for general provisioning and for medical supplies, shoes and leather for making-up here, shirts of standard and other patterns, soaps, linens, smocks, breeches, cloth for making clothes at reasonable prices and other things, such as preserves, which are not part of our rations but are good for the men's health. All such things the men here would gladly accept in lieu of part of their wages. And if the produce is bought over there by loyal servants whose concern is for their Highnesses' service, some saving will be made. Therefore you will learn their Highnesses' wishes on this matter, and if it should seem to them conducive to their service, then let it be put into effect.

Item: you shall also tell their Highnesses, in as much as at the parade which was held yesterday the men were found to be very ill-equipped, that I think this happened in part as a result of the change-around that was contrived in Seville or Puerto de Santa María, when the men who were seen to be well equipped were left out, and others were taken aboard who gave some bribe to those who substituted for them. It seems it would be as well to send out two hundred cuirasses and a hundred arquebuses and a hundred crossbows and plenty of stores, which are what we most need, and from all these weapons some can be issued to ill-equipped men in lieu of pay.

Item: in as much as certain artisans who have come here, including builders and men of other crafts, are married and have their wives over there and would like what is owed to them by way of wages to be paid there to their wives or to other persons to whom they can send messages asking them to buy the things which are needed here, I beseech their Highnesses to order them to be paid, for it will be conducive to their service that the men here should be supplied with their wants.

Item: apart from the things which have been sent for from there in the lists, signed by my hand, which you have with you, it would be as well to add fifty pipes of sugar syrup from Madeira, both for the sustenance of those whose health is good and for the men who are sick; for it is the best provender in the world and the healthiest, and it normally costs no more than two ducats a pipe, not counting the barrel. And if their Highnesses order a caravel to pass that way on its return journey, it can buy it, together with ten crates of sugar which is badly needed. And this is the best time of year – that is, between now and the month of April – to find it and get the best bargain. And it could be ordered, if their Highnesses so commanded, without letting anyone in Madeira know what it is wanted for.

Item: you shall also tell their Highnesses how, while the rivers contain gold in the amount which has been declared on the authority of those who have seen it, it is yet certain that the gold is not engendered in the rivers but in the earth, and the water, as it flows through the mines, carries it mixed up with the sands. And as we have found so many of these rivers, some of which are fairly big and others so small that they are rather springs than rivers with no more than two fingers' depth of water; and as the place where the flow of gold begins will soon be found; it will be useful for all this to have workers not only to pan the gold from the sands, but also others to dig it from the earth, which will yield the finest gold in the greatest quantity. And to this end it will be well for their Highnesses to send workers, including some of those who work over there in the mines of Almadén, so that one way or another the job gets done. However we shall not wait for them here, but with the workers we have already we hope, with God's help, once the men are fit, to get together a big consignment of gold for the caravels of the next sailing.

Item: you shall beseech their Highnesses very humbly on my behalf to treat Vilacorta as very highly recommended. For, as their Highnesses know, he has done much service in this business and with a very good will, and, from what I know, he is a diligent person devoted to their service. I shall be favoured if he is given some position of trust for which he is suited, and you shall make every effort so that

Vilacorta knows by deeds that what he has done for me in matters where I had need of him shall be to his advantage.

Item: the said Master Pedro and Gaspar and Beltrán and others who have remained here came as captains of caravels which have now returned and cannot now enjoy their salaries. But as they are persons of such sort as must be placed in important positions of trust, and no salary has been fixed for them to differentiate them from everybody else, you shall beseech their Highnesses on my behalf to decide what shall be given to them every year or on a monthly basis, or whatever will best be conducive to their service.

Dated in the city of Isabela on the thirtieth day of January of the year 1493.

.S.

.S.A.S.

X M Y

Xpo Ferens*

V

PREPARATIONS FOR
A THIRD CROSSING

Antonio de Torres returned late in 1494 with a summons from the
monarchs to Columbus to return to court. Ostensibly, this was so
that his services should be available for negotiations with the
Portuguese, and there was as yet no marked sign of royal disfavour.
The progress Columbus had made since his arrival in the New World
did not encourage him to return home. His explorations had revealed
no convincing evidence of the proximity of Asia and no new
exploitable lands. The garrison on Hispaniola was undermined in
health and rebellious in spirit; relations with the Indians had degener-
ated into open warfare. Columbus did not feel able to extricate
himself until March 1496, by which time the natives, at least, thanks
in large part to the energy of Alonso de Hojeda, had been reduced to
quiescence. He left his brother, Bartolomé, in charge.

The context of the next fragment, preserved in a copy made by Las
Casas, is the slave trade which Columbus organised prior to his
departure, apparently in a desperate effort to set up some sort of
viable trade which would attract merchants to Hispaniola and ensure
supplies for the troops. Evidently Columbus was troubled in his
conscience by recourse to this questionable remedy, as well as aware
that the enslavement of innocent Indians was rejected by the monarchs for reasons of conscience and policy alike. The travails of which
Bartolomé had apparently complained are likely to have arisen from
the problems of controlling the ill-disciplined and mutinous garrison.
Columbus addressed his brother with undeniable feeling, stirred, no
doubt, by his own experience of the same problems.

The Columbus who wrote this poignant letter was far from the
swaggering *parvenu* who had paraded before the world so proudly on
his return from his first voyage. The disappointments of the second
voyage had left him subdued and apprehensive. At court, he appeared
constantly in penitential garb; and he supplicated tirelessly for leave

to make a third voyage, which should vindicate his faltering claims, and transform the settlement on Hispaniola by establishing a stable colony with a systematic agrarian economy. By the time he wrote to Bartolomé, he was aware that his pleas were being heeded and that he would soon be given leave to sail again.

Fragments of a letter to Bartolomé Colón, Seville, February 1498*

... In this and in all else a very exact account has to be kept, without keeping anything from their Highnesses or anybody else. And in all things the demands of conscience must be looked to, for there is nothing good that is not to the service of God, to whom all the things of this world are as nothing and He is for everlasting ...

Our Lord knows how much anxiety I have suffered wondering how you are. So these problems, though I may seem to make heavy weather writing about them, have been far worse in reality: so much so that they made me weary of life because of the great trouble I knew you must be in, in which you should think of me as united with you. To be sure, although I have been away over here, I left and keep my heart over there constantly, without a thought for any other thing, as our Lord is my witness, nor do I believe that you will have any doubt of it in your heart. For besides our ties of blood and great love, the effects of fortune, and the nature of danger and hardship in places so far removed, embolden and oblige man's spirit and sense to endure any trouble that can be imagined, there or in any other place. It would be a thing of great advantage if this suffering were to be for a cause which redounded to the service of our Lord, for whom we ought to labour with a joyful mind. Nor would it be other than a comfort to remember that no great deed can be accomplished except with pain. Again, it is some consolation to believe that whatever is achieved laboriously is treasured and esteemed the sweeter for it. Much could be said to the purpose, but as this is not the first cause for which you have suffered or which I have seen, I shall wait to speak of it with more time to spare, and by word of mouth.

Before departing on his third ocean crossing Columbus, in his new role as a Castilian nobleman, made an entail of his estate. Such documents were regularly drawn up by notaries in accordance with well tried formulae. Columbus's, however, while influenced by professional help, bears the hallmark of his personal literary creation. Indeed, it appears to have been dictated to the notary. Some of its provisions are bizarre, and much of its language unprofessional. It is prolix and repetitive, even by the standards of Spanish legal documents of the time. Yet, like so much of Columbus's writing, it grips the reader's attention, as vivid glimpses of the writer's personality and mental world unfold.

Seven themes, all familiar from elsewhere in Columbus's work, emerge. First and foremost is the obsession with lineage. The document in which he creates his entail is for Columbus the foundation of an aristocratic dynasty. Succession shall be limited, in normal circumstances, to the nearest legitimate male heir and to those who 'call themselves and shall always have called themselves' by the name of Colón. Columbus stresses that the procedures he enjoins are normal 'for persons of title'. He repeatedly envisages the transmission of the entail 'in perpetuity' and 'from generation to generation'. He explicitly compares himself with Don Fadrique Enríquez, the hereditary Admiral of Castile. Egregious social ambition was one of the great driving forces of his life.

The second theme is constituted by his references to the terms of his bargain with his monarchs. Obviously, this was highly germane to his purpose: it was the basis of his claim to inheritable titles of nobility and to the material rewards on which he hoped to establish the greatness of his house. Columbus's insistence, however, seems to go beyond what the occasion required, and to betray his anxiety over his prospects of exacting performance of his contract in the future. Hence in part, perhaps, his dwelling on the extent of his discoveries, which was evidence that he had fulfilled his side of the bargain with his patrons, and the hint of divine authority for his claim to have discovered the Indies. Columbus's prospects of obtaining in practice the rewards to which he staked a claim were rendered more problematical by his extraordinarily generous estimate of what was due to him: according to the document in question, twenty-five per cent of all the yield of the New World. Ferdinand and Isabella were never prepared to admit that they had conceded more than a tenth part of their own share of one fifth of whatever might be obtained by conquest.

Though this in itself was enough to make any individual or family wealthy, the amounts of money with which Columbus juggled in his imagination were fantastic. Unrealistic pecuniary ambitions are the third great theme of the document. He envisages fortunes of millions being piled up by collateral branches of his family, the dowries of poor relations being provided for, charitable endowments lavishly accrued, and money accumulated for a campaign to liberate Jerusalem.

This esoteric reference should perhaps be considered in conjunction with the fourth theme – that of Columbus's cryptic signature which all his direct heirs were ordered to use. The Admiral pointedly fails to elucidate the meaning of this device. The mystery he contrived has continued to elude commentators. Alain Milhou has recently argued that the arrangement of symbols is meant to correspond to the iconography of the coronation of the Virgin, with each 'S' representing one person of the Trinity grouped around the Virgin's crown, and the 'X' and 'Y' standing for Saints Christopher and John the Baptist respectively – both, like Mary, 'bearers' of or for Christ to the world.* Columbus commonly signed himself 'Xpo ferens' – bearer for Christ; nor would it be inconsistent with his character for him to imagine himself in saintly company. If this interpretation is correct, it does not necessarily exclude other possible readings of the signature, which may well have been intelligible at a variety of levels.* Columbus dedicated the voyage he was to make in May 1498, his third Atlantic crossing, to the Holy Trinity. Together with the aggressively austere manners he adopted at the time, his effort to perpetuate the use of the mystic signature is strong evidence of his growing revulsion, under the influence of disillusionment, from worldly standards of success. His interests were shifting towards the evangelical possibilities opened up by his discoveries and towards his own potential role as a prophet.

This reflection has, however, to be set against the limited vision of the future of the Indies revealed in the document creating an entail. It was not, of course, an appropriate context for a detailed exposition of Columbus's plans for the colony he had founded; it is remarkable, however, that only three small religious foundations are specifically envisaged in the document; that these include substantial provision for masses for members of the Columbus dynasty, and only very modest provision for putting the evangelisation of the New World on a sound doctrinal footing; that the overall provision is so niggardly by comparison with the amounts bequeathed for the glorification of the Columbus dynasty; and that one of the major purposes to which

Columbus's proposed foundation of the Church of Santa María de la Concepción was to be consecrated was the display of the terms of the entail as a perpetual memorial. Similarly, the document provides for the division of tithes to the enrichment of Columbus's brother Bartolomé and his heirs, pending the accumulation of a substantial fortune.

Finally, the document is concerned with two themes which might have been linked in Columbus's mind: pride in his Genoese origins and implicit dissatisfaction with his Spanish sovereigns. The first is shown by Columbus's repeated asseverations of his Genoese birth, his praise of Genoa and of the Bank of San Giorgio, and his desire to maintain a house in Genoa, at the expense of his estate, for ever. Columbus's professed expectation that Genoa will help his lineage in the future may be intended to have, for the monarchs, an admonitory resonance in conjunction with his assurance that he came from Genoa to serve them. The implication is that the trajectory can be reversed and his services returned, if inadequately appreciated in Spain, to the city of his birth. The Admiral's reproach to the monarchs for their delay in adopting his plans inaugurates the note of bitterness which came to dominate his attitude to his patrons; and his insistence that 'they have gone on granting me favours and much increase' is transparently insincere: Columbus is not offering thanks for favours received but trawling for more. Attempts to heap coals of fire on the monarchs' heads, particularly by thanking them for unfulfilled promises, became a dominant technique of Columbus's supplications to Ferdinand and Isabella.

Document creating an entail: Seville, 22 February 1498*

In the name of the Holy Trinity, who put into my mind the thought, which later became perfect knowledge, that I could sail to the Indies from Spain by crossing the Ocean Sea to the west: And thus I informed our lord King Ferdinand and our lady Queen Isabella, and they were pleased to give me the means and equipment, in the form of men and ships, and to make me their Admiral in the said Ocean Sea, beyond a line which was drawn from pole to pole a hundred leagues beyond the islands of Cape Verde and those of the Azores, past which to the westward I should be their Admiral. And they ordered that in such mainland or islands as I might discover and find from there onwards, I should be their Viceroy and Governor in those lands, and that in the said appointments my eldest son should succeed me, and so on from generation to generation forever; and that I should have the tenth part of whatever should be found or had or yielded by way of profit in the said area over which my Admiral's role extended, and similarly the eighth part of the lands and all the other things, and the salary which it is proper to attach to the offices of Admiral, Viceroy and Governor in consideration of all the other rights pertaining to the said offices, according to all that is contained at greater length in the letter of privilege and contract which I have from their Highnesses.

And it pleased our Lord Almighty that in the year 1492 I should discover the mainland of the Indies and many islands, among which is that of Hispaniola, which the Indians who live there call Heiti [sic]. Afterwards I returned to Castile, to their Highnesses, and they returned the enterprise to me to undertake colonisation and make more discoveries. And so our Lord gave me victory, whereby I could conquer and impose submission on the people of Hispaniola, which measures six hundred leagues around, and I discovered many islands of cannibals and seven hundred islands to the west of Hispaniola, among which is that of Jamaica, which we call Santiago. And I explored three hundred and thirty-three leagues of the mainland, from the southern side towards the west, as well as a hundred and seven on the northern side which I had discovered on the first voyage along with many islands, as will be seen at greater length in my writings and nautical charts.

And WHEREAS we hope in the same high God that before very long there will be forthcoming a great and goodly profit from the islands and mainland, of which, for the reasons aforesaid, the said tenth part, eighth part, salaries and rights belong to me; and because we are mortal men it is well for every man to order his estate and leave for his heirs and successors a declaration of what he shall and may have and hold.

THEREFORE it came to me to compose an entail of this eighth part of lands and offices, as I shall say hereinafter.

First, that my son, Don Diego, shall succeed me, and, if our Lord should take him before he has a son, that my son, Don Fernando, shall succeed thereafter; and that if our Lord should take him without his having a son, then my brother, Don Bartolomé, and after him his eldest son; and if our Lord should take him without his having an heir, that my brother Don Diego shall succeed, being married or able to contract marriage; and that his eldest son shall succeed him. And so on from generation to generation perpetually for evermore — beginning with Don Diego, my son, and with his offspring succeeding him one after the other in perpetuity; or in the event of his direct heir's death, that my son Don Fernando should succeed, as aforesaid, and similarly his son; and that the succession should continue from son to son forever, both he and the aforesaid Don Bartolomé, should the title come to him, and the aforesaid Don Diego, my brother.

And if it should please our Lord that after this entail shall have passed at any time to one of the said successors, and it shall happen that the line of legitimate heirs shall have failed, then the nearest relative of the person who inherited it, and in whose possession it was at the time of the failure of the line, shall have and succeed to the said entail, provided he is a man of legitimate birth who shall call himself and shall always have called himself by the name of a father and ancestors called by the name of the house of Colón. The said entail shall in no circumstances be inherited by any women, unless here or in any corner of the world no man may be found of my authentic lineage who, together with his ancestors, shall call and have called himself by the name of Colón. And if this should occur, which God forbid, then the said entail shall be inherited by the woman most closely related by legitimate ties of blood to the person who would have succeeded thereto.

And this shall be subject to the conditions which shall hereinafter be specified, which shall be taken as applying equally to my son, Don Diego, and to all the aforesaid or whoever shall succeed, severally. The which conditions they shall fulfil; and whoever shall fail to fulfil them shall be deprived of the said entail and it shall pass to the closest relative of such person as shall have forfeited it through failure to comply with what I shall specify herein; the which successor shall also be charged, should he fail to comply with these conditions which I shall specify hereinafter, with the forfeiture thereof, and the person next closely related to my line shall succeed, provided he conform to the conditions which shall thus endure forever. And so it shall be, in the form aforesaid, in perpetuity. The which penalty shall not apply in minor matters which could be the subject of lawsuits, but only for some substantial cause which shall affect the honour of God and my own and that of my lineage, such as failure freely to carry out the dispositions made by me, fittingly in accordance with my words, all of which I commend to the courts of law.

And I petition the Holy Father now incumbent and all who shall succeed him in the Holy Church, now and as the occasion arises, that this my bond and testament shall be held binding under his holy ordinances and commands; that it shall be ordered by him subject to the obedience owed him and under pain of papal excommunication and that it shall never be in any way transgressed. And similarly I beseech the lord King and the lady Queen and the lord Prince Don Juan, their heir apparent, and all who shall succeed them, that it may please them, because of the services I have rendered them and because it is just, that neither they nor he nor any of them shall consent to any deformation of this my binding entail and testament, but rather that it shall remain as it is and in the fashion and form which I have ordered it to have for ever, so that it shall be for the service of our Lord God Almighty, and root and basis of my lineage, and a memorial of the services I have performed for their Highnesses. For I, who was born in Genoa, came to serve them here in Castile and for them discovered in the west the Indies and islands as aforesaid. And so I beseech their Highnesses that without initiation of any action at law and without further petition or any delay, they may summarily command that this my deed of gift and testament shall be valid and shall be executed, as is and shall be contained herein; and similarly I beseech all the great lords of the kingdoms of his Highness and the members of his Council and all others who have or shall have charge of justice or of government, that it shall please them not to consent that this my will and devising shall be void or unenforceable, and that it shall please them that it shall be executed as ordained by me. For it is very just that whatever shall be ordained and made by way of will or bond or entail or inheritance by a person of title, who has served his King and Queen and the realm, should be valid and should not be transgressed in any way in part or whole.

First, Don Diego, my son, and all who shall succeed me or descend from me, and similarly my brothers Don Bartolomé and Don Diego, shall bear my arms which I shall leave at the end of my days, without omitting any element of them, and my son, Don Diego, or whoever shall inherit this entail, shall use as his seal the seal thereof. And, having inherited it, and being in possession of it, he shall use as his own the signature which it is my present custom to use, which is an

.X. with an .S. above it and an .M. with a Roman .A. above it and above that an .S. and after it a .Y. with an .S. above, with the appropriate dots and obliques [*sic*], as I do at present and will appear in my signatures, examples of which can be found and will appear at the end of the present document. And he shall write no title save 'The Admiral', no matter what other titles he gain or be given by the King, and this is to apply to his signature but not to his designation, in which he may use all his titles according to his pleasure, but in his signature he must write only 'Admiral'.

The said Don Diego or whoever else shall inherit this entail shall have my appointments as Admiral of the Ocean Sea, which applies to the west of an imaginary line which their Highnesses ordered to be established a hundred leagues beyond the Azores and the same distance beyond the islands of Cape Verde, extending all the way from pole to pole. Beyond this line they ordered me to be and made me their Admiral in the sea, with all the rights and powers which belong to the Admiral Don Enrique in the office of Admiral of Castile, and they made me their Viceroy and Governor forever in perpetuity, in all the islands and mainland alike, discovered and yet to be discovered, for me and my heirs, as appears at greater length in my letters of privilege, which I have, and in my commission, as is said above.

Item: the said Don Diego, or whoever shall inherit the said entail, shall divide the income which our Lord shall be pleased to give him from it in this manner, subject to the said penalty:

First, of everything that the said entail shall yield now and in the future, and all that shall be had or gained from it or through it, he shall give one quarter every year to Don Bartolomé Colón, Adelantado of the Indies, my brother, and shall continue to do so until such time as this income amounts to one million *maravedis* for his maintenance and in consideration of the work he has done and continues to do for the benefit of this entail. He shall receive the said income every year, as is said, if the said quarter amounts to so much, provided he had no other income. But if he has part or all of this sum in income of his own, he shall not receive the said million nor part of it — assuming that henceforth the said sum of one million shall be contained in the said quarter if there is sufficient for it — but as much as he shall receive apart from this said quarter in clear income from returns on property or from hereditary offices shall be subtracted.

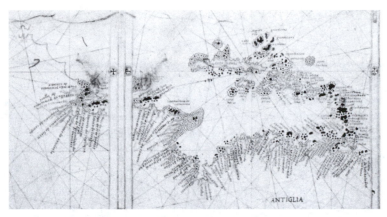

Chart showing the West Indies and north coast of South America
from a portolan atlas of c. 1508

Natives of the New World, detail of a map by Pedro Reinel c. 1519:
'People wear necklaces . . . around their heads and bracelets on their
arms and legs, all of thick gold'

One of the earliest representations of American cannibals: 'I have found no report even of any monsters, except for one island, which is "Carib" . . . which is inhabited by people who in all the islands are accounted very fierce and who eat human flesh'

And the said sum of one million shall be considered apart from any dowry or marriage portion which he shall have jointly with the woman he marries and shall have as his wife, so that whatever he possesses jointly with such said wife, it shall not be understood to imply that on that account anything should be subtracted from the said million, but only what he shall earn or have other than through his said marriage with his wife. And after it shall please God that he or his heirs or descendants shall achieve an income from property or offices under the crown of one million *maravedis*, as has been said, if God so will, then neither he nor his heirs shall receive anything more from the said quarter of the entail, and the said Don Diego, or whoever shall inherit it, shall have it.

Item: from the income of the said entail or a further quarter of it, Don Fernando, my son, shall have a million a year, if the said quarter amounts to so much, until such time as he is receiving an income of two million in the same manner or wise as is said above of Don Diego – or, rather, I mean Don Bartolomé – my brother, and this shall apply alike to him and his heirs, in the same way as to my brother Don Bartolomé and his heirs, and they shall also have the said million or the part thereof that shall correspond to their portion.

Item: the said Don Diego and Don Bartolomé will so dispose that of the income from the said entail my brother Don Diego shall receive as much as shall enable him to live honourably, in an estate befitting a brother of mine, which he is. I leave him no fixed inheritance of his own because it was his wish to enter the Church. And they shall give him what is reasonable and it shall be taken from the full amount, before anything is given to Don Fernando, my son, or Don Bartolomé, my brother, and their heirs, and it shall be proportionate to the total sum yielded by the said entail. And if there should be any disagreement about the amount, the matter shall in that case be referred to the arbitration of two persons of property, of whom one shall represent one side and the second the other, and if they should be unable to agree, the said arbitrators shall choose a third person of property who shall be suspect to neither party.

Item: all this income which I order to be given to Don Bartolomé and Don Fernando and Don Diego, my brother, shall be held by them and given to them, for as long as they remain loyal and faithful to Don Diego, my son, or their heirs to those who succeed him. And if it should be found that they were to go against him in a matter which adversely affected his honour and the increase of my line and which led to the diminution of my said estate, whether by word or deed that was or seemed to be to the shame or abasement of my line and the diminution of the said estate, or if any one of them were to do so, then from thenceforth he should no longer receive any portion, so that they might always remain faithful to Don Diego or to whoever shall succeed.

Item: whereas, when I began to make this my testament and the entail of my estate, I had intended that I or my son Don Diego or whoever else should succeed should distribute the tenth part of the income as a tithe for the worship of our eternal and almighty God and for needy people, and therefore I now declare that for the fulfilment and furtherance of my intention, and so that His Divine Majesty shall aid me and those who shall inherit my estate in this world and the next, the said tithe shall continue to be paid in this manner:

First, of the quarter of the income of this entail which I order and command to be given to and held by Don Bartolomé until such time as he is in receipt of an income of one million, it shall be understood that within that million shall be contained the whole of the tithe of the said entailed estate; and as the income of the said Don Bartolomé so rises that part or all of the yield from the said quarter shall be deducted, an inspection and account shall be made to establish the total of the income aforesaid in order to verify the amount which shall correspond to the tithe thereof, and as much of it as shall not fall within, or shall be surplus to, the portion belonging and due to Don Bartolomé towards his million, shall be received by needy persons of my line and charged against the said tithe; and these shall be the neediest and most urgent of such cases, care being taken to restrict the gifts to those who have incomes of less than fifty thousand *maravedis* a year. And if the person with the lowest income shall have as much as fifty thousand *maravedis*, the portion shall be received by whoever shall seem best to the two persons who shall be appointed hereinafter for this purpose with Don Diego or whoever shall succeed.

So, to make it clear, the million which I have ordered to be given to Don Bartolomé is and includes the aforesaid amount of the tithe of the said entail, which I wish and have ordered to be distributed from the total income of the said entail to persons related to me, in order of the proximity of their relationship to the successor in the said entail, who shall be most in need. And after Don Bartolomé shall have come to be in receipt of one million in income and nothing more shall be owed to him from the said quarter, then and in anticipation of such time, my said son, Don Diego, or such person as shall hold the said entail, with the other two persons whom I shall specify hereinafter, shall inspect and dispose the account in such a way that the tithe of the entire income shall continue to be given to, and shall be received by, the neediest persons of my line who shall be in this or any other part of the world, where they shall be sought with diligence. And this tithe shall be part of the said quarter from which the said Don Bartolomé shall have his million, which I give him without deduction of the said tithe, with the provision that if the said tithe should be surplus to his portion, then that surplus should also be deducted from the said quarter and should be received by the most needy as defined above, and if there is no such surplus, then Don Bartolomé shall continue to receive the tithe until such time as his own income shall come to be deducted from the said million leaving part or all of it intact.

Item: the said Don Diego, my son, or the person who shall succeed, shall have two persons of my line, from among those most closely related, who shall be persons of character and authority, and who shall inspect the said income and account thereof with all diligence and who shall ensure that the said tithe of the said quarter, from which the said million shall be given to Don Bartolomé, shall be paid to the neediest of my line who shall be here or in any other place, and they shall enquire to find them with much diligence and at their souls' charge. And since it may happen that the said Don Diego, or the person who shall succeed, may for some reason not wish them to reveal his wealth and the scale of his estate and the support yielded by the said entail, and may wish that the income therefrom should not be altogether known, I order that to whoever shall succeed the said income shall be given, and that they shall not divulge nor publish it, at their souls' charge, unless the said Don Diego or the person who shall succeed so wills, but should only ensure that the said tithe shall be paid in the aforesaid manner.

Item: so that no differences shall arise over the selection of these two very close relatives who must assist Don Diego or the person who shall succeed, I declare that I at once elect Don Bartolomé, my brother, to be one of them and Don Fernando, my son, to be the other, and as soon as they begin to take up this duty they shall be obliged to nominate two other persons who shall be the most closely related to my line and of the greatest reliability, and they shall choose two more when it shall be the time for them to begin to do this task.

And so one shall follow another, alike in this and in all else that pertains to the regulation and good and honour of the service of God and of the said entailed estate for evermore.

Item: I charge the said Don Diego, my son, or the person who shall inherit the said entail, that he should have and keep forever in the city of Genoa a person of our lineage who shall keep there his marital home; and that he should grant him an income with which to live honourably, as befits a person related to our house, and that he should establish roots and base in the said city like a native thereof; for help and favour may be forthcoming from that city in matters which are of concern to him, for I came from there and therein was I born.

Item: the said Don Diego or whoever shall inherit the said entailed estate shall send by way of bills of exchange or by any other means he can, as much of the income from the said entail which he shall save, and have purchases made in his name and that of his heir of certain investments which are called *luoghi* which are available in the Bank of San Giorgio, which at present yield six per cent and they are very secure investments; and this shall be for reasons I shall declare hereinafter.

Item: because for a person with an estate and income it is meet for the service of God and for the increase of his wealth that he should have the foresight to act for himself, and should be able to use his fortune so as to make it grow, there in the Bank of San Giorgio any money is very safe and Genoa is a noble city, powerful at sea. And this also because at the time when I was moved to go to discover the Indies, I went with the intention of petitioning the lord King and lady Queen that with the income their Highnesses would obtain from the Indies they should resolve to spend it on the conquest of Jerusalem. And I so beseeched them. And if they do it, may prosperous circumstances attend it. And if not, let the said Don Diego, or whoever shall succeed, continue to maintain the policy of increasing the money as much as he can so as to be able to go with our lord King to Jerusalem, if he should make an expedition to conquer it, or else to go on his own with as much force as he can raise and as shall be our Lord's pleasure; for if he maintains this intention, God will give him the means to undertake and accomplish it. And if he does not have enough for the conquest he will at least be given part of it. And so let him invest and accumulate his treasure in the *luoghi* of the Bank of San Giorgio in Genoa, and there let it multiply until he has an amount sufficient, as shall appear to him or as he shall know, to perform some good work in the matter of Oran.* For I believe that once the lord King and lady Queen and their successors see that this task has been resolved upon, their Highnesses will be moved to perform it or they will grant help or means to him who, as their servant and vassal, shall perform it in their name.

Item: I charge Don Diego, my son, and all who shall be my descendants, especially such as shall inherit this entail, which, as I have said, is composed of the tenth part of all that shall be found and had in the Indies and, in another connection, the eighth part of the lands and income, all of which with my rights belonging to my offices as Admiral and Viceroy and Governor comes to more than twenty-five per cent, and declare that the whole of this income and their persons and all the power at their command they shall commit and devote to the support and service of their Highnesses and their successors, well and faithfully, even to the loss and expenditure of their lives and wealth. For, under Almighty God, their Highnesses gave me the means and right to conquer and achieve this entailed estate, even though I came to these realms to offer this enterprise to them and they spent a long time without giving me the means to put the work into effect. Yet this is not to be wondered at, for this enterprise was something unheard of in all the world, and there was no one who would believe in it, wherefore I am all the more in their debt, and subsequently because they have gone on granting me many favours and much increase.

Item: I charge that if for our sins there should ever arise within the Church of God any person of whatever rank or estate, who, by some act of tyranny, shall seek to dispossess the Church of her estates or possessions, the said Don Diego, or whoever shall possess the aforementioned entail, shall, under pain of the penalty aforesaid, lay himself at the feet of the Holy Father – unless the latter should be a heretic, which God forbid – and resolve and be disposed to serve him in deed, with his or their person or persons, and with all his or their might and income and property, in the effort to free the Church from schism and prevent her from being dispossessed of her estates and possessions.

Item: I charge the said Don Diego or whoever shall possess the said entail always to work and labour for the honour and good and increase of the city of Genoa, and to venture all his goods and all his might in the defence and increase of the honour and welfare of the

Republic thereof, without doing anything contrary to the service of the Church of God and the high estate of the lord King and lady Queen and their successors.

Item: that at the time when Don Bartolomé and his heirs shall have saved their two million or part thereof and the aforesaid tithe shall be available for distribution among our relatives, from the income from the quarter which, as I said above, shall provide the tithe, the said Don Diego or the person who shall inherit or be in possession of the said entail, with the two persons who, being relatives of ours, shall join with him, shall be obliged to distribute and disburse this tithe for the marriage of young women of our line who shall be in need of such help, and they shall be obliged to favour them as much as they can.

Item: that at the time when sufficient funds shall be available, I charge that a church shall be built, which shall be called Santa María de la Concepción, in the most suitable place on the island of Hispaniola; and that a hospital shall be built, as well set up as may be, just like others which are in Castile and in Italy; and that a chapel shall be set up in which masses shall be offered very devoutly for my soul and that of our ancestors and descendants, and so that our Lord shall be pleased to grant us so great an income that all that I have declared above may be fulfilled.

Item: I charge the said Don Diego, my son, or whoever shall inherit this entail, that he should labour to maintain and sustain on the island of Hispaniola four good masters of sacred divinity, who shall intend and apply themselves to the work of providing for the attempt to convert all the peoples of the Indies to our Holy Catholic faith. And when it shall please our Lord that the income from the said entail shall have grown, then the number of masters and devout persons and the effort to impart their souls' health to this nation shall be increased accordingly; and to this end let there be no regret at the expenditure of whatever cost shall be required. And to preserve the memory of this my declaration, and of all that is written above, let there be a block of marble stone in the said church of Concepción, in the most conspicuous position, to bring my declared will to mind continually to the said Don Diego and all other persons who shall see it, on the which stone shall be an inscription which shall declare it.

Item: I charge Don Diego, my son, or whoever shall inherit the said entail, that each and every time he has to go to confession, he shall first show this binding document, or a copy of it, to his confessor, and shall ask him to read the whole of it, so that he shall have a basis of information on which to examine him concerning the observance of it, and may it be a source of much good and solace for his soul.

Dated the 22nd of February of 1498.

.S.
.S.A.S.
X M Y
El Almirante

VI

THE THIRD
ATLANTIC CROSSING

Columbus has left two accounts of his third ocean crossing: the first is in the form of a partial copy by Las Casas of a letter written to Ferdinand and Isabella on arrival in Hispaniola and sent to Spain in October 1498; the second survives in a few fragments extracted from a journal and included in a work of Las Casas. Both documents capture a period of concentrated change in Columbus's life, when religious priorities were coming to dominate his way of perceiving and presenting himself and when his geographical ideas seem briefly to have been returned to the crucible because of genuine doubts of his own about the true nature of his discoveries.

The letter* opens with a transparent attempt to rewrite the history of Columbus's lobbying at court in line with his new way of presenting himself as the hero of an evangelistic enterprise. Material considerations are waived; gold and Asia go unmentioned. The 'riches' to be expected from the Indies are reduced to a regrettable but necessary adjunct to the argument. The emphasis is on the 'word of God' legitimising Columbus's enterprise through prophetic scripture. The two friars referred to are probably the Franciscans, Juan Pérez, one of the Queen's confessors, and Antonio de Marchena, a court cosmographer, whose support for Columbus is confirmed elsewhere. It is typical of Columbus's way of dramatising his life from this time onwards that he should single out one or two heroic exceptions in an otherwise hostile world. He ignores other known backers of long standing – the members of the entourage of Prince Juan; the treasury officials of the crown of Aragon; Fray Diego Deza, whose constancy he praised on other occasions; the Genoese financiers at court; the ingenious manipulator of royal finances, Alonso de Quintanilla; the Duke of Medina Celi – all of whom contributed to the gradual growth of a party that favoured Columbus and helped to bring his ideas to fruition. The image of Columbus as an isolated figure, whose visionary greatness triumphs over hostility and derision, is one of the most successful elements of the explorer's own propaganda. The letter includes a claim that Columbus had brought allegedly prophetic texts about his discovery to the monarchs' attention on his return from the second voyage, in an attempt to counter the calumnies of his enemies. This seems to mark a further stage in the evolution of his interest in divination and of his sense of himself as an instrument of Providence.

The account of the third voyage made by the Admiral Don Cristóbal Colón on the third occasion of his coming to the Indies, when he discovered the mainland, as it was sent by him to the King and Queen, from the island of Hispaniola, between 31 August and 18 October 1498

Most Serene and Very High and Mighty Princes, our Lord and Lady, King and Queen, The Holy Trinity inspired your Highnesses to undertake the enterprise of the Indies and by His infinite goodness made me His messenger thereof, wherefore I was moved to bring the mission vouchsafed to me before your royal presence, as well as to the highest princes of Christian people and those who laboured mightily for the faith and the increase thereof. The persons who looked into it regarded it as impossible; and they set their store by the fruits of material success, and there the matter stuck. I spent six or seven years of terrible anguish on this, showing as best I could how much good service could be rendered thereby to our Lord, by spreading His Holy Name and Faith among so many people, all of which was a cause of very great excellence and good repute, and great and enduring fame for great princes. It was also necessary to argue on secular lines, and so the writings of many trustworthy authorities were cited, who wrote works of history in which they said that there were great riches in these parts of the world. And likewise it was necessary to bring to bear on this the sayings and views of those who had described the geography of the world in writing.

At last your Highnesses resolved that it should be put into effect. In this you showed the great heart you always put into every great cause, for all those who had looked into it and listened to the debate regarded it as a joke, without exception, save for two friars whose constancy never failed. Weighed down as I was by weariness, I felt well assured that no less would happen, and I remain convinced, for the truth is that all things shall pass away but not the Word of God, and all that He has said shall be fulfilled. He spoke so clearly of these lands through the mouth of His prophet Isaiah in so many places in His Scriptures, announcing that His Holy Name would be spread abroad from Spain.*

If there seems a hint of paranoia in Columbus's picture of himself as a victimised loner, the emphasis of the passage which follows, with its denunciations of unnamed enemies, its aggressive self-vindication, and its pointed reproaches of the monarchs (who are compared unfavourably with their Portuguese rivals), tends strongly to convey an impression of a writer embittered to the point of self-delusion. The speculation that he had found Solomon's Ophir introduces a line of thought to be developed later in this letter and throughout the rest of Columbus's life. There is a quixotic as well as an exotic touch about the reference to Alexander – not the classical hero but the character from chivalric romance – and in the emphasis on princely deeds of renown.

Columbus's statistics – the numbers of islands, the size of Hispaniola – are wildly exaggerated, just as the language is grossly inflated. By expressing his achievements in terms which emphasise the aggrandisement of the monarchs, Columbus seeks to indemnify himself against his enemies' calumnies. Capturing the monarchs' smiling assurances to him in a vivid vignette, he reminds them of their obligations to him. (The square brackets indicate lacunae in the original text, the phrases in italics within them are my efforts to supply them.)

And I departed in the name of the Holy Trinity and very soon I returned with proof of all I had said in my hand. Your Highnesses sent me back and in a short time, I declare, not [a long one], by the power of Divine help I discovered 333 leagues of the coast of the mainland at the end of the Orient, and gave names to 700 islands, in addition to what had been discovered on the first voyage. And I charted the island of Hispaniola, which has a longer coastline than

Spain, and in which there are people without number [*and I made them all submit to your Highnesses*] and all pay tribute. Evil words arose in Spain and belittlement of the enterprise which had been begun there, because I had not at once despatched ships laden with gold: no allowance was made for the brief time that had elapsed nor all else I had said of the many problems. And in this business – I believe it must have been for my sins or for my salvation – I was placed in abhorrence and obstacles erected against whatever I said or asked.

Therefore I decided to come before your Highnesses and express my incredulity at all this, and show you how I was right about everything; and I told you of the peoples whom I had seen whose many souls – some or all of them – could be saved. And I brought you the submissions of the people of the island of Hispaniola, by which they committed themselves to pay tribute and regarded you as their King and Queen and lord and lady. And I brought a sufficient sample of gold to show that there are very big mines and deposits of gold-dust, and likewise of copper; and I brought you specimens of many kinds of spicery which would take a long time to list; and I told you of the great amounts of brazil wood and an infinity of things beside. Not all this was good enough for some people, who had a fancy to speak ill of the enterprise and had begun to do so – not even when I began to speak of the service to be done for our Lord in saving so many souls, nor when I said that for the greatness of your Highnesses this was an enhancement of the highest calibre that ever a prince had attained: for the effort and expense were for spiritual as well as material gain, and it could not be but that Spain would have great advantages from this land as time went on, since the indications were so clear of what had been written of these regions that the rest was sure to be seen to be fulfilled.

Nor did it avail to point out the things which great princes customarily did in this world to increase their fame, such as Solomon, who sent from Jerusalem to the ends of the Orient to see the mountain of Sophara [Ophir], where his ships tarried for three years and which your Highnesses now possess in the island of Hispaniola; or Alexander who sent an expedition to see the government of Taprobana in the Indies; or the Emperor Nero to the sources of the Nile and to find out the reason why they increased in summer when water is scarce;* or many other great deeds accomplished by princes, for it is to princes that it is given to perform such things.

The third Atlantic crossing

Nor did it avail to say that I had never read that Princes of Castile had ever before won territory outside Spain, and that these lands over here are another world which the Romans and Alexander and the Greeks had striven to conquer, with great exercise of arms; nor to point out the present achievements of the Kings of Portugal, who had the heart to persevere in Guinea and in the discovery thereof, and who spent so much of treasure and of manpower that whoever counts the entire population of the kingdom will find that something like half their number have died in Guinea. And yet they continued with the enterprise until they got the results which now appear. They began it all a long time ago and only recently has it begun to yield revenue. They also ventured to make conquests in Africa and to persevere in the enterprises of Ceuta, Tangier, Arcila, and Alcazar and continually to make war against the Moors, and all at great cost, solely to accomplish what is proper to princes: to serve God and enlarge their realms.

The more I said, the more these calumnies they uttered were doubled and abhorrence shown, with no consideration for how well it appeared to the rest of the world and how well men spoke of your Highnesses throughout Christendom for having taken this enterprise in hand. For there was no one, old or young, who did not want an account of it. Your Highnesses answered me, smiling, and saying that I should not be anxious about anything, for you gave no heed or credence to those who spoke ill to you of this enterprise.

In contrast to the route adopted for his first two crossings, when Columbus had exploited the trade winds, he chose on this voyage to drop down to the equatorial zone, presumably in the hope of increasing his chances of finding gold – for he would then be on the same latitude as the auriferous regions of West Africa* – or of establishing the shortest possible route to the Orient. The results of this strategy were almost disastrous, for Columbus found himself becalmed in the doldrums.

I departed in the name of the most Holy Trinity on Wednesday, 30 May, from the town of Sanlúcar, after a journey which left me very weary, for, while I was hoping for some rest when I left the Indies, in fact my afflictions multiplied. And I sailed to the island of Madeira by an unaccustomed route to avoid any upset that might have occurred with a French fleet that was lying in wait for me off Cape St Vincent.

And from there I continued to the Canary Islands, from whence I departed with one round ship and two caravels; and I sent the other ships straight to the Indies, to the island of Hispaniola. And I sailed south with the intention of reaching the equator and then continuing westwards until the island of Hispaniola should lie to my north. And having arrived at the islands of Cape Verde – a misleading name for they are all so dry that I saw no green thing on any of them – with all my men sickening, I did not dare to tarry on them and sailed 480 miles to the south-west, which make 120 leagues, to a point where, at nightfall, I found the North Star was at an angle of five degrees. There the wind ceased to favour me and I began to experience a heat so great and so intense that I thought all my ships and men would be consumed by burning. And all at once everything became badly disordered for there was no man who would dare to go below deck to mend the casks or see to the stores. This heat lasted for eight days. On the first the sky was clear and on the seven following days it was raining and overcast. And we found no [*sic*] relief withal, for I think it certain that if it had remained clear, like on the first day, there would have been no hope for escape.

I recalled that in sailing to the Indies I found that each time I passed one hundred leagues to the west of the Azores the environment changed for the better all over, in both the more northerly and more southerly latitudes. And I decided, if it should please our Lord to grant me wind and fair weather to enable me to get away from where I was, that I would no longer attempt to go further south nor yet turn back, but sail westward until I reached that line, in the hope of finding there the same easing of conditions that I had found when sailing along the parallel of Gran Canaria; and that if it should so prove, I should then be able to head further south. And at the end of those eight days it did please our Lord to give me a fair east wind and I proceeded westward; but I did not dare to drop down towards the south, for I found a very great change in the sky and the stars, but no improvement in the weather. And so I settled for a continued course ahead, always straight towards the west, on the same parallel as Sierra Leone, with no intention of altering course until I got to where I had been expecting to find land. There I would make repairs and, if possible, put the stores to rights and take on water, which I was short of.

And after seventeen days on which our Lord gave me favourable winds, on Tuesday, 31 July, at midday, land was revealed. And I had been expecting it on the previous Monday and had been following my westerly course until that day at sunrise, when because of the shortage of water I decided to steer for the cannibal islands and took that route. And as Divine Majesty has always used me mercifully, a seaman climbed to the top of the mainsail to look out and he saw three mountains joined in the west. We said the *Salve Regina* and other canticles and all of us gave many thanks to our Lord. And then I left the northerly course and turned back towards the land, which I reached at the hour of compline, by a cape which I named Cape of La Galera, after having given the island the name of Trinidad. And there would have been a good harbour there, if it had been deeper, and there were houses and people and very fair fields, as handsome and green as the gardens of Valencia in March. I was sorry not to be able to enter the harbour and ran along the coast to the westward. And after five leagues I found a bottom of suitable depth and dropped anchor. And the following day I set sail on the same course, seeking a harbour where I would be able to caulk the ships and take on water and see to the corn and victuals I was carrying. At the first anchorage I took on only one pipe of water, with which I went on until I came to the farthest point of the coast, where I found shelter from the east wind and a good bottom [Erin Bay].* And so I ordered anchors to be lowered and the tackle pitched and wood and water to be taken on and the crews disembarked for a rest from the long time they had spent in discomfort.

Columbus's account of the people he found on this crossing dwells on their differences from the Blacks with whom, as they lived on the same latitude, they might have been expected to be comparable. Instead, Columbus seeks to give the impression that they are more like oriental peoples: they look like Moors, wear turbans, and display commercial sagacity.

I called this point the Punta del Arenal [Icacos Point], and all the land there looked as if it was smothered with creatures who had hooves like those of goats; and though there were a lot of them, to judge from appearances, we saw not one that was dead. The following day there came from the east a big canoe with twenty-four men aboard, all young and well equipped with weapons – bows and arrows and small shields – and all of them young men, as I said, of goodly appearance and not black but rather whiter than others I have seen in the Indies, and very fair of face and with handsome bodies and long, lank hair cut in the fashion of Castile. And they wore their hair tied with a cotton handkerchief, woven with patterns and colours, which I believed to be a turban. And they wore another similar strip at the waist and covered themselves with it instead of drawers.

When the canoe arrived, it hailed us from far off and neither I nor anyone else could understand them but I ordered signs to be made inviting them to approach. And two hours were taken up with this and if ever they drew a little nearer, they would back off again at once. I had tin pots shown to them and other shiny objects to attract them to come on, and after a long spell they drew in closer than they had been. And I badly wished I had had an interpreter, for by then I had nothing left that I could think of that might persuade them to approach us, except that I ordered a tambourine to be taken aloft on the forecastle to beat time while some young lads danced, hoping that they would come in closer to see the fun. And as soon as they saw the playing and dancing, they all laid down their oars and reached for their bows and strung them, and each of them took cover behind his shield and they began to shoot arrows at us. The playing and dancing stopped right away and I ordered crossbows to be got out at once. And they left my ship and went on further towards another caravel and suddenly darted under its bows. And the pilot got in with them and gave a cloak and bonnet to a man who appeared to be a leader among them. And he arranged that he would go to parley there on the beach, where they then went with the canoe to wait for him. And when they saw him come to my ship in his boat, because he was unwilling to go to his rendezvous without my leave, they got back into their canoe and went away, and I never saw them or any other people of this island again.

When I arrived at the Punta del Arenal, I observed that the island of Trinidad forms a large bight, two leagues broad from west to east, with a land I called the Tierra de Gracia, and that in order to get into it to complete the circuit of the island to the north, there were some currents to take into account, which crossed that bight and made a very loud crashing noise. And I supposed that there was probably a reef of rocks and shoals which would make it impossible to enter the bight and that behind it was another and another again, all of which caused the loud crashing noise, like a wave that goes and breaks and dashes against rocks. I dropped anchor off the aforesaid Punta del Arenal, outside the said bight, and I found that the current was flowing from east to west with all the fury of the Guadalquivir in flood. And it went on continuously, day and night, so that I thought I should be unable to get back, because of the current, or go forward, because of the reefs. And during the night, when it was already very late, and I was up on deck on my ship, I heard a terrible roar which was approaching the ship from the south, and I stopped to look, and I saw the sea arisen from west to east, like a broad hill as high as the ship. And still it came on towards me, little by little, and on top of it I could see the trend of the current, and on it came roaring with a mighty crash, like the fury of the crashing of those other currents which, as I said, seemed to me to be like waves of the sea that dashed against rocks. For to this day I can feel the fear in my body that I felt lest they should capsize the ship when they got underneath her. And it passed by and reached the mouth of the bight where it seemed to teeter for a long time.

And the following day I sent out boats to take soundings, and I discovered that in the shallowest part of the bight there were six or seven fathoms' depth, and that those currents were continuous, some flowing in and others out. And it pleased our Lord to grant me fair wind and I crossed into the bight, where I found the surface was calm and we took a sample of the water from the sea to see what it was like and found it sweet. I sailed northward as far as a very high range which must have been twenty-six leagues from the Punta del Arenal; and there were two promontories, both very high: one on the eastern side, which belonged to the island of Trinidad itself; and the other, on the western side, which belonged to the land I called Tierra de Gracia. And the bight at that point was very narrow, more so than at the Punta del Arenal; and the same currents were there and the same strong roar of the water as there was at the Punta del Arenal, and there too the water tasted sweet.

The first recorded European landing on the American mainland was made on 5 August, at an unknown site, apparently a small bay on the southern coast of the Paria peninsula: Ensenada Yacua is a probable candidate.*

And up to that time I had still had no speech with any of the people of these lands and I desired it greatly. And for that reason I sailed along the coast of this land, the Tierra de Gracia, to the westward, and the further I went the more I found the water sweet and palatable. And a long way on I reached a place where the fields seemed to be cultivated, and I anchored and sent the boats to the shore. And they found that people had recently gone away and they found all the woods full of wild cats. They came back. And while it was hilly there, it seemed to me that the ground was more level further to the west and that it would be settled country, for it would be settled for that reason. I ordered the anchors to be weighed and ran along the coast as far as the end of the range of hills, and there I anchored in the mouth of a river [River Guiria].* And a lot of people came at once, and they told me that they called the land Paria and that further west from there it was more densely settled.

I took four of them aboard and then set sail to the west. And a further eight leagues to the west, beyond a point which I named Punta del Aguja [Punta Alcatraz], I found lands which were the fairest in the world and very densely peopled. I arrived there one morning at the hour of terce and when I saw the greenness and the beauty of the place I decided to anchor and see the people. Some of them then came to the ship in canoes to invite me to come ashore in the name of their king. And when they saw that I was not on my guard against them, endless numbers of them came to the ship in canoes, and many of them wore pieces of gold round their necks, and some had some pearls threaded round their arms. I rejoiced greatly when I saw them and took great pains to find out where they found them, and they told me that it was there and in the northern part of that land.

I should have liked to linger, but the provisions I was carrying for our people over here, corn and wine and meat, which I had procured over there with so much trouble, were getting ruined; and for that reason my only purpose was to make way to get them delivered and not to linger for any reason. I did try to obtain some of those pearls and sent the boats ashore.

The people of this place are very numerous and all of very goodly appearance, of the same colour as those we saw before and very easy to deal with. Our men who went ashore found them very agreeable and were very honourably received by them. They say that after their boats reached the shore, two of the leading men came with the whole population – they believe that these two were father and son – and they took them to a very large house, built between two streams, and not round like a campaign tent as the others are. And they had plenty of chairs there, where they invited them to sit down, and others where they sat down themselves, and they had bread brought and fruits of many kinds and wines of many kinds, red and white, but not made from grapes. These must be made in various ways, one from one sort of fruit and another from another; and some again must be made from maize, which is a kind of grain which grows in a spiky cob resembling a spindle, and some of which I took over there to Castile, where there is now a lot of it. And it seemed that the best of the wine was served with greater ceremony and received with higher esteem. All the men sat together at one end of the building and the women at the other. Both sides felt great sorrow at not being able to understand one another, for the natives wanted to ask about our homeland and our men wanted to know about theirs.

And after they had been given that meal there in the older man's house, the younger took them to his and gave them another one. And after that they got into their boats and came to the ship. And I raised anchor at once, because I was in a great hurry to attend to the stores which were getting spoiled and which I had collected with so much effort; and also to put myself to rights, for I had become ill through never closing my eyes; for though I had gone thirty-three days without a thought for sleep during the voyage I made to explore the mainland,* and then lost my sight for the same length of time, my eyes did not give me so much pain then, nor did blood break out of them as much or as painfully as now.

These people, as I have already said, are all of very goodly stature, tall of body and fair of face, their hair very long and lank; and they wear their hair tied with cotton handkerchiefs, embroidered, as I said before, and attractive, which from a distance look like silk turbans. Others have a longer sash with which they cover themselves instead of wearing drawers, men and women alike. Their colour is paler than any other I have seen in the Indies. They all wore something after the fashion of these lands around their necks or arms, and many wore pieces of gold dangling from a necklet. Their canoes are very big, better built than these others here on Hispaniola, and lighter, and in the middle of each there is a cabin with a cubicle, in which I saw that the leading men travel with their wives.

I called this place Jardines, because its appearance suits the name 'gardens'. I put a lot of effort into finding out where they get that gold and they all pointed me towards a land bordering theirs to the west. It was very high, but not far away. But they all told me not to go there because there the inhabitants eat people; and then I understood that they were saying that the people were cannibals and that they must be like the others. And since then it has occurred to me that their meaning was that there were wild animals in that land. I also asked them where they got the pearls, and they again signed to the west and to the north, beyond the land they lived in. I deferred putting this to the test because of this business of the supplies and the pain in my eyes; and it would not be the sort of job for a big ship like the one I have with me.

And as the time available was short, it was all taken up with queries, and they returned to the ships, as I said, at what must have been the hour of vespers. I then weighed anchors and sailed to the west and the same the next day until I found that there were no more than three fathoms to the bottom, still expecting that this land would be an island and that I would be able to find a way out to the north. And having seen the soundings I sent a nimble caravel ahead to see if there was a way out or if it was enclosed, and so she went a long way as far as a very big gulf, within which there seemed to be four others of middling size, and from one of them a huge river led inland. They found five fathoms' depth throughout and everywhere water that was most sweet and so much of it that I never saw the like. I was very unhappy about it when I saw that I would be unable to get away to the north, nor could I now turn south or continue west, for I was hemmed in by land on those sides. And so I weighed anchor and went about the way I had come to find a way out to the north through the bight I mentioned above and I could not go back through the settlement where I had been because the currents had led me away from there. And always at every turn I found the water sweet and clear, and it bore me very strongly eastward towards the two bights which I mentioned above.

And then I conjectured that the visible lines of the current, and those walls of water that rose and fell in the bights with that roar that was so loud, must have been the effects of the clash of the fresh water with the salt water; the fresh water pushed against the salt to prevent it from entering; the salt water thrust against the fresh to stop it flowing out. I conjectured that where there are now those two bights, there must at one time have been continuous land joining the island of Trinidad with Tierra de Gracia, as your Highnesses will be able to see from the depiction of it which I am sending with this letter. I got out through this bight to the north and I found that the fresh water always won this struggle; and when I emerged it was with the force of the wind. When I was on top of one of those walls of water I found that in the stream of the current the inner channel was of fresh water and the outer of salt.

The third Atlantic crossing

The volume of fresh water discharged from the mouth of the Orinoco seems to have alerted Columbus to the immensity of the hinterland through which so mighty a river must flow. Unfortunately, this observation was occluded by the effects of others, less accurately made and productive of some fantastic inferences.

First, Columbus added an inaccurate observation about the climate. He seems always to have exaggerated the merits of the climate, wherever he was: in a marginal annotation to one of his books he claimed to have found the Gold Coast very healthy.* He insisted throughout his career that the climate improved as one got further into the Atlantic and, in particular, that the boundary of his own jurisdiction as Admiral, one hundred leagues beyond the Azores, marked the frontier of a temperate climatic zone. On this voyage, he claimed to find that the same effect was discernible even in the depths of the tropics, and that the neighbourhood of Trinidad was characterised by an equability inexplicable, according to the usual conventions, at such a latitude.

Secondly, he took into account observations of the variation of the Pole Star and of the magnetic compass which were a misleading blend of the accurate and the bizarre. He was quite right about magnetic variation,* but in supposing that he could measure accurately the angle of elevation of the Pole Star, aboard a moving ship with a simple quadrant, he was flattering himself. His finding – that the angle diminished irrespective of latitude – must have been a delusion. Instead of blaming imperfect observations or faulty instruments for the observed variations Columbus, like the doctrinaire empiricist he was, accepted the data and sought an explanation: he concluded that he must be sailing uphill.* In conjunction with his observation of the climate and the fact that the Orinoco had four mouths, reminiscent of the four rivers of Eden, he went on to infer that he must be approaching the earthly Paradise. He claimed to have written tradition on his side, for the earthly Paradise was almost universally acknowledged to lie 'at the end of the Orient'.* It was, however, a 'modern' conclusion, which arose from Columbus's conviction that observed reality was more trustworthy than written authority or unaided reason. In complimenting himself on having improved on the geographical knowledge of Ptolemy and Aristotle, Columbus was bestowing on himself what he must have regarded as the highest possible intellectual accolade.

When I have sailed from Spain to the Indies, I find that as soon as a line one hundred leagues west of the Azores is passed, a great change comes over the sky and the stars and the mildness of the air and in the waters of the sea. And I have put a great deal of effort into testing this. I find that as soon as the said hundred leagues from the said islands are traversed, in the more northerly and more southerly latitudes alike, the compass needles, which until then tended to vary to the north-east, turn a full quarter of a point to the north-west, and this begins to occur as one draws near to that line, like someone cresting the brow of a hill. And again I find that the sea is full of a weed of a kind that resembles pine branches very heavily laden with a growth like that of the mastic plant. And so thick is it that on my first voyage I thought it was a shoal and that I would run aground with my ships; and until one reaches that line not a single little branch of it is found. I have further found, on reaching that line, that the sea is very smooth and calm and although the wind may be strong, the sea never rises. Again, I have found that beyond the line to the west the weather is very mild and the temperature does not vary much, be it summer or winter. When I am there, I find that the North Star describes a circle of five degrees in diameter, and that when the Guards are in the right arm, it is at its lowest point, and then goes climbing until it appears on their left; and the angle of elevation is then five degrees; and from there it goes descending until it comes to return again to the right-hand side.

On this voyage I made for the island of Madeira from Spain, and from there to Gran Canaria and thence to the Cape Verde Islands. From there I undertook to make my voyage to the south until I was on the equator, as I have said. When I was close to the parallel of Sierra Leone in Guinea, I found the heat so intense, and the sun's rays so hot, that I expected to burn, and though the rain fell and the sky was very overcast, I remained in a state of exhaustion, until our Lord provided a fair wind and made it His will that I should sail to the west; and it was with this source of hope, that when I arrived at the line of which I was speaking above, I should there find a change in the atmosphere. Once I reached this line, I then found the state of the heavens very calm and the further I went, the more so it became, but I did not find that the stars conformed to this change.

There I found that as night fell I had the North Star at a height of five degrees, and at that time the Guards were directly above it; and later, at midnight, I found the star was ten degrees high; and at dawn, when the Guards were at its feet, fifteen.

I found the sea was as smooth as I expected, but there was no seaweed.

Over this matter of the North Star I was profoundly puzzled, and so for many nights on end I again took sightings with the quadrant and each time I found that the plumbline dropped a point. I take it to be a new discovery – and as such, perhaps, it will be taken – that the heavens should alter so much within so short a distance.*

I have always read that the world – land and sea together – was spherical. This appeared from the authorities and from experiments which Ptolemy and all the rest who wrote on this subject recorded and deployed to the purpose; their proofs were eclipses of the moon, and other phenomena which can be observed from east to west, and the consistency with which the angle of elevation of the Pole Star diminishes as one goes from north to south. Now I observed the very great variation which I have described and because of it began to ponder this matter of the shape of the world. And I concluded that it was not round in the way they say, but is of the same shape as a pear, which may be very round all over but not in the part where the stalk is, which sticks up; or it is as if someone had a very round ball, and at one point on its surface it was as if a woman's nipple had been put there; and this teat-like part would be the most prominent and nearest to the sky; and it would be on the equator, in this Ocean Sea, at the end of the Orient. By 'end of the Orient' I mean where all land and islands end.

To suggest this I would adduce all the reasons given above concerning the line that runs from north to south one hundred leagues west of the Azores; how in passing beyond it to the west, the ships begin gradually to ascend towards the heavens, and thereafter enjoy calmer weather; and how the compass needle moves; and how temperate the climate is in this quarter of the wind; and how the further one goes and the higher one climbs, the more the needle drifts to the north-west. And this climbing causes the North Star, in relation to the Guards, to vary and describe a circle. And the further one goes along the equator, the higher the ships will climb and the more variation there will be in the said stars and in the circles they describe.

And Ptolemy and the other sages who wrote of this world believed that it was spherical, believing that this hemisphere on this side was as perfectly round as it was back there where they lived, which took its central point as the island of Arin,* which is on the equator, between the Arabian Gulf and the Gulf of Persia. And its periphery touches

Cape St Vincent in Portugal on the west and passes through Catigara* and the land of the Chinese in the east. In that hemisphere I see no reason to believe that it is other than perfectly round, as they say. But of this other hemisphere I declare that it is as if it were the part of the otherwise perfectly round pear which has its stalk sticking up, as I said before; or like a female nipple on a round surface.

So Ptolemy can have had no knowledge of this hemisphere, nor did any of the other ancients who wrote about geography, for it was very much unknown. They took as the basis of their writings the hemisphere in which they lived, the surface of which is perfectly rounded, as I said above. And now that your Highnesses have ordered this part of the world to be sailed and sought and uncovered, it is being very fully revealed. For on this voyage I have been twenty degrees north of the equator, on a straight line from Arguim and lands of that sort, where the people are black and the land is badly scorched; and from there I went to the Cape Verde Islands, in parts where the people are far blacker still, and the further south they go the nearer they get to the extreme, so that right down there on a straight line from where I was, which is on the latitude of Sierra Leone, where at nightfall the North Star appeared to me at an altitude of five degrees, the people are as black as can be. And from that point I sailed westward, through heat of extreme intensity and once I had passed the line mentioned above, I found that the temperance of the climate increased manifold.

And I sailed on so far that when I reached the island of Trinidad, where at nightfall the North Star was still to be seen at an altitude of five degrees, there and in the land I called Gracia I found the most gentle climate. And the land and trees were very green and as fair as in April in the gardens of Valencia; and the people there were of very handsome appearance and of a whiter colour than any others I have seen in the Indies, with hair that is long and lank; and the people are more astute and of greater ingenuity and are not timid. At that point the sun was in Virgo, directly above our heads and theirs. And so from all the foregoing it appears that the very mild climate which is to be found there is a result of being higher up in the world, closer to the refined atmosphere which I am describing.

And therefore I affirm that the world is not spherical, but has this modification which I have explained and which is to be found in this hemisphere where the Indies are and in the Ocean Sea. And the highest part of it is on the equator. And it very much conduces to the same conclusion that the sun, when our Lord fashioned it, was positioned above the easternmost point of the world, at the very place where the highest point of the bulge of the world is located. And although it was Aristotle's opinion that the South Pole, or, rather, the land at the South Pole, is the loftiest part of the globe and the closest to heaven,* there are other authorities which disagree, stating that this is at the North Pole. It therefore appears that they understood that there must be some part of the world which is loftier and closer to heaven than the rest. But they did not hit upon the fact that it was on the equator in the form I have described. And their failure should not be wondered at, because they had no certain information of the existence of this hemisphere, except for shadowy speculations inferred by reason alone; because no one had been here or sent a mission to seek it until now, when your Highnesses ordered sea and land alike to be explored and discovered.

My finding is that these two river mouths, which, as I said, both touch the same meridian that runs from north to south, are separated by a distance of twenty-six leagues; and there can be no error about this, because the measurements were checked with the quadrant. And from these two river mouths in the west, eastward as far as the meridian of the gulf which I named Gulf of Las Perlas [the Pearls], there are sixty-eight leagues, each of four miles as is customary with us seafarers; and from there, at that gulf, the current runs fiercely and continuously towards the east; and that is why the water flowing from the river mouths has that clash with the salt water. In the more southerly river mouth, which I named La Sierpe [the Serpent], I found at nightfall that I had the North Star at an altitude of almost five degrees, whereas at the more northerly of them, which I named El Drago [the Dragon], it was at almost seven degrees. And it is also my finding that this Gulf of Las Perlas is to the westward of Ptolemy's limit of the west by almost 3,900 miles, equivalent to almost seventy degrees at the equator, reckoning each degree at fifty-six and two-thirds miles.

Columbus could not claim to have tested empirically his hypothesis about the location of Paradise; indeed, he regarded it as strictly unverifiable. He therefore suspended his empirical reasoning at this point in favour of an appeal to a rag-bag of written traditions, some of which Las Casas abbreviated to 'etc.' The range of authorities cited even in the mutilated text is, however, extensive enough. With few exceptions, the texts cited are Columbus's usual favourites, to which he appeals for any point he happens to be making at any moment. Most of them he knew only through intermediate authorities, particularly Pierre d'Ailly's *Imago Mundi* and the *Historia Rerum* of Pope Pius II. Thus Columbus made his little learning go a long way. And, as usually befell him when he tried to ape academic habits, he became distracted by irrelevancies – collecting, for instance, testimony in support of the canonical status of the prophecies of Esdras which had no bearing on the point he was here seeking to establish. Throughout the discussion, however, Columbus remained true to his empirical epistemology, citing texts in support of observations, not in place of them, and appealing at last to proverbial wisdom: 'as one goes, one's knowledge grows' ('*andando más, más se sabe*').

Holy Scripture bears witness that our Lord made the earthly Paradise and placed there the Tree of Life and that from it flows a fountain from which issue the four chief rivers of this world: the Ganges in India, the Tigris and Euphrates in . . . which divide the mountains and create the land of Mesopotamia and flow into Persia, and the Nile which rises in Ethiopia and joins the sea at Alexandria.*

I cannot find, nor have I ever found, any writings of Latins or Greeks which authoritatively claim that the earthly Paradise is anywhere else, save in this world. Nor have I seen it located in any world map, other than in a position justified by argument rather than experience. Some authorities locate it in Ethiopia, where the sources of the Nile are; but others have travelled all over those parts and found nothing, whether in the mildness of the atmosphere or in the elevation of the land towards the heavens, to suggest that the earthly Paradise was there, nor any evidence that the waters of the flood had reached there, which rose above, etc.* Certain pagan writers sought to argue by the use of reason that the earthly Paradise was in the Fortunate Isles, which are the Canary Islands, etc.*

St Isidore and Bede and [Walafrid] Strabo and the Master of the *Historia Scholastica* and St Ambrose and Scotus and all holy theologians agree that the earthly Paradise is in the Orient, etc.*

I have already stated my findings concerning this hemisphere and how it is shaped. And I believe that if I were to continue along the line of the equator, as I climbed further into the higher part, I would find the mildness of the atmosphere very much enhanced and much greater variation in the positions of the stars and a change in the nature of the waters. Not that I suppose that it would be possible to sail to where the altitude attains its highest point, nor that one could ever climb up there. For I believe that is where the earthly Paradise is, which no one can reach save by God's will.

And I believe that this land which your Highnesses have now ordered to be revealed must be very big, and that there must be many other such lands in southern parts, of which nothing has ever been known before.

And I am not supposing that the earthly Paradise has the form of an abrupt mountain, as is confirmed by what has been written about it. Rather, my view is that it is located at the summit, where, as I suggested, the likeness of the stalk of a pear is to be found, and that as one approaches, little by little, from a great distance, one finds oneself climbing towards it. And I believe that no one would ever be able to reach the summit, as I said. And I think it possible that the rivers I saw could rise from there, even though it must be a very long way away, and end up at the place I came to, and form the body of fresh water offshore.

These are powerful signs of the presence of the earthly Paradise; for the place accords with the opinions of those holy and sacred theologians. And what is more the indications are very persuasive, for I never read nor heard of so great a quantity of fresh water flowing into the sea and forming a continuous mass in the midst of it. And the same conclusion is supported by the very mild climate. And if it is not from Paradise that it flows, the marvel is even greater, for I do not believe that any river so big or so deep is known anywhere else in the world.

When I emerged from the Dragon estuary or Dragon's Mouth, as I called it, which is the more northerly of those two river mouths, on the feast of the Assumption of Our Lady, I found the current was flowing so strongly from west to east that from the hour of mass, when I set off on my way, until the hour of compline, I covered sixty-five leagues of four miles each, and the wind was not particularly strong, but rather very gentle. And this fact reinforces my realisation that as one goes south from there one is going uphill and that in heading north, as I was doing, one descends.

I take it to be a well known fact that the waters of the sea tend to flow from east to west with the course of the heavens. And over there, in the region I am speaking of, they flow more rapidly as they pass; and that is why they erode so much of the land, and as a result there are so many islands there; and the islands themselves attest this, for every one of them is stretched out in an east–west direction, and from north-west to south-east rising and falling only a little, and all are very narrow from north to south and from north-east to south-west, which is against the winds I have recorded. And in all of them precious products occur because of the mild climate which they derive from their proximity to the heavens, because they are close to the loftiest part of the world. It is true that in some places the waters do not seem to flow thus, and this is only in certain places where some piece of land is in the way and makes it look as if the currents are flowing in different directions.

Having added this empirical evidence of the proximity of the world's hump, Columbus turns to summarise his written authorities on behalf of his theory of a narrow Atlantic. Though strictly speaking irrelevant in the present context, this material was presumably introduced by Columbus because his claim to have discovered the approach to the earthly Paradise rested on the further claim that he was in the vicinity of Asia, which, he supposed, depended in turn on the narrowness of the ocean. Columbus was not the only believer in a narrow Atlantic in his day: Toscanelli appears to have shared a similar view. It was also cultivated in Nuremberg in a circle which included Martin Behaim and Hieronymus Münzer: these three were all highly respectable if rather avant-garde cosmographers.

Columbus's citations are almost all borrowed from Pierre d'Ailly, who in his turn was passing on authorities first collected by Roger Bacon. The cardinal's purpose was to argue that most of the surface of the world could be covered by land rather than sea: the narrowness of the Atlantic was a necessary inference. Like Chinese whispers, the authorities amassed here by Columbus had become garbled as they passed from one intermediate source to another. The opinion attributed to Aristotle, for instance, by d'Ailly, and adopted by Columbus, that 'the sea is small between the western extremity of Spain and the eastern part of India' is unconfirmed in any genuine surviving text of Aristotle's, whose known view seems rather to suggest the opposite.*

Pliny writes that all the sea and land together form a sphere, and he states that this Ocean Sea constitutes the major body of water and that it is placed towards heaven, and that land is below it and upholds it, and that the two are combined like the meat of a walnut with the thick covering which goes around it.* The Master of the *Historia*

Scholastica, on the Book of Genesis, says that the sum total of the waters in the world is very small, for although they covered the earth when they were created, they afterwards tended to evaporate like clouds and that subsequently, compacted and forced together, they took up very little space.* And Nicholas of Lyra concurs in this.*

Aristotle says that this world is small and its waters slight and that the passage from Spain to the Indies can be easily accomplished. This is confirmed by Averroës and cited by Cardinal Pierre d'Ailly, who gives authority to these statements, and another of Seneca's, which agrees with them, pointing out that Aristotle could have known many secrets of geography because of Alexander the Great, and Seneca similarly because of the Emperor Nero, and Pliny as a representative of Roman learning – for all of these expended much wealth and many lives and invested much trouble in their efforts to learn the world's secrets and pass them on to their people.* The said cardinal gives a great deal of weight to these authorities, more than to Ptolemy or any other Greeks or Arabs. And in support of the statement that the amount of water must be small and the extent of the earth which it covers must be small, despite the authority of Ptolemy and his followers, there is a text of Esdras which can be cited, from his third book, where it says that of seven parts of the world six are uncovered and the seventh is covered with water. The authority of this text is approved by holy men, who regard the third and fourth books of Esdras as canonical, such as St Augustine and St Ambrose in his *Exameron* where he says, 'There shall come Jesus, my son, and there shall my son, Christ, die'. And these state that Esdras was a prophet, as did Zacharias, the father of St John, and the Blessed Simon, who are authorities cited by Francisco Mairones.* As for this matter of the span of the earth, it has been demonstrated experimentally that it is very far removed from what is commonly supposed; nor is this to be wondered at, for 'as one goes, one's knowledge grows'.

I now turn back to my main subject, which is the Tierra de Gracia and the offshore body of fresh water I found there, which is more of the dimensions of a sea than a lake. For a lake is a place full of water and when it is particularly big it is called a sea, like the Sea of Galilee or the Dead Sea. And it is my opinion that, if that river does not flow from the earthly Paradise, then it must come from and rise in an enormous land, to be found in the south, of which until the present time nothing has been known. But I feel very settled in my own mind that there, where I have said, is the earthly Paradise, and I rest my case on the reasons and authorities aforesaid.

May it please our Lord to give long life and health and repose to your Highnesses, so that you shall be able to proceed further with this very noble undertaking, in which, it seems to me, our Lord is well served and Spain grows greatly in glory, and all Christian people gain much satisfaction and contentment because our Lord's name is here proclaimed. And in every land to which your Highnesses' ships travel, and on every cape, I am ordering a tall cross to be planted. And to all the people I encounter, I give notice of the estate of your Highnesses, and of how your justice is established in Spain; and I tell them all I can of our Holy Faith, and of the creed of our Holy Mother Church, which has members in all the world; and I tell them of the civilisation and honourable status of Christian people and of their faith in the Holy Trinity. And may it please our Lord to recall this to the memory of those who have impugned and do impugn so excellent an enterprise and impede it, and formerly did impede it, in an attempt to prevent it from going ahead, without considering how much honour and greatness it contributes to your Highnesses' royal estate in all the world. They cannot think of what calumnies to put in its way, save that it is a cause of expense and that ships laden with gold were not sent back at once; but they do not consider how little time has been available, or how many difficulties have arisen here; nor do they consider how in Castile, from your Highnesses' household, there are people who go forth each year who by their merits have each gained more from this enterprise in a single year than needs to be spent on it; nor, similarly, do they consider how no princes of Spain ever conquered any land beyond Spanish territory until now, when your Highnesses have here a new world, where our Holy Faith can be greatly increased, and whence such great profits can be derived. Although ships laden with gold have not been sent, enough samples have been forthcoming – of gold and other valuable products alike. From this it can be inferred that in a short space of time a large return can be expected – and all this without looking at the example of the greatness of spirit of the princes of Portugal, who have persevered for so long in the enterprise of Guinea and have persevered in that of Africa, where they have spent half the manpower of their kingdom. And today their king is more firmly resolved upon it than ever. May our Lord provide in this matter as I have said, and may He put it in their minds to consider all this which appears here in writing, which is not the thousandth part of all I could write of the deeds of princes who devoted themselves to acquiring knowledge and conquests and persevered therein.

All this I have said, and not because I have any doubt that your Highnesses' will is to persevere in this as long as you live. And I take as very sure what your Highness said to me once by way of reply when I spoke to you of all this by word of mouth. Nor is it that I have observed any alteration in your Highness, but only that I am afraid of what I have heard from the people to whom I have referred. For a drop of water can wear a hole even in a stone. And your Highness's reply to me, made with that greatness of heart which all the world knows you have, was that I should have no worries on this score; for your will was to continue in this enterprise and to sustain it, even if it were all bare rocks and crags; and that the expenditure it cost you was reckoned at nought, for your Highnesses spent much more on things of less account; and that you regarded it all as well spent, both past and future expenditure, because your Highnesses believed that our Holy Faith would be spread and your royal sway enlarged; and they who spoke ill of this enterprise were no friends to your royal estate.

And now, while this news is on its way, of these new lands which I have newly discovered, where I feel in my heart the earthly Paradise is, the Adelantado will go with three ships well equipped for the purpose to reconnoitre ahead; and they will discover all they can towards those parts. In the meantime I shall send your Highnesses this report and my depiction of the land; and your Highnesses shall decide what ought to be done about it, and will send me further orders, which shall be carried out with all diligence and with the help of the Holy Trinity, in such a manner as your Highnesses shall be served and shall be content. Thanks be to God.

Although not as extensive as the fragments from the first crossing, Las Casas's extracts from the third voyage are perhaps more revealing. They were written in an introspective mood; they provide a means of tracing the evolution of the thoughts Columbus collected for the monarchs' benefit in the last extract; and they reveal Columbus's debate with himself on the nature of his discoveries. In his letter to the monarchs, Columbus wavered between a characterisation of his latest find as an antipodal continent 'previously unknown' and 'another world which the Romans and Greeks strove to conquer' – a land, that is, both unknown and Asiatic. The journal shows that at one point, at least, on 13 August 1498, Columbus had a clear perception of what he had done and that he recognised America for what it was: 'an enormous continent, of which until now nothing has been known.'

Columbus is as self-congratulatory as ever in this text; the superlatives flow as freely. Yet his assurances lack conviction because of his evident desire to evade the obligation to give a factual account of what he has seen and done. He takes refuge in reminiscence: recollections of Portuguese achievements are included to taunt the monarchs into a livelier sense of their duty; memories of his treatment at court spill out, perhaps without contrivance, because they are so deeply felt. He escapes into geographical speculation and theory. He turns to self-pity and affected contrition: it is hard to resist the impression that his reflections on the superiority of spiritual goals are an act of penance for his own material cupidity. Throughout the text Columbus, while clinging to his former hopes, seems to ease himself away from reliance on the monarchs' patronage towards dependence on God. What Las Casas calls a digression is included here, although it can only be given in the Dominican's paraphrase, because it includes a powerful expression of the solace Columbus claimed to find in the certainty of divine favour.

Passages from the Log of the Third Voyage, extracted by Las Casas*

[31 July 1498. He decided to change course and from his present westward course veer to starboard and go to land at Dominica or another of the Cannibal islands . . . and so he ordered the course to be set to the north and by north-east and he followed that course until midday] but as His Divine Majesty [he says] has always been merciful to me, a mariner from Huelva, a servant of mine, called Alonso Pérez, climbed to the crow's nest by chance, just to check, and saw land to the west, and it was fifteen leagues away and all that could be seen of it were three hummocks or mountains [these are his own words. He called this land the Island of Trinidad, because he had decided that the first land he sighted should be so named.] And it pleased our Lord [he says] that thanks to His Divine Majesty the first sighting was of three hummocks, or I should say three mountains, all seen at once in a single glance. May His lofty power guide me for His mercy's sake [he says] in such a fashion that He is well served and your Highnesses well contented. For certain it is that the discovery of this land, on this voyage, was a great miracle, as much as the discovery made on the first voyage. [These are his words. He gave untold thanks to God, as he usually did, and the whole company praised God's goodness and, in great happiness and rejoicing, they sang out the *Salve Regina*, with other devout versicles and canticles that contain praises to God and our Lady, after the custom of mariners, or our mariners of Spain, at least, whose custom it is to offer them in trouble and gladness alike.

Here he digresses and summarises the services he has performed for the King and Queen and the good will that had always burned in him to do them service.] Not as evil tongues have said [he says] and false witnesses inspired by envy. [... he speaks again of the heat he endured, and how on that day he was still sailing along the same parallel, only in order to find land by the route he took when he ordered his course to be set to the west.] Because the land emits cool breezes which arise from the springs and rivers, whose waters make the atmosphere mild and temperate, [he says] it is for this reason that the Portuguese who go to Guinea are able to make the journey, because, according to common report, they keep close to land and inshore. [He further says that he was now on the same parallel as the place from where they carry gold to the king of Portugal, wherefore he believes that whoever searches those seas shall find things of value.

Here he confesses that there is no man in the world to whom God has granted so much favour and he beseeches Him to vouchsafe to afford something with which their Highnesses and the whole of Christendom shall rest well content. And he says that even if no other exploitable product is found, apart from these lands so fair, they are so green and so full of woodland and palm trees that they are better than the gardens of Valencia in May and are bound to be highly prized ... He says that it is a miraculous thing that the King and Queen of Castile should have territories so close to the equator while Isabela lies twenty-four degrees (*sic*) to the north of that line.]

8 AUGUST 1498

Although my mariners had not gone with any intention of going ashore, two leading men came with all their people and made them leave the boats and took them to a large house, built between two waters, rectangular and not round like a campaign tent, as those they have in the islands are. There they received them very well and put on a feast for them and gave them a meal of bread and many kinds of fruit. And to drink they had a white beverage which the people hold in high esteem and which they traded throughout the time we were there; there is a red version of it, too, and some kinds are better than others, as with wine among us.

The men were all together at one end of the house and the women all together at the other. After the meal had been eaten in that house, which belonged to the elder chieftain, the younger took them to another house and offered them another of the same type. It seemed that the elder must have been the chief and the lord and the other must have been his son. Afterwards, the seamen returned to the boats and, with the boats, to the ships, very favourably impressed by the people. [All these are the Admiral's words. He says further:] They are all of very fair appearance and all, without exception, tall and paler in colour than any other people I have seen in the Indies [and he says that the previous day he had seen many who were as white as ourselves, with better hair, well cut, and very well mannered.] As for the lands, there can be none greener, nor fairer, nor better populated in the world; as for the climate, the same; so that all the time I have been on this island (*sic*) [he says] I have felt the cold every morning, I declare, enough to put on fur-lined clothes, close though this place is to the equator. The water in the sea still tastes fresh. They call this island (*sic*) Paria. [All these are the Admiral's words.]

Columbus has decided to make directly for Hispaniola and leave his brother, the Adelantado, to resume the work of exploration.

10 AUGUST 1498

May our Lord guide me for His mercy's sake and afford me something with which He shall be served and your Highnesses well contented. And so you shall be, to be sure, for here you have a noble and regal possession, worthy of great princes. And it is a great mistake to believe those who speak ill of this enterprise; rather they should be abhorred. For there is no record of any prince who has had so much favour from our Lord, nor so great a victory over so remarkable a conquest, which has added so much honour to his high estate and kingdoms and where God eternal can be so greatly served, while the people of Spain receive so much help and advantage. For it has been seen that the things of value here are infinite.

And although what I am now saying may not yet be recognised, the time will come when this enterprise shall be accounted a thing of great excellence, and when the persons who speak against it to your Highnesses shall be held in great contempt. For although it may have cost your Highnesses something, it has been in the most noble cause, of the highest status, of any undertaken by any prince until the present day. Nor was it something to be abandoned peevishly but to be sustained, with help and favour granted to me. For the kings of Portugal spent, and had the courage to spend, money and manpower in Guinea for four or five years before they saw any return. And after that God granted them gains and gold. And, indeed, if a count is made of the population of the kingdom of Portugal, and of the men who have died in the course of the enterprise of Guinea, it would be found that more than half the active manpower of the realm has been lost. And, to be sure, it would have been a most glorious act to earmark some income in Spain to be expended on this enterprise. For nothing more worthy of renown shall your Highnesses leave behind you. And consider how there has never been any prince of Castile – at least, I have never encountered any in writing or by word of mouth – who ever made any conquests outside Spanish territory. And your Highnesses have won these lands, which are so extensive that they make up a new world; and here Christendom shall have so much reason to rejoice and, in time, our faith shall be so much increased.

All this I declare with a very healthy intent, and because it is my desire that your Highnesses shall be the greatest lords in the world – indeed, lords of the whole of it. And may all be to the great service and pleasure of the Holy Trinity, so that at the end of your days your Highnesses may enjoy the glory of Paradise, and not for the sake of my own personal interest, for I hope in His Divine Majesty that your Highnesses shall soon see the truth of it and what it is that I most desire. [All these are the Admiral's exact words.]

Columbus's inference, from the amount of fresh water discharged from the mouth of the Orinoco, that the land of Gracia must be a continent, was recorded in Las Casas's abstract from the log under 13 August 1498.

'The Catholic Kings' by Santa Cruz: Ferdinand and Isabella with Prince Juan (*bottom left*) and Princess Juana (*bottom right*)

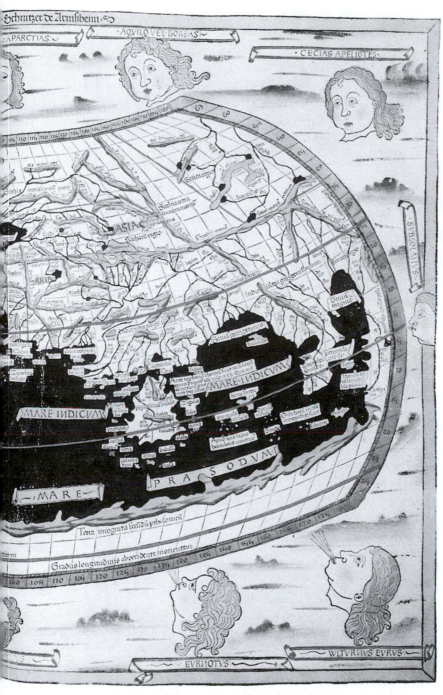

Map of the world according to Ptolemy,
from the fourth earliest printed atlas, 1482

'The Virgin of the Navigators' by Alejo Fernández. Columbus may be the figure dressed in friar's habit, *centre right*: 'they sang out . . . devout versicles and canticles that contain praise to God and our Lady, after the custom of mariners, or our mariners of Spain, at least, whose custom it is to offer them in trouble and gladness alike'

I have come to believe that this land is an enormous continent, of which until now nothing has been known. And reason is on my side because of this very big river and this body of fresh water; and I am further assisted by the saying of Esdras in the sixth chapter of his fourth book, which states that six parts of the world are covered by dry land and only one part by water. This book is approved by St Ambrose in his *Exameron* and St Augustine in that passage *Morietur filius meus Christus*, as cited by Francisco de Mairones.* And further to this, I am assisted by what many of the cannibal Indians whom I captured on previous occasions have said, to the effect that to their south there was a continent; and at that time I was on the island of Guadelupe and I also heard others from the islands of Santa Cruz and San Juan say the same; and they said there was a great deal of gold there.

And, as your Highnesses know, it was only a little while ago that no other lands were known than those Ptolemy wrote of; and in my time there was no one who would believe that it was possible to sail from Spain to the Indies. I spent seven years in your court on this matter, and there was no lack of experts to look into it. And at the end, it was only thanks to the very great courage of your Highnesses that it was put to the test experimentally, against the opinions of those who spoke against it. And now the truth has been revealed. And it will appear more fully before long. And if this is a continent, it is an admirable thing, and so it will appear to all men of learning, since so great a river flows from it as to form a body of fresh water forty-eight leagues across. [These are his words.]

The notion of total dependence on God, which Columbus seems to have imagined as a suitable estate for himself, was prominent in Franciscan thought. It may have been to reproach the monarchs with their own unreliability, compared with the Divine Provider, that Columbus had affected Franciscan garb at court. The companion of this notion was the mendicant ideal of poverty. Columbus ventures direct criticism of the material wealth of the secular church in his recommendations for the evangelisation of his discoveries. The passage was extracted by Las Casas from an entry made later on 13 August.

Those people [he says here] are no friends to your Highnesses, nor do

The third Atlantic crossing

they seek the honour of your high estate, who have spoken ill to you of so noble an enterprise. Nor was the expense so great that it could not be borne, although there could hardly be enough profit to repay it so soon, for the service rendered to our Lord in spreading his Holy Name in unknown lands was very great. And what is more, it would serve as the greatest monument that any prince, ecclesiastical or lay, had ever left for his commemoration. [And the Admiral says further:] And for such a purpose the income of a good bishopric or arch-bishopric would be well spent, indeed, say I [he says], the best in Spain, where the bishops enjoy so many rents yet none of them – though they have heard of the innumerable people here – has resolved to send learned persons of intelligence, friends of Christ, here, to attempt to make Christians of the natives or at least to make a start. I am very confident that the expense incurred, being pleasing to our Lord, would soon be recovered from here and a surplus would soon be yielded which could be taken to Spain. [These are his words.]

Among the other reasons which obliged him to leave exploring and make for Hispaniola was the pain in his eyes, brought on, he claimed, by long sleepless periods on the watch.

May it please God to free me of them [of the pains in his eyes, he means], for He well knows that I do not endure these hardships to gather treasure nor find riches for myself, for, to be sure, I know that all is vanity that is accomplished in this world, save what is to the honour and service of God, which is not to build up riches or causes of pride or many of the other things we use in this world to which we are better affected than to the things that can save our souls. [These are his words.]

Columbus arrived in Hispaniola to find a chaos which excelled even the disorder encountered on his last visit. In an act of tergiversation such as was becoming typical of those who attracted Columbus's confidence, Francisco Roldán had rebelled against the rule of Barto-lomé Colón and had withdrawn with followers of his own to live off the Indians and defy orders. Roldán had been entrusted by Columbus with an important role as deputy magistrate of Hispaniola: this suggests that his qualifications and character were better than we might suppose from Columbus's subsequent denunciations.

The two documents which follow present contrasting accounts of the rebellion, both from Columbus's hand. The first, addressed to Roldán himself, was deliberately dissembling, as Columbus later admitted, designed to lure the recipient into custody. In the second, addressed to the monarchs, Columbus declares his view of Roldán without modification. The main purpose of the account, however, is to anticipate and rebut the charges Columbus's enemies were laying against him at court. It includes a frank admission of his own unpopularity and an attempt to attribute it to the deficiencies of character of his opponents. It also reveals Columbus's capacity for mendacity – or self-deception – in the glaring imbalance between the accounts of his own comportment and that of others. Most conspicuously, his insistence on the salubrious merits of the malarial swamplands around Isabela, which he had selected as the site of the garrison, fails to command conviction. His justification is characteristic: Isabela must be a good site, because God took him there 'by a miracle'.

Letter to Francisco Roldán, 20 October 1498*

My dear friend, I have received your letter. I asked after you as soon as I arrived, after enquiring about the lord Adelantado and Don Diego, believing in you as one in whom I had placed total confidence and whom I had left in utmost certainty that you would do your best to deal with and settle whatever problems were needful. And everyone was at a loss to find a way of telling me about you, except that they all, with one voice, declared that, because of certain differences which had arisen, you were waiting anxiously for my return, as if your soul's health depended on it. And I of course believed it, for even if I were to see the evidence with my own eyes, I should never believe that you would go so far as to risk your life in an affair inconsistent with your obligations to me. And, with this in mind, I talked it over at length with the Alcaide [Miguel Ballester, commander of the Fort of Concepción], fully convinced that you would report here promptly, in accordance with the words I used to him, which he passed on to you.

Apart from expecting you to arrive in person, I also supposed that, even had there been graver incidents than can have happened in this case, everything would be well resolved when you reported to me and gave me willingly an account of your responsibilities – as was done by all the others whom I left in charge, and as is, of course, the normal and honourable procedure. If there were reasons to prevent this being done in person, it could be accomplished in writing, and there could be no need for any prior assurances or safeguards. Immediately on my arrival I said that I could assure everyone that he could come to me and say whatever he liked, and I now repeat it and give the same assurance again. And as for the other matter you raise, of whether you may return to Castile, I have delayed the departure of the ships for eighteen days on your account, and that of the men who are with you, some of whom, I believe, also wanted to leave. And I would have been willing to detain the fleet longer, except that the Indian slaves they are carrying were causing a lot of expense and were dying on board. It seems to me that frivolous reports ought not to be credited. And you and your men ought to have a greater regard for your honour than appears from what I am told of your conduct, for no one's reputation is more likely to be affected than your own; nor should you give those who wish you ill, here or in your own land, something which can be held against you; and it should be your care to spare our lord King and lady Queen disappointment in matters with which they expected to be pleased. For truth to tell, when their Highnesses asked me who were the persons here to whom the lord Adelantado could look for counsel and loyalty, I put your name at the head of the list, and I rated your services to them so highly, that it pains me now that the present fleet shall take them opposite tidings. Consider now what can be done or what would be appropriate to the case and let me know accordingly, for the ships have sailed. Our Lord preserve you in His keeping. Santo Domingo, 20 October.

*Fragment of an Account of Roldán's Rebellion, addressed to Ferdinand and Isabella, May 1499**

When I arrived with such a large force and such extensive powers from your Highnesses, and he departed from his previous intentions and declared his challenge, I wanted to go after him, but I found that it was true that most of my men sympathised with him. For although they were working men, and I had contracted with them as such, this Roldán and his followers and supporters had a way of inducing them to take their side, by promising them no work, a loose rein, plenty of

174

food and women and, above all, licence to do as they fancied. And so I was obliged to dissemble. And at length I came to an agreement by which I would give them two of the three caravels which the Adelantado had intended to take exploring, which were ready to sail, with letters for your Highnesses saying they had served well and with their salaries and many other improper concessions. And so I sent the caravels over to the western end of the island where they had their camp. And thus have I endured anxiety from the day I came and do so to the present, which is in May of 1499, for he has still not sailed away and he is keeping the ships there and every day he launches raids and plagues me. May our Lord resolve it as may best be for His service.

Very High Princes, when I came here, I brought a large number of men to conquer these lands. I welcomed them all importunately, telling them that they would serve in very good conditions and do better than anybody else. And the opposite has turned out to be true, for they came only in the belief that the gold and spices which were said to be found here could be gathered by the shovelful, and that the spices were ready-made in bundles all on the sea-shore, and that nothing was wanting but to fling them aboard the ships. To such a degree did covetousness make them blind. Nor did it occur to them that, though there might be gold, it would be in mines, and so would the other metals; and that the spices would be on the trees; and that the gold would have to be dug for and the spices gathered and cured.

I proclaimed all this to them in Seville, for so many men wanted to come and I knew what was in their minds, that I had it explained to them, as well as warning of all the hardships customarily endured by those who go to colonise remote lands for the first time. To which they all replied that that was what they were going for, and to gain honour thereby. But the reverse proved to be the case, as I have said; and as soon as they arrived and saw that what I had told them was true and that their greed had no chance of being satisfied, they all wanted to go home at once, without understanding that this would make the conquest and subjection of this land impossible. And because I would not consent they began to hate me; but they were in the wrong, for I had brought them at their own urgent clamour, and I had told them clearly that I was coming, not to go back home again straight away, but to carry out a conquest, as one who had experience of such things and whose intentions were well known. And again they hated me because I refused to let them go up country, split into little groups of two or three or so, or some on their own – in which event the Indians would have killed more if I had not put a stop to it, as I have explained. And the dissidents' boldness got to such a point that they would have thrown me out of the country without a word, if our Lord had not intervened.

I suffered great grief over this. And then there was the business of the victuals I had to provide for them; for there were some who would not have been capable of maintaining a serving-boy in Castile and who wanted to have six or seven manservants over here, and expected me to take responsibility for them and pay their wages. And there was no way in reason or justice to make them content. Others – I should rather say, a quarter of the total – had come without pay, having stowed away aboard the ships, and I had to satisfy them along with the rest. The result is that I have had more trouble from the Christians than the Indians, and am still not at the end of it.

But, if on the one hand, the problems are increasing, there is another respect in which they are getting easier. They are increasing because of that ingrate Roldán, a nobody whom I had in my household, and the men who are with him whom I treated so honourably; and I gave that Roldán, who had nothing before, so much in so short a time that he was worth more than a million *maravedís*; and I had given money and good fellowship to those others who have just joined him as soon as they got here together from Castile. That is why they have caused me this grief. On the other hand, I am relieved because the rest of the men are sowing crops and are now well supplied with victuals and have got to know the customs of the land and are beginning to appreciate its splendour and fertility, very much to the contrary of what has been said hitherto. For I believe there is no land in the world better fitted for idlers than this, and it is very much the best for someone who wishes to build up an estate (as I shall explain later so as not to get things out of order). And so has it been with our people here, once they saw they could not glut their greed. And that greed has been so out of all proportion that I have even been moved many times to ponder and believe that it has been the reason why our Lord has kept the source of the gold and other things concealed from us.

For as soon as I went out into the hinterland, I had the Indians put to the test to see how much gold they could gather. And I found that some of them, who knew the techniques well, could gather in four days an amount that contained an ounce and a half. And so I arranged with all the people of this province of Cibao that each of them, male and female, between the ages of fourteen and seventy years, would pay tribute of one of these measures which I mentioned every three months. And I collected this tribute until the time of my departure for Castile. That is why it has occurred to me that greed has been the reason why it has been lost. But I am convinced that our Lord for His mercy's sake will not consider our sins and that when He sees a time meet for it he will restore it with advantage.

Those men of ours, once they saw that their expectations were not turning out as they had imagined, were thereafter always full of demands to return to Spain. And so I gave them space to return with each sailing, and good luck to them. Although they had been well and honourably treated by me, as soon as they arrived over there, they spoke worse of me than you would of a Moor, without putting forward any good reason for it. And they swore a thousand false depositions against me. And it is still going on. But our Lord, who knows my purposes and the truth of it all, will preserve me, just as He has done hitherto. For to this day no one who has risen against me maliciously has escaped punishment by Him; and for this reason it is well to put all one's care into His service, for He will guide it.

Over there they said that I had settled the people in the worst place on the island. And yet it is the best place, and confirmed as such by the word of mouth of all the Indians of the island. And many of those who made this complaint have never ventured further than a lombard shot beyond the town stockade: I know not what credit they can have. They said that they were dying of thirst; and the river flows by the town there, no further away than from Santa Marta to the riverside in Seville. They said that the place was the most unhealthy; and it is the most salubrious, though the whole of this land is of the healthiest, with the most waters and best air of any under heaven. And this is to be expected, since the land is on the same latitude and the same distance from the equator as the Canary Islands, which are comparable in situation (albeit not in their topography, for they are all covered with very high, parched mountains, without water or fruit or any green thing) and which used to be praised by sages for their very good climate, under so goodly a part of the heavens, and because of their distance from the equator as I have said. But this Hispaniola is enormous, with a circumference bigger than Spain's, and very full of meadows and dales and woodland and mountains and enormous rivers and many other sources of water and harbours, as will clearly appear from the depiction of it which will accompany this letter. And the whole of it is very thickly populated with very industrious people, so that I believe that under heaven there is no better land in the world.

They said that there was no food, yet there are meat and bread and fish and provender of many other kinds in such abundance that since the arrival of the peasants who were brought from over there to work here without wages, they have been able to support themselves and their Indian servants. And the same can be shown by the case of that man Roldán, who has been at large in the country for more than a year with one hundred and twenty people, who have more than five hundred Indian servants, and all are provided for with plenty to spare.

They said that I had taken the livestock away from those who brought some here and that no one received any payment, except me for eight pigs; but these belonged to a number of other people. And because these pig-owners were people who wanted to go straight back to Castile and were killing their animals, I forbade it in order to breed from them, no matter who owned them. As a result it can now be seen that there are pigs without number here, all of which came from this bloodstock-line from animals I bought on board the ships: and I reimbursed the owners' costs, except for the initial purchase price, which was seventy *maravedis* a head in the island of Gomera.

They said that the land at Isabela, where the settlement is, was very bad and would not yield grain. I harvested it and we ate bread made from it and it is the fairest land a man could desire: a grassland fourteen leagues long and two leagues wide, extending to three or four, set between two mountain ranges; and a very abundant river flows through the middle of it, with two others which are not big, and there are many streams besides which flow from the mountains to join them. Nor does anyone here pine for wheaten bread, because this other sort is plentiful and better for over here and can be made with less trouble.

Of all this I stand accused contrary to all justice, as I said; and this is so that your Highnesses should turn away from me and from this enterprise. But it would not have happened had the idea for it come from one of the convert Jews; for the *conversos* are enemies to your Highnesses' prosperity and that of Christian men. It was they who started these rumours and tried to find a way to achieve the ruin of the whole enterprise; and according to reports, most of the men who are with this Roldán, who is at present in arms against me, are of their number. They accused me of the abuse of justice, which I have always administered in the fear of God and of your Highnesses, without fearing the criminals or their ugly and brutal misdeeds, for which our Lord has punished them so severely in this world; and the magistrates here have the records of their trials.

They have made innumerable other depositions about me and about the land, which our Lord can be seen to have granted by a miracle. And it is the fairest and most fertile land there could be under heaven. In it are gold and copper and so many kinds of spices and so great a quantity of brazil wood. The merchants who have been here told me of the latter that, using slave labour alone, we could harvest annually forty million *maravedis'* worth, and they have produced accounts to prove it, for over there every year a load goes for three times as much. And in this land people can live with much ease, as shall very soon appear. And it is my belief, in view of the exigencies of life in Castile and the fertility of Hispaniola, that a large population is bound to come here very soon from over there. And the settlement will be at Isabela, where it started, because it is the most suitable place, better than any other in the land – which we ought to believe since our Lord took me there by a miracle, which was that I could not go forward with my ships nor turn back, but only disembark and establish a camp.

And this was the reason that moved me to write this down. There will be some who will say of it that it was not necessary to repeat facts from the past and who will regard this account as prolix, and yet it is so short. But I was aware that it was necessary to set everything out like this for your Highnesses, as well as for others who had heard the calumnies uttered with so much malice and deceit, which have been voiced over all the items recorded here, not only by the people who have been here but also, very cruelly, by some who have never been outside Castile, who have leave to try their malice out at your Highnesses' ear and can contrive to do so with every artifice, and all to do me harm, because of their hatred for a poor foreigner. But He who is everlasting has succoured me and does succour me throughout, and has always shown mercy to me, very great sinner that I am.

Like other worldly afflictions, Roldán's rebellion turned Columbus's thoughts to the consolations of religion. In a very brief but important fragment preserved in the biography attributed to his son, Columbus records a further apparition or experience of the direct presence of

Christ. The sense of personal contact with God is more distinct here than in the first such occurrence, on the way home from the first voyage (above, p. 95), and much less so than on the last occasion, which would occur at the worst moment of the fourth crossing (below, p. 226). The elements, however, are always the same: Columbus is isolated and alone, spiritually and even physically; he is facing a crisis and impending death; he is in repentant mood, abjuring his worldly greed in favour of the blessings of heaven; he has a strong sense of the confrontation of enemies – variously courtiers, savants, Indians, mutineers and rebels. In these circumstances he feels overwhelmed by the conviction that he is enduring a test of faith; and in the access of faith that accompanies that feeling he senses the presence or hears the voice of our Lord. The shift of Columbus's priorities from the secular to the spiritual, which seemed to overshadow his thinking throughout the third voyage, was crystallised in this experience on 26 December 1499.

Fragment extracted from the Historie*

The day after Christmas Day, 1499, when all had abandoned me, I was assailed by the Indians and the wicked Christians. I found myself in such a pass that in an attempt to escape death I took to the sea in a small caravel. Then our Lord came to my help, saying, 'Oh, man of little faith, be not afraid. I am with thee.' And he scattered my enemies and showed me the way to fulfil my promises. Miserable sinner that I am, to have put all my trust in the vanities of this world!

Roldán's rebellion was not the only problem that faced Columbus during his stay on Hispaniola. The colony was ungovernable and, except by recourse to slaving, unsustainable. Columbus's reactions are preserved only in a few fragments from undated letters to the monarchs, collected by Las Casas, and here set out in what seems the most rational sequence possible.* Columbus's familiar obsessions and tireless attempts at self-justification characterise these fragments. They raise, however, three new themes. First, there is Columbus's plea to be assisted or replaced by 'a well educated man, a person equipped for judicial duties'. Columbus's failure as a colonial administrator was altering his perception of himself. It was a commonplace in Spain that 'arms and letters' were diverse, if not incom-

180

patible, talents, and that both were needed for the discharge of the duties of government. Don Quixote would summarise the tradition crisply in his advice to Sancho Panza:

'You, Sancho, must dress in a mixture of a graduate's gown and a captain's armour, for in the island I shall give you to govern arms shall be required as well as letters, and letters as well as arms.'*

Parvenu though he was, Columbus was now coming to see himself as an old-fashioned aristocrat, whose great virtue was his prowess. From now on he designated himself increasingly as a 'captain' – a military term – rather than a mariner, and his discoveries as 'conquests'. His failure in administration was thus a proof of his nobility rather than a blot on his competence. As we shall see, when he got the professional judge he asked for, the consequences for his own career were to be disastrous.

The second new theme is Columbus's unease at the way the Spaniards of Hispaniola have come to acquire the personal services of Indians, particularly in concubinage. Columbus has traditionally been thought to have originated the system, later known as *encomienda*, of exploiting the Indians by apportioning their services among the colonists. Alternatively, the practice has been regarded as an implantation of old-world 'feudalism' into America. Columbus's own account, however, seems to show that it arose almost naturally, as Spaniards acquired Indian services, along with other traditional obligations of kinship, when they took Indian women. The labour-system that prevailed in the early Spanish Main thus becomes neither the brain-child of a single man, nor an example of the 'continuity' of colonial history, but an innovation attributable to a cultural encounter in a peculiar environment. Columbus's unease may have been genuine or may have been affected for the monarchs' benefit: Ferdinand and Isabella could not approve of concubinage, or of anything that smacked of unlawful slavery.

The last of the new themes of these pages is Columbus's increased willingness to ascribe his failures and frustrations to diabolic interference.* In these fragments, the devil is held responsible for the derision of Columbus's critics at court, for the faint-heartedness of the monarchs, and for the delays in extracting gold from Hispaniola. Columbus represents the history of his discoveries as a trial of faith, expressly likened to the sacred history of the Old Testament. The divine origin of his mission is confirmed by the evidence of devilish opposition to it.

Fragments of Letters to the Monarchs of 1498–1500, extracted by Las Casas

Your Highnesses already know how I spent seven years in your court, importuning you to support this enterprise. Never in all that time could any pilot or mariner be found, nor philosopher nor man of any other science, but all said that my proposal was false. For I never had any help from anybody, save from Fray Antonio de Marchena, apart from that of God eternal.

Devout friars are badly needed here, more to renew the faith within ourselves than to teach it to the Indians, for they have conquered us with their customs and we have become worse than they are. And at the same time we need a well-educated man, a person equipped for judicial duties, because without support from royal justice I do not think the friars will do much good.

There will soon be permanent settlers here, because this land is abundant in all things, especially bread and meat. There is so much bread here of the kind the Indians grow that it is a wonder; and our men are fitter on it, to judge from what they say, than on wheat. And our meat comes from innumerable pigs and fowl, and there are some animals which are all but like rabbits but with better meat, and there are so many of them all over the island that an Indian boy with a dog can bring in fifteen or twenty every day for his master. So that only wine and clothing are lacking. For the rest it is a land for the biggest idlers in the world, and there is not one of our men here, good or bad, who does not have two or three Indians to serve him and dogs to hunt for him, and, though it is not something to speak of, women so pretty that it is a marvel.

I am very unhappy about this practice, because it seems to me that it does no service to God; nor can I do anything to put it right, as with the eating of meat on Saturday [*sic*] and other evil customs which are not those of good Christians. For these problems it would be greatly to our profit here to have a few devout friars, more to reform the faith of the Christians than to teach it to the Indians. Nor shall I ever be able to impose suitable punishment, unless men are sent to me from over there, fifty or sixty of them in every sailing, and I send back the same number of idlers and recalcitrants, as I am doing on the present occasion. And this is the biggest and best punishment, with least charge upon my conscience that I can discern . . . I have been blamed over settlement policy, over the treatment of the people and in many other things, like a poor hated foreigner.

I always feared the enemy of our Holy Faith, for he has set himself to obstruct this great enterprise with all his might. He was so much against me before the discovery was made, that all those who looked into it took it for a joke. Afterwards he contrived that the men who came here with me uttered a thousand depositions against the enterprise and against me. And now he has been at work over there to strew so much delay and so many obstacles in the way of my mission, and to sow a lot of darnel, so that your Highnesses should begin to have fears about the cost of the project. The present cost could be as little as shall appear in the final account – or could even be nothing – if it so pleases Him who granted this enterprise and who is above the enemy and the world. And He will bring the project to an end, because it was He who began it, and of Him it can be seen very clearly that He sustains it and makes it prosper. For it is certain that if the things that have befallen here are examined, it could be said of them, 'How much they resemble the experiences of the people of Israel!' . . . I could write a reply to all the devil's calumnies, but I think there is no need for I have written about it at length enough times: how it must be believed that the land which God has now newly given to your Highnesses on this voyage is infinite; and how for this and for this land of Hispaniola you are bound to feel great joy and give boundless thanks and abhor whoever says that you should invest no expenditure in it, for they are no friends to the honour of your high estate. For apart from the many souls which, it may be hoped, shall be saved (of which your Highnesses are the cause and which is the chief of the benefits that flow from this enterprise), I wish to address myself to the vainglory of this world, which must be reckoned at nought, since almighty God abhors it. And I invite any man to answer me, of any who have read the histories of the Greeks and of the Romans, if at so slight a cost they ever expanded their empires so greatly as now your Highnesses have done with Spain's territories by the addition of the Indies. This island alone encompasses more than seven hundred leagues. Then there is Jamaica, with seven hundred other islands besides, and so great a portion of the mainland – which was well known to the ancients and not unknown as the envious and ignorant wish to claim – and many other large islands besides from here towards Castile, and now this one, which is so excellent. I believe among all Christians there must be talk of it for a marvel, with gladness.

Who, if he were a man of sense, would call this ill spent, or say that the expenditure involved was not worthwhile? What greater memorial, whether spiritual or temporal, was ever left or could ever be left by any prince? I feel astonished and my senses reel when I hear and see that this is overlooked. And let no man say that your Highnesses should amass silver or gold or any other thing of value, but rather press on with so high and noble an endeavour, from which our Lord will derive so much service and which will bring so much rejoicing to your Highnesses' successors and your peoples. Let your Highnesses examine it well: in my opinion this enterprise will exalt you more than those French or Italian affairs [. . . Las Casas omitted the context of the next remark, which is perhaps about the crops] For I always said that it would be necessary to keep up the effort on them for three or four years, until they become well established, because it was obvious that this would make them stronger . . . For if the natives realised how few of us there were, they would withdraw their obedience; and it is they who sow our grain for us, and the cassava, and all their other provender; and the Adelantado has three hundred cassava plants here, which are used for bread, already planted . . .

I beseech your Highnesses' approval henceforth for the reprovisioning of the people here every year or two, until this business gets on to a sound footing. For now that it is going well, your Highnesses can see that the mariners who are here, and almost all of the landsmen, are contented. And two or three ships' masters recently came out and posted forms at our gate for anyone who is willing to undertake to pay them 1,500 *maravedis* in Seville for carrying so many slaves there at their own expense – the payment to come out of what the slaves sold for. This was acceptable to all the men and I accepted it on their behalf and have protested the bill of exchange. And so the merchants will come back and bring supplies and things which are needed here, and this business will show a profit for our enterprise, which is at a low ebb because the men have not been working and the Indians have not been paying tribute, because of the trouble we have had and my being away. And the Adelantado could not do any more about it because he had no one with him except men whose mien was such that they could not be trusted; for they were all complaining and speaking ill, saying that they had been here five years and had not enough to buy a shirt. Now I have revived their morale and they apparently see the reasonableness of what I have told them, which is that they will soon be paid and will be able to get back pay.

VII

TOWARDS THE
FINAL VOYAGE

Columbus had begged for a lettered administrator to be sent to Hispaniola. The arrival of Francisco de Bobadilla in response to those pleas on 24 August 1500 was his undoing. Bobadilla was prejudiced in advance by what he had heard, or what the monarchs relayed, from Columbus's detractors. His brief was to conduct a judicial inquiry into Columbus's conduct – an unjust proceeding, in the Admiral's submission, since Bobadilla had a vested interest in an outcome that would keep him in power, but one which was normal in the Spanish bureaucracy at the time. Motivated by self-interest or excessive zeal, Bobadilla clapped Columbus in irons with his brothers Bartolomé and Diego, gathered depositions against them, and shipped them back to Spain.

The document which follows is, according to Las Casas, one of a number of letters to the monarchs and persons of influence, despatched by Columbus as soon as he got back to Spain, from Cadiz, in November 1500.* None of the others has survived. Copies of this particular letter, however – with slight variants, which my version attempts to reconcile – were bound up with Columbus's collected charters, letters of privilege, and other contractual letters, perhaps because Columbus thought it contained a persuasive statement of his case.* The addressee, Doña Juana de Torres y Ávila, was Antonio de Torres' sister and, as nurse to the heir to the throne, an important figure in the royal entourage: her significance for Columbus was as a reliable channel of communication with the monarchs, and the entire contents of the letter can be regarded as intended for the royal ears. It is well drafted with many rhetorical touches and more fluency and craftsmanship in the use of language than Columbus customarily showed. On the voyage home in fetters he doubtless had plenty of time to work on it.

The text has more to say about the deficiencies of Bobadilla than the

186

merits of Columbus himself. It does, however, reveal some intriguing new details. At the time, Columbus was savouring his humiliation, which he knew how to exploit for the maximum theatrical effect. He refused, for instance, to allow the manacles to be struck from his wrists until he had confronted the monarchs in person. By representing his adversities as a trial of faith he presented a Job-like image of himself as a man particularly favoured by God, whose travails were evidence of peculiar grace. In this temper, he let slip the fact that the patronage of Ferdinand and Isabella had raised him up 'from naught' – in sharp contrast to his more usual attempts to hint at a lofty lineage for himself. He also confides the admission that he exceeded the proper limits of his authority and the law in attempting to suppress the rebels of Hispaniola; his self-defence on this point is essentially practical: a savage frontier cannot be regulated with the decorum appropriate to one of the monarchs' European possessions. He also displays a changed attitude to the Indians: his disillusionment resounds in his picture of a wild and warlike people, when compared with the admirable, almost lovable images of peaceful natives, naturally good, which was generated by his first encounter with them.

Though diplomatically expressed, his implied reproaches to the monarchs fall thick and fast. God, he says, for instance, has promised to compensate him – for the monarchs' broken promises, he implies. He would have been better off, he claims, in the service of other princes or of himself – which contains a veiled threat to take his services elsewhere. Columbus seems also to have felt let down by the Franciscan advisers who accompanied Bobadilla. Perhaps because of his close relationship with other members of the Order, he expected justice or favour from them. In fact, though their reports have not survived, it is evident that they were sharply critical of Columbus.*
When he got back to Spain, his closest confidant among the clergy was the Carthusian Gaspar de Gorricio, although his special devotion to the Franciscan Order seems to have survived this crisis.

The letter shows signs of having been written under the influence of a mood of spiritual exaltation kindled by the apparition of St Stephen's day, 1499. The two references to the vision provide more details than the account in the *Historie*, adding particularly the information that Christ had assigned to Columbus a term of seven years to gather gold from Hispaniola: that, at least, is the plain and obvious meaning of the text, though it may have a mystical significance which is unclear.

At the start of the letter, Columbus strongly voices his growing conviction that his discoveries had been the subject of biblical prophecy, and closely associates this with a claim that the inspiration of the Holy Spirit underlay his enterprise and the Queen's endorsement of it. Emphasis on the special relationship with the Queen which Columbus claims is also strong in this text. Isabella is singled out, rather as Fray Juan Pérez or Fray Antonio de Marchena were singled out at other times, as a constant friend and support. Columbus clearly felt some special rapport with this patroness and at times evinced firmer expectations of her than of the King. In practice, however, it is impossible to show any particular way in which Isabella can be said to have favoured the transatlantic enterprise. Rather, it is the indulgence her husband showed to Columbus after her death that seems remarkable: above all, Ferdinand's willingness to allow Columbus's titles to pass to his heir, and the appointment of the explorer's elder son, Don Diego Colón, as Governor-General of the Indies in 1509, were remarkable tokens of esteem for a royal servant who had been almost entirely discredited at the time of his death.

Letter to Doña Juana de Torres

Very virtuous lady, If my complaint against the world is new, its habit of using me ill is well established. In a thousand combats it has engaged me and I have fought back until now, when neither advice nor arms avail me. Cruelly, the world has cast me down to the depths. Hope in Him who created all sustains me. He was always a very present help. Once before, and not from afar, when I was further downcast, He raised me up with His right arm, saying, 'Oh, man of little faith, rise up, for I am here. Do not be afraid.'

I came here with so heartfelt a desire to serve these Princes and I have served them with such service as has never been heard of nor seen before. Of the New Heaven and New Earth of which our Lord spoke through St John in Revelation (having formerly spoken through the mouth of Isaiah)* He made me His messenger and revealed those places to me. Everywhere I was met by disbelief, and to my lady the Queen He gave the spirit of understanding and great strength, and He made her receive it entire, like a very dear and beloved daughter. I went to take possession of that whole legacy in her royal name. They who had been left behind in their ignorance tried to make up for it by passing hurriedly over the limits of their knowledge to talk about practical difficulties and costs. None the less, her Highness approved the enterprise and supported it in every way she could.

I spent seven years in debate and nine performing signal deeds, worthy of renown, during the whole time of my service. None of it made much impression. I reached my goal. And today no man is too lowly to think of ways of vilifying me.* Anyone who demurs at it will be accounted virtuous by the standards of this world.

If I were to snatch the Indies from the altar of St Peter, together with the continent that is now known to lie nearby, which people are now talking about, and hand them over to the Moors, people in Spain could hardly evince more hostility towards me. Who would believe such a thing of a land once so generous of heart?

I should dearly love to be rid of the business, if I could do so without dishonouring my obligations to my Queen. The strength given me by our Lord and her Highness made me carry on; and to bring her some relief from the sufferings which Death had inflicted upon her, I undertook a new voyage to the heaven and earth which until then had lain hidden.* And if that discovery is not held in much esteem at court, like the other discoveries of the Indies, it is no wonder, because it was an achievement that seemed to come from my exertions.

I thought that voyage of mine to Paria would bring me some peace, thanks to the pearls and the finding of gold in Hispaniola. I ordered the pearls to be fished and gathered by the people with whom I contracted for the purpose on my return; and, as I understood, they would get them by the bushel. The result, as far as I was concerned, was the same as in many other matters: if I had sought my own good, or left Hispaniola to its ruin, or if my rights and contracts were respected, I should not have suffered such losses – in particular, to my honour. And I could say the same of the gold which I have now collected, which is at last complete, thanks to God's strength and help, after many travails and deaths. When I arrived from Paria, I found half the men on Hispaniola up in arms, and they have gone on making war upon me as if I were a Moor, while the Indians attacked on another front, and grievously. At that point Hojeda arrived and threatened to cap it all; and he said that their Highnesses had sent the men with promises of land-grants and fiscal exemptions and wages. He attracted a sizeable gang, for in all Hispaniola there are few men besides the freebooters, and none with a wife and family. That Hojeda gave me no end of trouble and when it became necessary for him to go away, he left saying that he would be back soon with more ships and men and that by that time our lady the Queen would be near to death. At that point Vicente Yáñez [Pinzón] arrived with four caravels. This caused a hubbub and some distrust but no damage.

The Indians claimed later that six more caravels had arrived bringing one of the Alcalde's [Roldán's] brothers, but it was a wicked lie. And that was afterwards, when all hope that their Highnesses would ever send another ship to the Indies was in ruins, and common rumour was that her Highness was dead.

A certain Adrián [de Múgica] at about this time attempted another uprising like the one before, but our Lord would not allow his evil design to come to pass. It had been my resolve not to touch a hair of the head of any of my men, but in this case I wept at the impossibility – thanks to his ingratitude – of keeping the resolution I had made. I would do no less to my own brother, if he tried to kill me and steal the lordship which the King and Queen had placed in my trust.

It was now six months since I had sent a despatch asking leave to report to their Highnesses with the good news about the gold and to resign from governing dissolute men, who had no fear of their God or of their King and Queen, and who were full of vice and malice.

Before my departure the previous time, I had many times beseeched their Highnesses to send someone over at my expense to take responsibility for the administration of justice. And after I found the Alcalde up in arms, I made the same request again, and asked for more men or at least some official messenger with royal letters; for my reputation is so low that if I were to build churches and hospitals, people would call them dens of thieves. At last provision was made, but the man appointed was the very opposite of what the nature of the job demanded. A fat lot of good came of it, after I had spent two years on the island awaiting his pleasure and without being able to get any provision in my favour or that of the men who were there. And he had a chest full of gold. Whether it all ended up in his pockets, God alone knows. Now, as a start, he has granted rights of gold-gathering for twenty years at a time, which is the time it takes to grow to manhood, while there was one man who collected five marks' worth in four hours, as I shall explain more fully another time.

It would be a mercy to me if their Highnesses would publicise the facts as related by those who know what I have been through; for I have suffered more harm from the evil reports of men than I have gained in recompense for all my service and husbandship of royal resources and rights. And if I were restored to an honourable estate, men would talk of it in all the world, for this enterprise is one of quality, and ought every day to be more renowned and held in higher esteem.

This was the enterprise the Comendador Bobadilla joined when he came to Santo Domingo. I was away in the Vega Central and the Adelantado was in Jaragua, where that Adrián fellow had raised his head, but by that time everything had been smoothed out and the land was prospering and all at peace. The day after his arrival he proclaimed himself Governor and appointed officials and issued orders and decreed exemptions for gold-mining and from tithes and pretty well everything else for a term of twenty years, which is as long as it takes to grow to manhood; and he announced that he had come to settle every man's pay, even though they had not done a proper job up to then. And he gave out that he would ship me off in chains, and my brothers with me, as indeed he has done, and that neither I nor any other member of my lineage would ever return. And he uttered a thousand things dishonourable to me and unbecoming to a gentleman. All this was on the day after his arrival, when I was far away and without news of him or his arrival.

He filled out some blank charters from their Highnesses, which he had with him in bulk, and sent them to the Alcalde and his gang with favours and appointments. To me he has sent not a word, written or spoken, to this very day. Imagine what anyone in my position would think. Giving honours and favours to someone who tried to rob their Highnesses and did so much wrong and harm, while dragging down a man who went through such great perils to do his duty!

When I heard about it, I supposed that he would turn out to be like Hojeda or one of those others. I felt cautious, however, because I had heard from the friars about someone whom their Highnesses were sending. I wrote to him saying that his coming was opportune and that I had applied to go to court and was putting up all my goods for auction; in the matter of conceding immunities, I told him not to be in too much of a hurry and that I would hand over my powers and rule to him directly, as smoothly as the surface of a palm-leaf. And I wrote to the friars in the same sense. Neither he nor they gave me any reply. Instead, he acted belligerently and gave rewards to anybody who went to take an oath to obey him as Governor – for twenty years, according to what I was told. As soon as I heard about the exemptions he was handing out, I thought that I had better do something to patch up so serious a mistake, and that he would not object; for they were conceded needlessly, for no reason, to a bunch of vagabonds, and conferred advantages so enormous that they would have been excessive even for family men who brought wives and children with them. I announced by word of mouth and in writing that he was debarred from using his powers, because mine were superior, and I published the charters of privilege carried by Juan Aguado.

Everything I did was to gain time for their Highnesses to learn the state of the country and to have an opportunity of commanding that whatever pleased them should be done there. It is out of the question to issue such extensive exemptions in the Indies. For those who claim rights of residence it represents pure gain, because they are being given the best lands and soon – by the time their rights as residents expire after four years – they will be worth 200,000 *maravedis* without the new owners having so much as stuck a spade in them. I would not make this objection if those claiming residents' rights were married men, but there are less than half a dozen among the whole lot of them who are not there simply to grab what they can and leave as quickly as possible. It would be a fine thing if permanent settlers could go out there from Castile – and better still if one could find the men and the means to do it; and then the land would be settled with honourable men. I had agreed with those claiming residents' status that they would be liable to pay tax of one third on their gold, and their tithes: and this was at their request and they were glad of it as a great favour from their Highnesses. And I called them to account when I heard of any defaulters. And they were expecting that the Comendador would do the same; but he did the opposite. He raised their indignation against me by saying that I wanted to take from them what their Highnesses were willing to give. And he put a lot of effort into getting them to throw out their agreements with me; and he was successful and prevailed on them to write to their Highnesses asking that I should not be sent back to my post; and my plea was the same, for my own sake and the sake of everything dear to me as long as the people out there were no different. And he subjected me to official inquiries into iniquities they charged me with, more wicked than have ever been heard of, even in Hell. Our Lord is above us, who rescued Daniel and the three young men,* with all the wisdom and strength at His command, and He shall be as ready again, if it please Him, as His will may be.

I could easily put all this right, and everything else that has been said and has happened since I have been in the Indies, if I were willing in conscience to put my own interests first and if it were honourable for me to do so. But to uphold justice and augment their Highnesses' sway has till now been all my care.

Today, when so much gold is being found, opinion is divided about how to make most gain: by going robbing or by working the mines. Meanwhile, for a woman they have to find a hundred *castellanos* – as much as for a smallholding, and the practice is widespread, and there are plenty of traffickers abroad looking for girls; the nine- and ten-year-olds are the priciest at present. A good price can be had for one of any age.

I have said that the malcontents' power to spread evil rumour has caused me more harm than my services have brought me gain. It is a poor example for the present and future ages. I take my oath that plenty of men have gone to the Indies who were not worth so much as a dismissive nod – not for God or the world – and the like are still going back there today. Bobadilla made these his allies against me and it is clear enough that this started – as one can judge from what happened and how – as soon as he was on his way. And, of course, it is well known that they say that he put up a lot of money to be able to join this enterprise: I know nothing of this except what I have heard. Never did I hear of a judge appointed to conduct an official inquiry siding with the rebels and taking testimony from them against the person responsible for the government – and not just from the likes of them but also from others who had no credit and deserved none.

If their Highnesses were to order a general inquiry over there let me tell you that they could think it a great miracle that the island has not sunk beneath the waves.

I think your Grace will recall how, when that storm drove me into Lisbon under bare poles, I was falsely accused of having gone there to give the Indies to the King of Portugal. Afterwards their Highnesses learned that the contrary was true and that it had all been the product of malice. Ignorant I may be, but I cannot believe anyone would think me so stupid as to fail to realise that even if the Indies were my own I should be unable to keep them without help from some prince. If this is so, where could I find better support and security than with our lord King and lady Queen who from naught have raised me to so much honour and are the greatest princes in the world by land and sea? And they know that I have done them good service and they respect my privileges and charters of grace; and, if any man transgresses against my rights, their Highnesses restore them to me with increase, as was seen in the case of Juan Aguado, and they order much honour to be done me. And, as I said, their Highnesses have been served by me and have my sons to serve them in their households, the like of which could never have come to pass with any other prince, for where there is no charity all else passes away.

This I have said here in reply to an evil report uttered with malice and contrary to my very nature, for it is something which would not occur to my mind even in dreams. The Comendador Bobadilla wants to gloss over his own wicked deeds and methods by this means. But I shall make him see, even with my right arm tied, that his ignorance and cowardice and intemperate greed have tumbled him into a mistake this time.

I have already said how I wrote to him and the friars. And then I set off, just as I had told him I would, quite on my own, partly because all my men were with the Adelantado, and also in order to give him no grounds for suspicion. When he heard of this, he flung Don Diego as a prisoner, loaded with fetters, on to a caravel; and to me, on my arrival, he did the same, and again to the Adelantado when he arrived later. I said no further word to him and he has forbidden anyone to talk to me up to the present. And I take my oath that I cannot think why I have been made a prisoner.

The first duty he performed was to seize the gold, which he did without measuring or weighing it, while I was away. He said that he wanted to pay the men out of it and, from what I heard, he paid the first portion to himself. And he sent out new requisitioners to get some more. I had set aside certain samples of this gold – very large nuggets, like the eggs of geese, hens, pullets and many other fowl, which had been rapidly gathered by certain of us, and which would have gladdened their Highnesses and helped them to understand the potential of this enterprise – and a quantity of big stones full of gold. That man assigned these to himself right at the start, with the wicked intention of preventing their Highnesses from having a high regard for this enterprise until he had feathered his own nest, which he is doing quickly enough. The gold that goes to the foundry seems to diminish in the heat: a chain worth as much as twenty marks has disappeared from sight. I have been grievously wronged over this gold

– worse even than over the pearls that I have been prevented from laying before their Highnesses.

Whatever the Comendador could think of to inflict harm on me was at once put into effect. Six hundred thousand *maravedis* would have been enough for him to pay wages to everybody, without cheating anyone, and just the tithes and the profits of justice together amounted to more than four million *maravedis*, without touching the gold. He performed some acts of largesse which have to be laughed at, though I believe he was quick to give the best part to himself. Their Highnesses will learn this when they order accounts to be taken from him over there, especially if I have anything to do with it. All he says is that a large sum is owing: but the amount is as stated by me, and not as much as he has appropriated. I have been most unjustly treated in that the judge sent to investigate my conduct was aware that if he turned in a very adverse report he would take over the government himself.

I could wish it had pleased our Lord to move their Highnesses to send that man or some other two years back, because I know that I should then be free of scandal and infamy, nor would my honour be lost or forfeit. God is just and I am sure He will make it known why and how this has come to pass. Over there at court men judge me as if I had been sent as Governor to Sicily or to some town or city that was subject to orderly government, where the law can be upheld in its entirety without fear of losing everything. And I am greatly wronged there: I ought to be judged as a captain sent from Spain to conquer a warlike and numerous people, of rites and customs very much opposed to our own, as far away as the Indies, where, by God's will, I have reduced a new world to the lordship of our lord and lady, King and Queen; thanks to which Spain, which was once called poor, has become the richest of kingdoms.*

I must be judged as a captain who has carried his arms on his back for so long, until the present day, without laying them down for a single hour: one of the cavaliers who go forth to conquer; practical men, not men of letters (except perhaps for some of the Greeks or Romans or some others of modern times, of whom there are so many of such nobility in Spain). Otherwise I should be grievously mis-judged, for in the Indies there are no settled people and no established colony.

To the gold and pearls the gate is now open, and we can confidently expect a great quantity of all – precious stones and spices and a thousand other things. As I hope for heaven, I swear that everything I have gained, including on my first voyage, shall, with our Lord's help, be offered to Him in equal measure for the expedition to Arabia Felix, even to Mecca, according to the plan I wrote for their Highnesses when replying to the enquiry Antonio de Torres brought about how to divide the land and sea with the Portuguese. And after that, I should be able to undertake the expedition to Calicut, as I projected by word of mouth and in writing when I was staying at the friary of La Mejorada.*

The news of gold, which I said I should give, is that on Christmas Day, when I was sorely afflicted by the war waged against me by wicked Christians and by Indians, and on the point of giving everything up and escaping, if I could, with my life, our Lord came miraculously for my solace and said: 'Have strength. Be not afraid. I shall provide in all things. The seven years appointed for you to share in the gold are not yet passed, and in this and all else redress shall be made to you.' That day I learned that there were eighty leagues of land, along the whole length of which were gold mines. At present it appears that it is all one deposit. Some men have gathered 120 castellanos' worth in a single day, others ninety, and as much as 250 have been collected in a day. And between fifty and seventy – or, in a great number of cases, between twenty and fifty – is reckoned a good day's work and there are many men who are carrying it on. The common mean is from six to twelve and anyone who gathers less than that is left dissatisfied. It seems, too, that these mines are like others: they do not yield the same amount every day. These mines are new and the miners new to the work. It is everyone's opinion that even if the whole of Castile were to go out there, however lazy any particular individual was, he would still not get less than one or two castellanos a day, despite being a novice in the business. It is true that they have an Indian or two to help but the success of the operation depends on the Christian. You can see how sensible Bobadilla was to give everything away for nothing and squander four million maravedis in tithes without cause, and without being asked, and without first notifying their Highnesses. And that is not the only harm he has done.

I know that if I have erred it has not been with any evil intent. And I believe that their Highnesses accept what I have said. And I know and can see that they are merciful even to those who serve them with malice. I believe, and hold for certain, that they will treat me with far better and greater mercy, for my fall was innocent and forced, as they shall know fully in due course. And I am their creature, and they will behold the service I have performed and will learn each day how much they have gained. They will weigh all in the balance, as Holy Scripture tells us shall be done on the Day of Judgement with the evil and the good. If it is still their command that I should be judged by a third party – which is not what I hope – and that it should take the form of an inquiry in the Indies, I humbly beseech them to send there two persons of conscience and of honour, at my own cost, who will now easily find that five marks' worth of gold can be got in four hours. Whether in this connection or not, it is essential for some such provision to be made.

When the Comendador arrived in Santo Domingo, he stayed in my house. Just as he found it, he appropriated it to himself. Good luck to him. Maybe he needed it. No pirate ever thus used a merchant. My more serious complaint is about my papers, for he has taken them from me so that not one sheet could ever be wrested from him. And those which would have been most useful to me in my defence are the ones he has most effectively hidden. See what a just and honourable investigator he is! From what I hear, not one of the many things he has done has been within the bounds of justice – not one. Our Lord God is above in His power as ever He was, and to the ends of the earth He shall punish wrongs, especially those inflicted in ingratitude.

The following autograph fragment covers more briefly some of the same ground as the letter to Juana de Torres and presumably belongs to the same context.

Fragment of a Memorandum apparently addressed to the Council of Castile late 1500?*

My lords, It is now seventeen years since I came to serve these princes in the enterprise of the Indies. I spent the first eight locked in dispute and at the end of it my advice was treated as a joke. I persevered in it with a full heart and I turned away approaches from France and England and Portugal with the reply that those lands and lordships were for the King and Queen, my lord and lady. The promises I made were neither few nor vain. Over here our Redeemer smoothed my path. Over there I have reduced to their obedience more land than is contained in Africa and Europe and more than seven thousand islands, besides Hispaniola, which has a longer coastline than Spain. It is believed that the Holy Church will flourish there greatly. As far as the material gains are concerned, it is common report what can be hoped for.

I carried out this conquest in seven years, by God's will. At a time when I was thinking of retiring with the favours granted to me, I was suddenly seized and dragged away loaded with chains, much to my dishonour and hardly to their Highnesses' advantage. The case against me was trumped up in malice. It rested on the testimony of civilians who had risen in rebellion and were trying to take the country over. And the man who was sent to look into it had a commission to stay on as Governor, if he found a serious case against me. Is there anyone anywhere who would ever regard such a thing as just? In this business I have foregone my youth and lost the share of these gains which is due to me, as well as the honour of the discovery – unless this is put right in Castile, where my deeds shall be judged, and I shall be judged as a captain who went from Spain to make conquests as far as the Indies, and not to govern a city or town or people that was already well ordered, but rather to reduce to their Highnesses' sway savage peoples who are warlike and live in mountain ranges and forests.

I beseech your lordships that, with the commitment proper to very faithful Christians in whom their Highnesses repose so much trust, you will look at all my papers, and at how I came to serve these Princes from so far away, and left my wife and children, whom I never saw in consequence, and how now, at the end of my life, I am stripped of my honour and estate without cause and how neither justice nor mercy has been respected therein. When I said 'mercy', I did not mean to refer to their Highnesses, for the fault is not theirs.

Columbus's claim to a special relationship with the Queen, together with most of the other preoccupations of his time in Spain between 1500 and 1502, is expressed in a letter in his own hand in the royal archives.* It is a curious letter which disclaims artifice but is full of literary contrivance, with its rhetorical inversions of word order and its coquettish, courtly tone.

Most Christian Queen, I am the servant of your Highness. The keys to my desires I gave to you in Barcelona. If you try a taste of my good will, you will find its scent and savour have only increased since then, and

198

not by a little. My constant concern is for your peace of mind. If it should be your pleasure to put my efforts to the test, it could be that some evidence of my sincerity might have a chance to emerge. My very great trust in that pious Redeemer of ours is what gives me the courage to say so, not any strength or skill that might be ascribed to me.

I dedicated myself to your Highness in Barcelona without holding back any part of me, and as it was with my spirit, so it was with my honour and estate. Fray Juan Pérez will confirm this and so will the [Prince's] nurse. And I remain in the same path and ever more steadfast.

My thoughts on my own life I gave to your Highness in a memoir written in my own hand. If I could believe that your Highness is aware that it was written without malice or artifice, I should be very happy.

I see this enterprise of the Indies as a very great affair. Because of your Highness's many other undertakings, and your ill health, the management of it is not running perfectly. This saddens me on two accounts: first, because of the matter of Jerusalem, which I beg your Highness not to treat lightly, nor to believe that I spoke about it with any ulterior motive. The second reason is that I am afraid this enterprise is heading for ruin. I beseech your Highness not to suppose in this or any other connection that I am anything but at your service and to believe that, without dissemblance, I am disposed with all my strength to seek your repose and contentment and to increase your lofty sway.

May your Highness now consider whether it would be your pleasure to put this commitment of mine to the test in this matter of the Indies or the other business of the Holy House. And as I have said, let this be as to a servant and not an opponent. For my God pardon them who have tried to make your Highness believe otherwise.

The order can be given and the matter put in hand at once without any serious difficulties. And if your Highness were pleased to heed my advice, it would be done right away and I believe that it will be very much to your Highness's satisfaction.

It appears from the letter to Juana de Torres that Columbus had written from Hispaniola, after the return of Antonio de Torres, with a project for an expedition to Mecca. The reconquest of Jerusalem, which Columbus seems to have advocated as a practical undertaking since before his first voyage, must have been connected with this plan, not only because of the relative geographical proximity of the two places, but also because of the link in prophetic tradition between the extirpation of Islam and the creation of the Last World Empire in Jerusalem.

The document which follows appears to have been written in justification of the scheme in reply to a demand from Ferdinand and Isabella that Columbus explain his reasons for believing in the practicability of the project.* It survives in two copies, one of which is in a compilation, made by Columbus, of prophetic texts and random pieces, which he apparently intended to work up into a systematic exposition of the providential origins of his plans; letters exchanged between him and his Carthusian friend, Fray Gaspar de Gorricio, whose help he enlisted for the editing of the collection, show that it was in progress in September 1501. A further reference proves that it was still being worked on after Columbus's return from his last voyage in November 1504. The surviving text, however, is no more than an ill-ordered draft, and it is not clear why the letter which follows forms part of it. Nevertheless, Columbus's lucubrations among divinatory scriptures seem genuinely to form the backdrop against which this letter was composed.

In some ways, the letter is an impressive piece of writing, full of vivid images and successful rhetorical devices. The structure, however, is disorderly and the arguments feeble and obscure. Columbus seems to have three main 'reasons' to cite in favour of the expedition to Jerusalem. The first is that the idea comes from the Holy Spirit. As evidence in favour of this elusive proposition he cites the previous interventions of the Paraclete in his life: in providing him with an education in inauspicious circumstances; in inspiring his transatlantic design; in influencing Ferdinand and Isabella to take it up; and he represents himself as a suitable vessel for the outpourings of the Spirit on the grounds that he is essentially an unlearned man, like the evangelists and the children and innocents whom God commonly favoured as His mouthpieces. This emphasis on the irrelevance of erudition may owe something to the influence of Franciscan tradition, which assigned a high value to holy simplicity and was mistrustful of the vanity of unnecessary learning; it also clearly matches the main theme of Columbus's long-maintained war with the courtly savants, against whom he had so many times cited his own practical wisdom. In the letter to the monarchs he seems to hesitate between two mutually exclusive self-appraisals; he repeats his oft-asserted claim to the authority that is due to practical experience, but plumps rather for a self-characterisation as an ignoramus unencumbered by worldly learning of any sort and wholly dependent on God.

His second argument, compressed into a brief allusion, is that success will attend an expedition to Jerusalem if the monarchs (and their subjects, who will provide the resources) have sufficient faith. The third is that success is prophesied by two divinatory traditions: that derived from scripture and that derived from astrology. This part of the letter seems to anticipate his anthology of prophetic texts. He does not get around to citing any scriptures that foretell the recovery of Jerusalem; the texts from Isaiah to which he alludes seem to have been read by him as prophecies of the discovery of the Indies. It is clear enough, however, that in the prophecies with which he is chiefly concerned at the time of writing this letter, the event predicted is the end of the world. Columbus regards the recapture of Jerusalem as a necessary precondition of this consummation, because the establishment of Jerusalem as the court of the Last World Emperor and the cosmic struggle of that hero with Antichrist were seen, in the tradition of prophecy that went back to Joachim of Fiore, to precede the last days. Thus Columbus claims that St Augustine's calculations of the age of the world suggest that only 155 years are left; that the discovery of the New World is part of the divine acceleration of history that must precede the end; that a great change, including some of the expected prerequisites of the end of the world, could be anticipated from astrological data; and that Joachim associated the recapture of Jerusalem with a Spanish initiative.

It has to be said that Columbus was as inattentive a reader of prophetic as of geographical literature. For example, a cycle of ten revolutions of Saturn described by Pierre d'Ailly had come to an end in 1489; it might therefore be alleged as a portent of the discovery of America, but cannot also have been relevant to Columbus's projected conquest of Jerusalem.* He fails to make use of Pierre d'Ailly's texts on planetary conjunctions; his references to d'Ailly's passages on Antichrist, which were highly germane to Columbus's views, are left vague and unexploited; nor does Columbus seem aware that in those passages the cardinal was reporting the views of Roger Bacon.* And the text he attributes to Joachim seems to be an invention of his own, or a mistaken tradition of the time.*

Not only does the letter show us Columbus wrestling with esoteric literature; it also gives us his retrospect on his own life at a moment of intense anxiety and self-examination. In this brief chapter of autobiography he discloses that he took to the sea at an early age; that practical experience preceded and inspired book-learning; and that he regarded his achievement as owing nothing to 'reason or mathematics or mappamundi'. This last point was demonstrably false, since, by his own account (above, p. 45) he tried to navigate by the aid of a marine chart on his first voyage; but it better suited Columbus's need to present himself as divinely guided to forget or ignore that fact. And there recurs that familiar image of the lonely and derided Columbus, which may have been imagined rather than real.

Letter to Ferdinand and Isabella, 1501?

Most Christian and very exalted Princes, The reason I have for believing in the restoration of the Holy House to the Holy Church Militant is as follows:

Very exalted King and Queen, From a very young age I began sailing on the sea and I have continued to do so to this day. This same art inclines all who follow it to wish to know the secrets of this world. It is now more than forty years since I began this way of life. Every sea so far traversed have I sailed. I have conversed and exchanged ideas with learned men, churchmen and laymen, Latins and Greeks, Jews and Moors and many others of other religions. To that wish of mine I found that our Lord was very favourably disposed, and for it He gave me the spirit of understanding. He endowed me abundantly in seamanship; for astrology He gave me sufficient aptitude, and for geometry and arithmetic too, with the wit and craftsmanship to make representations of the globe and draw on them the cities, rivers and mountains, islands and harbours, all in their proper places. Throughout this time I have seen and studied books of every sort – geography, history, chronicles, philosophy, and other arts – whereby our Lord opened my understanding with His manifest Hand to the fact that it was practicable to sail from here to the Indies. And He inspired me with the will to put it into effect. And aflame therewith, I came to serve your Highnesses. All those who heard of my proposal made fun of it as they smilingly turned it down. All the sciences I mentioned above, and all the authorities who had written about them, availed me nothing. Only in your Highnesses did faith and constancy prevail. Who can doubt that your enlightenment came from the Holy Spirit, the same as mine?

With miraculous rays of light He came to your help, and with His Holy Scriptures, most lofty and luminous. With forty-four books of the Old Testament and four Gospels and twenty-three epistles of those blessed apostles, He came to encourage me to persevere; and continually since then, without a moment's pause, they rapidly put new heart into me.

It was our Lord's will to send a most evident miracle in the form of the voyage to the Indies to give me and others hope for this further expedition to the Holy House. I spent seven years here in your royal court debating the merits of the case with very many persons of much learning and authority in all the arts, and in the end they came to the conclusion that it was all futile, and with that they gave the matter up. Afterwards, it happened as our Lord Jesus Christ had said and had said before through the mouths of His holy prophets. And so we must believe that this other enterprise shall be fulfilled in the same way, in witness thereof, if what has been said does not suffice, I call on the Holy Gospel, in which God said that all things would pass away, save His own marvellous Word. And by this He meant that all would certainly be fulfilled as was written by Him and the prophets.

I said that I would declare the reason I have for believing in the restoration of the Holy House to the Holy Church. Let me say that I leave on one side all my navigational experience from an early age and all the discussions I have had with so many people in so many lands and from so many religious traditions; and I leave on one side all the many arts and writings which I referred to above. I rely entirely on holy, sacred Scripture and certain prophetic te ts by certain saintly persons, who by divine revelation have had something to say on this matter. It could be that your Highnesses and all others who know me and to whom this paper shall be shown, will admonish me publicly or privately with various reproaches: as a man ungifted in scholarship, as a lay seafarer, as an earthy, practical fellow, etc. I reply in St Matthew's words: 'Oh Lord, Who wouldst hide these things from the clever and learned and reveal them to little innocents!' And St Matthew again: when our Lord entered Jerusalem, 'the children sang out, "Hosanna to the Son of David!"' The scribes to test Him asked if He heard what they were saying, and He answered saying, '"Yes. Have you never heard that out of the mouths of babes and sucklings the truth has been brought forth?"' Or I would appeal more generally to the example of the apostles who uttered such well founded truths, especially St John: '*In principio erat Verbum et Verbum erat apud Deum*,' etc. – such exalted words from men who had never had any higher learning!*

It is my opinion that the Holy Spirit works through Christians, Jews, Moors and all others of whatever religion; and not just through the learned but also the ignorant. For in my time I have seen a villager who could give an account of the night sky and the stars and their courses better than others who had spent money to learn it. And let me say that not only does the Holy Spirit reveal future happenings to rational beings, but He shows them to us by signs in the heavens, and the air and the beasts when it so pleases Him, as in the example of the ox of which He made use in Rome in Julius Caesar's time, and in many other ways which would be tedious to relate and which are well recognised throughout the world.*

Holy Scripture bears witness in the Old Testament, through the mouths of the prophets, and in the New through our Redeemer Jesus Christ, that this world shall come to an end. The signs of when this shall be were given by Matthew and Mark and Luke. The prophets, too, had predicted it amply. St Augustine says that the end of this world must come in the seventh millennium after its creation. Our holy theologians follow him, especially Cardinal Pierre d'Ailly in his eleventh chapter* and other places which I shall specify below. From the creation of the world or of Adam until the advent of our Lord Jesus Christ there elapsed 5,343 years, and 318 days, by the reckoning of King Alfonso, whose is considered the most reliable (Pierre d'Ailly, *Elucidarium astronomice concordiae cum theologia et historia*, chapter X).* Adding to them 1,501 which is not yet finished, makes in all 6,844, rising 45. By this account, only 155 years are wanting to complete 7,000 when, it is said, by the authorities mentioned, the world must come to an end.

Our Lord said that before the end of this world all that had been written by the prophets would have to be fulfilled. In their writings, the prophets used various means to speak of the future with reference to the past and the past with reference to the future, as well as of the present, and they said many things with figures of speech, others symbolically and others entirely literally; and one might use such devices more than others, and another less so and some better than others. Isaiah was the one most praised by St Jerome and St Augustine and the other doctors of the Church and all endorse him and hold him in great reverence. Of Isaiah they say that he is not just a prophet but an evangelist: he spared no effort to write down what was to come and to call all men to our Holy Catholic Faith.

Many holy doctors and sacred theologians wrote about all the prophecies and other books of the Holy Scriptures. They cast much light on what was formerly unknown to us, even though they disagreed in many things. There were some matters which it was not given to them to understand.

I must come back again to repeat my claim not to be dismissed as unlearned and presumptuous and I still rally to that text of St Matthew, who said, 'Oh, Lord, Who wouldst hide these things from the clever and learned and reveal them to little innocents!' And with this I make my reply, and with the practical experience which has been seen to confirm it. A very great part of the prophecies and Holy Scriptures has now been fulfilled. The Scriptures tell of it and Holy Church proclaims it in a high voice unceasingly, and no other witness of it is needed. I shall speak of one instance, because it touches my case and gives me relief and makes me content whenever I think of it. I am a most grievous sinner. The pity and mercy of our Lord have covered me entirely whenever I have called on them. Most sweet consolation have I found when I have placed all my care in the contemplation of His wonderful countenance. I have already said that to carry out the enterprise of the Indies I made no use of reason or mathematics or mappamundi. What Isaiah had prophesied was amply fulfilled.

And that is what I wanted to write here, to bring it to your Highnesses' notice and to help you to find gladness in what I have to tell you of the other matter of Jerusalem, relying on the same authorities. For in that enterprise, if there is faith, you shall have a most certain victory. Let your Highnesses remember the Gospels and the many promises which our Lord made to us, and how all has come to pass in practice. St Peter, when he leaped into the water, could walk on it as long as his faith held firm. Whoever has so much faith as a grain of wheat shall find that the mountains obey him. Whoever asks in faith, all shall be given unto him. Knock and it shall be opened unto you.* No one need fear to undertake a great enterprise in our Saviour's name, as long as it is just and of a healthy purpose in His holy service. He succoured St Catherine when He saw how her faith was put to the test. Let not your Highnesses forget how you undertook the conquest of this kingdom of Granada with little money in hand. Our Lord leaves our decisions in all things to our free will, even though He may give many men warnings. Nothing shall be wanting for this that is in your people's power to give. Oh, how the Lord is good, Who desires that deeds be done in His service with the means which He provides! Day and night and at all times all people ought to give Him their devoutest thanks.

I said above that much remained to be accomplished before the prophecies were fulfilled, and let me say that they are great things in the world and that it is a sign that our Lord is hastening them on. The preaching of the Gospel recently, in so many lands in so short a time, suggests it to me.

Cardinal Pierre d'Ailly writes at length about the extinction of the sect of Muhammad and about the coming of Antichrist in a treatise of his, *De concordia astronomiae veritatis et narrationis historicae,* in which he treats of the opinions of many astronomers concerning the ten revolutions of Saturn, especially towards the end of the book in the last nine chapters.* Abbot Joachim of Fiore said that he who would rebuild the House upon Mount Sion would be sure to come from Spain.

Columbus's compilation of prophetic texts, the *Book of Prophecies,* consists mainly of texts copied without comment. There are some jottings of an apparently casual nature and a fragment of what appears to be a copy of a passage on eclipses observed by Columbus with calculations of longitude arising from the observations, essentially similar to material discussed below (p. 270). In addition, three fragments of verse appear. There are eight lines on the propriety of keeping one's promises, which may have been relevant, in Columbus's mind, to the suits he addressed to his monarchs. A verse of twelve lines celebrates the feast of St John the Baptist, to whom Columbus may be presumed to have had some special devotion (above, p. 131). Along with some rough drafting attempts, the following long and introspective poem appears in the margins of a leaf at the end of a book; copies of the first two verses of it are also transcribed on a page towards the middle of the collection. Although included in a document substantially of 1501, the verses could have been written much later, to judge from the use of the margins for the finished version. In its ballad-like verse form and sententious message, the poem resembles the genre, popular at the court of Ferdinand and Isabella, of moral philosophy in verse, in which Franciscan writers specialised.* Each verse begins with a Latin term; read sequentially, these yield the message: *Memorare novissima tua et in aeternum non peccabis.* In the Middle Ages this legend, based on a text of Ecclesiasticus, was associated with images of St Jerome and was interpreted as an exhortation to penitence: in this

Frontispiece to Giuliano Dati's *La lettera dellisole che ha trovato nuovamente il Re dispagna*, 1493, the verse translation of Columbus's letter to Luis de Santángel: 'The people of this island . . . all go naked, men and women, as their mothers bore them, although some of the women cover themselves up in just one place with a leaf of grass'

The port of Seville in the mid-sixteenth century

tradition, it could be translated, 'Be mindful of thy most recent actions and thou shalt avoid sin in eternity.' For Columbus, the phrase seems to have had a different, triumphant and self-righteous meaning which I have tried to reflect in the translation given here, where the terms originally in Latin are capitalised. I do not think there can be any doubt that for Columbus they formed a self-referential sentence, just as the lines on the fate of the malicious must have referred to his enemies; and the entire poem seems expressive of his state of mind in the period following the third Atlantic crossing.

Verses from the Book of Prophecies, *after 1501?*

REMEMBER, Man, in time of trial,
To hold, whoever thou mayst be,
Steadfast to God without denial,
If thou wouldst reign, within due while,
With Him in immortality.
Our end in death we all shall see.
Give thought to making thy provision
To clear the way for thy last mission,
When the time comes to sail that sea.

UNHEARD OF DEEDS have been provided
By holy saints, time and again,
Who fled the world, its ways derided,
Upon Christ's service ay decided.
By travails wracked, enduring pain,
They spurned the motley and the strain
Of flesh, which is all vanity.
So thou in due humility
Must now thy passion's frenzy rein.

OF THINE OWN deeds the contemplation
Must be thy very urgent case,
And if thy wrongs shall lead apace
To wicked men's last destination
Or whether to that blessed station
Attained by just men, who have paid,

To God and Caesar, duly weighed,
Their ultimate consideration.

AND thou must raise uplifted thought,
Henceforth to heaven and must flee
The coarse world's dull depravity,
In wisdom seeking glory's court,
Ever resolved to set at nought
The vicious sins that would enslave thee.
Follow the counsel that shall save thee
And learn to shun the other sort.

EVER shall they joyful sleep
Who embraced good without alloy
And ever, too, shall others weep
Who feed the fires of the deep.
Because their lives they did employ
Maliciously, and did enjoy
The pleasures of the world and greed,
Forever forfeit is their mede
Of riches that can never cloy.

SINLESS BE, and contemplate
The agonies of those who die,
How grief and terror are the fate
Of sinners in their wretched state.
Think well, as far as in thee lie,
Upon the just, released at last
From travails suffered in the past,
Into the light eternally.

At this remove of time, Columbus's efforts at self-vindication make
fascinating reading. For contemporaries, however, they probably
seemed a bore. For two years after Columbus's arrival in chains, the
monarchs had to endure his implied reproaches, veiled threats, embittered claims and fantastic proposals. By early 1502 both he and his
patrons seem to have tired of it. In February Columbus sought and
obtained leave to make a further voyage across the Ocean Sea. Before
leaving he loosed off a volley of business letters and also wrote a
general account of his career so far, addressed to the Pope, with a

request for members of religious orders to be appointed to evangelise the new discoveries.*

The letter to the Pope is characterised by some of the same preoccupations as are to be found in the documents of 1500–1501, including the *Book of Prophecies*, in its early draft. The discovery of the whereabouts of the earthly Paradise, the projected reconquest of Jerusalem, the interest in making calculations of longitude from observations of eclipses, the insistence on the Salmonic geography of the lands Columbus discovered: these themes intrude with Columbus's characteristic pertinacity. Satan's manoeuvres are mentioned, nor does Columbus forget his treasured pearl fishery. The discoveries are described with compressed hyperbole: the familiar expansive epithets are omitted but a barrage of fantastic statistics is calculated to impress the reader.

It is hard to resist the impression that Columbus was preparing an appeal over the monarchs' heads to a rival potential patron. For an ordinary subject to request the appointment of clergy directly, without reference to the monarchs, was an irregular and perhaps treasonable proceeding. Columbus breaks off with a promise to lay his complaints against the monarchs before the Holy Father privately. It is not clear, however, whether the letter was ever finished or sent.

Letter to Pope Alexander VI, February 1502

Most Holy Father, When I undertook this enterprise and went to discover the Indians, it was my intention to come personally at once into your Sanctity's presence to give an account of it all. At that time a dispute arose between the lord King of Portugal and my lord King and lady Queen when the King of Portugal asserted that he too wished to discover and conquer lands along the same route, towards the same regions. And it was referred to arbitration.

My lord King and lady Queen sent me hurriedly back to the enterprise in order to discover and conquer all there was, and so my visit to your Holiness could not take place. Along this route I found and took possession of 1,400 islands and 333 leagues of the mainland of Asia, without counting other islands of great repute and large size, well to the east of Hispaniola, on which I established a foothold and around the coast of which I sailed for 800 leagues of four miles each. And it is very well populated. In a short time I made all the people of it tributaries of my lord King and lady Queen. In it are mines of every sort of metal, especially gold and copper. There are brazil wood, sandalwood, aloe wood, and many other spices. And there is incense: the tree on which it grows is of the mastic family.

This island is Tarshish. It is Qittim. It is Ophir and Ophaz and Cipangu, and we have named it Hispaniola.* On this voyage I sailed so far to the west that when the sun set at night, there were two hours' difference to the end of the Orient; for, counting from Cadiz in Spain, I had sailed through ten hours' time difference into the western hemisphere. And there could be no mistake about this, for at the time, on 14 September, there was an eclipse of the moon.*

Afterwards it was necessary to return hurriedly to Spain and I left behind two brothers with a large number of men in great need and peril.

I returned to them with help and made a new voyage towards the south, where I found immeasurably vast lands and fresh water in the sea. I believed and do believe what so many saints and teachers of sacred theology did and do believe – that in that region is the earthly Paradise. The needy state in which I had left my brothers and the men was the reason why I could not linger to learn more of those areas by experience or return to travel further among them. I found there a very great pearl fishery.

And in the island of Hispaniola half the men were up in arms and wandering at large waywardly. And when I was hoping for some peace – for in all the time that had passed since I began, death had not let me out of his clutches for a single hour – my perils and hardships were renewed.

My spirit would rejoice and be at rest if now at last I could come to your Holiness with my writings, which I have made for the purpose and which are in the form and fashion of the commentaries of Caesar. I have been at work on them from the first day until the present, when my plan has been interrupted by the need to make another voyage in the name of the Holy Trinity. It shall be for your glory and the honour of the Holy Christian Faith. This thought consoles me and helps me have no fear for dangers and set at nought the many travails and deaths I have witnessed in the course of this enterprise, with so little gratitude from the world. I hope from our everlasting God for victory this time as always in the past. And, to be sure, after I return here, I shall not rest until I come to your Holiness, with word of it all and my writings, for you are great-hearted and zealous for the honour and increase of the Holy Christian Faith.

Now, most Holy Father, I beseech your Sanctity, for my own repose and for other reasons which touch so holy and noble an enterprise as this, to help me with the persons of some priests and religious who I know are ideal for the purpose; and by your letters patent give orders to all ministers of the Orders of St Benedict, of the Charterhouse, of St Jerome, of the Friars Minor, and of Mendicants generally, to enable me, or someone with authority from me, to choose up to six of them. And these shall go about their business wherever they may be needed on this holy enterprise. For I hope in our Lord to spread His Holy Name and Gospel throughout the world. Therefore let your order be that the superiors of those religious whom I shall choose, from whatever house or monastery of the Orders aforenamed or to be named hereafter, shall not impede or deny them, neither by virtue of such privileges as they may possess nor for any other reason, but rather speed them on their way and help and succour them as far as they are able, and be pleased to give their assent, obedience and best endeavours to so holy and Catholic an enterprise and undertaking.

To this end may it please your Holiness to dispense them from spiritual duties, 'no reason withstanding', etc., granting and ordering on their behalf, moreover, that when they shall wish to return to their monasteries they shall be welcomed and as well treated as before, or better if their efforts so merit. I shall receive this favour as a great mercy from your Holiness and I shall be very much consoled by it and it will be greatly to the advantage of the Christian faith.

This enterprise was undertaken with the aim of spending any profit there might be from it on garrisoning the Holy House for the Holy Church. Once I had been there and seen what the land was like, I wrote to my lord King and lady Queen, promising that within seven years I would pay for 50,000 foot and 5,000 horse for the conquest of the Holy House, and within five years more another 50,000 foot and another 5,000 horse, which would add up to 10,000 horse and 100,000 foot for this purpose. Our Lord clearly showed that I would be able to keep my promise, showing in practice that this year I should be able to give their Highnesses 120 quintals of gold with the assurance that another like sum would be forthcoming after another period of five years.

Satan has upset all this and with his powers has set affairs in train so that neither purpose shall be accomplished, unless our Lord ties him down. The overall governorship was granted to me in perpetuity, but now I have been ejected from it in anger. It seems very certain that this was a result of the malevolence of the enemy of mankind, to prevent so holy a purpose from emerging into the light. It will be well to leave all this to be spoken of rather than briefly written.

Of the business letters Columbus wrote on the eve of his last voyage, only the following one, addressed to the directors of the Bank of San Giorgio in Genoa, and written in his own hand, contains any self-revelations.* In his disillusionment with his royal patrons in Spain his thoughts turned not only to the Pope as a potential protector, but also to the sovereign republic in which he was born. Ostensibly, the purpose of the letter is to inform the bank that Columbus has ordered his son to deposit money with them: this is consistent with the advice the explorer had included in the document entailing his estate. Additionally, however, Columbus seems anxious to assure the Genoese bankers of his own credit-worthiness. He mentions that he has deposited his contracts for safe-keeping with the Genoese ambassador in Spain, Niccolò di Oderigo, and declares his anxiety that the bankers should see this proof of his title to wealth and honours; by adding the assurance that he still enjoys royal favour, Columbus displays a concern that his fellow-countryman may be aware of his fall. The inflated signature, which expands on Columbus's titles by calling him 'Almirante mayor' rather than just 'Almirante' and adding a reference to Asia which was not part of the official title, seems to betray similar anxiety, or, at least, to show that Columbus was keen to write himself up in extravagant terms.

The purpose for which he claimed to be sending money to Genoa is unclear. It has commonly been supposed that it was intended for relief of the Genoese poor, but the language of the letter suggests to me rather that Columbus was instructing the bank to hold it against the cost of supplies for his own undertakings. In a memorandum to his son of about this time, Columbus enjoins that a tenth of the family income be set aside for charitable purposes, but makes no mention of Genoa. The reply of the directors of the bank, which survives, salutes Columbus's achievements in appropriate terms but does not suggest that Columbus's deposit was interpreted as an act of charity.* In a further letter to Oderigo, of 17 December 1504, Columbus refers to a deposit he had intended to make 'of a tenth of my income against the dues on corn and other provisions'.*

212

Letter to the Bank of San Giorgio, Genoa, 2 April 1502

Very noble Sirs, Although my body wanders here, my heart is always in Genoa. Our Lord has shown me more mercy than He ever showed to anyone since David. The deeds of the enterprise I undertook now shine forth and would cast a great light but for the overshadowing darkness of the way government is being run out there.* I am returning to the Indies in the name of the Holy Trinity and shall come back at an early date. And as I am a mortal man I am leaving my son, Don Diego, with orders to send you a tenth of all the income that may obtain every year for an indefinite period, to be charged against the cost of corn and wine and other victuals. If this tithe amounts to anything, please receive it; if not, accept my assurance of the good will I bear. I beg you as a favour to esteem this son of mine as one who is well commended.

Master Niccolò di Oderigo knows more of my deeds than I do myself and to him I have sent the notarised copy of my charters and privileges, for him to keep well secured. It would please me for you to be able to see them. My lord King and lady Queen desire to do me honour, more than ever.

The Holy Trinity guard your noble persons and augment the very illustrious office you hold.

Given at Seville on the 2nd day of April of 1502.

The Grand Admiral of the Ocean Sea and Viceroy and Governor General of the Islands and Mainland of Asia and the Indies for the King and Queen, my lord and lady, and their Captain General of the Sea and Member of their Council.

.S.

.S.A.S.

X M Y

Xpo FERENS

VIII

LAST VOYAGE
AND DEATH

When the new Governor of Hispaniola, Nicolás de Ovando, left for the Indies in February 1502 his fleet numbered thirty vessels. When Columbus followed in May, he had four caravels. His plan was to resume the explorations which had been interrupted by his misadventures on Hispaniola after the third ocean crossing. As the early biographer who was said to be his son Fernando wrote, 'The Admiral's intention, as he crossed the Ocean, was to go and reconnoitre the land of Paria.'* It was known that the continental part of the New World, which Columbus had discovered at Paria in 1498, occupied a large part of the South Atlantic, but its northern extension was unknown. Columbus believed that it would be possible to sail through the gap between the islands he had found on his earlier crossings and this new continent, across what is now the western part of the Caribbean Sea. Thus he would reach the elusive land of gold and spices and, he supposed, perhaps meet up with Vasco da Gama, who, at the same time, was making a voyage to India by his proven route to the east.

Columbus hoped from this voyage for the realisation of all his frustrated ambitions, the negation of all his failures, and the vindication of his successes in one crowning triumph. He had been sustained since his fall from favour by a mood of exaltation and a climate of hope is apparent in his letters. He was thus ill prepared mentally for the disappointments that lay in wait. For this voyage, in which his hopes were so lofty, was to be the most manifest failure of his life. It would end not in Asia but in the depths of misery and the vicinity of despair. Struck by a hurricane, taxed almost beyond endurance by adverse winds, enfeebled by malaria, attacked by hostile Indians on the Panama coast, marooned at last on Jamaica, threatened with starvation and repudiated by many of his men, Columbus was to be driven into a mental refuge compounded of wishful thinking, mysticism and fantasy.

214

The crossing was the most rapid he ever enjoyed – twenty-one days from Gran Canaria. But there the plain sailing ended. He scarcely encountered a favourable wind or current for the rest of the journey. The monarchs had warned him not to disturb Ovando on Hispaniola or even to put in to that island on the outward journey. But this was not an instruction Columbus was disposed to obey. He was anxious to know how Ovando was managing the colony and to claim the moneys belonging to him which had accumulated there. Moreover, Santo Domingo was the only permanent port on that side of the ocean, and it was sensible, as well as amenable to his crew, to stop there before continuing with exploration. Moreover, when he arrived off Hispaniola, it became urgently necessary to put in to port, for a hurricane was blowing up and Columbus, who knew these waters better than anybody, accurately read the signs. He sent word to Ovando, asking to be admitted to the harbour and warning him of the coming storm. The Governor ignored his request and scorned his warning. Part of the fleet that had brought Ovando from Spain set off for home in the face of the hurricane, while Columbus's vessels sought shelter in a small natural harbour he knew nearby.

That night, while his flagship held fast, his other caravels broke their cables and survived only by luck and daring seamanship. The fate of the larger fleet was a tribute to the might of the storm. Nineteen ships went down, with more than five hundred hands. Among the dead was Francisco de Bobadilla, incarcerator of Columbus. The records of Columbus's and Bobadilla's administration were lost, and so was the largest shipment of gold yet despatched for Spain. The only ship to reach Castile was one that bore part of Columbus's own revenues.

Opposed by southerly winds, Columbus could not resume his explorations on the coast of Paria. He had no option but to head west, until, towards the end of July 1502, he came against the coast of Belize, near Bonacca at the eastern end of the Bay islands. It had taken nearly twice as long to cross the Caribbean as to cross the Atlantic. The coast of Honduras was continental in appearance, with an obvious hinterland of high mountains. This was confirmed by the natives, who impressed Columbus as more civilised than the islanders, better clothed, with skill in working copper and access to long-range trade. The coast trended east–west. The question was whether this land was continuous with the continent in the south which Columbus had discovered at Paria. If so, it would have been consistent with the explorer's earlier intentions to continue along his westward course and look for India in that direction. But Columbus decided to turn east and sail against the wind in the direction of his former discovery.

The explanation of this conduct seems to be that Columbus was misled by information received from the natives. He understood that on the course he adopted lay a strait which led across an isthmus to a large ocean. He made at least a tentative identification in his mind of this strait with the Straits of Malacca, through which Marco Polo had travelled at the foot of the Golden Chersonese (or Malay Peninsula, as it is now more prosaically called). If this were correct, India should lie beyond. The biography attributed to Columbus's son says that the confusion arose because native informants indicated a 'strait' or narrow strip of land – that is, the isthmus of Panama – which Columbus took to mean a strait of water 'in its usual sense, according to his great wish'.*

For nearly four months the Admiral and his men suffered the hardships, as they chased the chimerical strait, first of a gruelling beat against the wind and later, where the coast turned southwards at Cape Gracias a Dios, of a malarial coast in wretched weather and frequent torrential rain. The ships were damaged and the men sick. In Cariai – a region around the tenth parallel on the coast of modern Costa Rica – he found rumours of civilised and auriferous lands, apparently on the far coast of the isthmus. By late October 1502, at the end of a few weeks' more of unrewarding and unhealthy navigation along the coast, Columbus really was in gold-bearing country – the province of Veragua, near the modern border of Costa Rica and Panama. The availability of gold called a temporary halt to the quest for a strait. Columbus, wishful as ever, harboured hopes that this would prove to be his most profitable discovery so far, to enrich his sovereigns and silence his detractors. But the malevolent weather would not allow him to make so great a conquest easily. He was suffering from fever, like many of his men, and his ships were driven by the gales and battered by the rain further along the inhospitable coast as far as the mouth of the Culebra River. There they languished on 'a sea of blood that bubbled like a cauldron on a great fire'. Columbus may have exaggerated his tribulations, or depicted them over-vividly under the influence of fever and continuing adversity, but it was late November before he was able to begin his return to Veragua. And even then bad weather delayed his progress, so that it was not until the Feast of the Kings, 6 January 1503, that the little fleet arrived at the mouth of the river which Columbus called Belén – Bethlehem – in honour of the day.

Veragua proved to be a poor return for so much suffering. At first, signs were good: the Guaymis Indians appeared friendly and disposed, at least, to trade. An expedition under Bartolomé Colón found rich gold deposits up-river. In fact the gold was plentiful, but the steepness of the place and the volume of rain which falls there makes exploitation almost impossible, even today. The Spaniards soon experienced the deterrent effects of the torrents of water that cascade down the mountain-sides, carrying all the detritus before them, and even striking the sea and breaking against the Spanish ships with such force that their cables were strained or sundered. What was worse, relations with the Indians rapidly deteriorated, as was always the case when the cupidity and rapacity of the rank-and-file explorers was revealed. Columbus intended to leave his brother and a garrison in a fortified post on the banks of the River Belén, to open trade and prepare a large-scale exploitation of the gold, while the Admiral took the news to Hispaniola and prepared to mount the shipment of supplies and tools from there. But the hostile attitude adopted by the Indians, and the low water which delayed the departure of the fleet, clearly jeopardised this plan. Columbus was anxious to leave as soon as he could make deep water, for all the ships had developed worm-holes after such a time afloat in torrid waters, and he was afraid they would not remain seaworthy for long.

In April, at the blackest moment of this protracted ordeal, three factors – isolation, despair, fever – combined to produce in Columbus one of his experiences of the presence of God.

The account of this experience, offered by Columbus in the next document, is the fullest he gives of the celestial voice that communicated with him at so many pregnant intervals of his career. Was the experience genuinely felt, or was it a device wielded for a rhetorical purpose? There is an air of literary contrivance throughout. The language is saturated in biblical allusions, many of them worked into the text with a subtlety unusual in Columbus's writings. The parallels evoked – with Daniel and St John – as Columbus undergoes his transcendental experience alone, seem self-conscious. His climb to the top of the rigging, where he will hear the angelic voice, seems symbolic of a mystical ascent. He is careful never explicitly to claim a divine origin for the voice, even though the Spanish Church at the time was generally sympathetic to lay apparitions.* Whether genuine or not, the voice was a suspiciously convenient medium for conveying criticisms of Ferdinand and Isabella which Columbus might not have dared to offer in his own character. On the other hand, Columbus's capacity for self-delusion was so vast and the mystical experience – with its millenarian discourse and its egotism – so characteristic that the entire episode has a ring of truth.

As soon as he recovered, he set about evacuating his brother and the short-lived garrison from their dangerous stockade before the Indians could finish them off. As on his second voyage, Columbus witnessed the collapse of his hopes, which brought on something like a temporary derangement, but from which he recovered sufficiently to extricate himself and his men from immediate danger. The problem of the worm-eaten ships' hulls, however, made any escape fraught with new danger. Their only hope was to make for Hispaniola with all speed. Pumping and bailing, they worked their way eastward along the coast. Columbus estimated their position accurately and realised that they still had a considerable easting to make before getting upwind of Hispaniola, but the Admiral's prestige in the fleet can no longer have been very high, and the consensus was that they were much further east than he estimated, and that they ought to turn away from the mainland as soon as possible. Perhaps the men suspected Columbus of continuing the search for a passage to India, or of attempting to establish whether the coast they were sailing was continuous with that of the land of Paria. In fact by the time they left the coast on the Darien peninsula on 1 May 1503, they had reconnoitred almost as far as the previously known northern extension of the South American continent. It therefore seemed that the mainland must indeed be continuous from Brazil to Honduras.

As Columbus had predicted, they had sought the north too soon, and their course brought them up on the coast of Cuba. A last desperate effort to reach Hispaniola, before the leaking vessels should sink, landed them short (for the wind was against them) on the Jamaican coast, at the modern St Ann's Bay. They were effectively castaways, since their ships were unusable and the nearest Spanish settlement, at Santo Domingo, was over 450 miles away including more than a hundred miles of open water.

Such was the inglorious end of Columbus's last command. The account which follows was written on Jamaica on 7 July 1503, at a time when Columbus seems to have recovered some of his mental equilibrium: certainly, he made a remarkably good job of preserving the lives and morale of most of his men during a long and at times, it seemed, hopeless wait for rescue. On the other hand, the letter betrays signs of the old syndrome of paranoid introspection in the face of adversity, which has earned its Italian translation the nickname of 'Lettera Rarissima', meaning, in this context, 'the very odd letter' rather than the literal 'very rare letter'.

As always when things went wrong – only more intensely this time – the familiar elements of febrile self-deception flowed from Columbus's distraught brain in a flood, mingled this time with the fear of old age. In Veragua, he claims, he had found the mines of Solomon; now he would not only recover Jerusalem, but also convert the Emperor of China to Christianity. He even repeated his claim to have discovered the earthly Paradise. The themes of other digressions in the letter – pride in and anxiety for his sons, obsession with the monarchs' unfulfilled promises of favour, complaints about his usurped rights and income, fear of his enemies at court, vindication of his geographical theories, divagations on millenarian prophecies – are all familiar and all particularly associated with documents written at the crises of his life. He adds the revealing disclaimer that by the time of this last voyage he was no longer animated by the urge 'to win status or wealth – for by then all hope of such was dead'.

The most disturbing feature of Columbus's mental state at this time was that he sought to circumvent the fact of his failure by senselessly affirming that he had succeeded. All the mistakes he had made and errors he had discarded, he now reasserted with the insistence that he had been right from the first. His own great achievement in recognising the true nature of the American continent and exploring its northward extension as far as Honduras was submerged beneath the fallacious assertions that Cuba was a part of China, that all his discoveries were Asiatic, and that all the elements of his original theory about an Atlantic crossing, even down to the false value assigned to the length of a degree, were right. As long as good luck kept Columbus lucid, he had been able to transcend these mistakes to demonstrate his genius as a navigator and his deserts as a discoverer. This obstinate reversion to falsehoods marks the virtual end of Columbus's intellectual development, the triumph of obsession under the influence of ill fortune.

Letter to Ferdinand and Isabella,
Jamaica, 7 July 1503

Most Serene and very High and Mighty Princes, our lord King and lady Queen, From Cadiz I made the passage to Gran Canaria in four days, and from there to the Indies in sixteen, whence I wrote to say that it was my intention to hasten on my journey, while I still had ships in good condition, men and supplies and that my staging-post would be the island of Jamaica. And it was in Dominica that I wrote this. Up to that point I had had the best weather you could ask for. The night I arrived there it was blowing a great storm, which followed me everywhere thereafter.

When I arrived off Hispaniola I sent ashore to deliver the mail-bag and to request as a favour a ship to transport my moneys, for one which I had brought was unhandy and would not bear sail. They took the letters in and presumably they know whether they were delivered. Their reply to me was to send a message on your Highnesses' behalf that I should not berth or come ashore. Spirits fell among the men I had with me, for fear that I would have to take them a long way away; for they said that if any peril befell them they would find no remedy there but would be more likely to suffer some great affront. It was also said that the Comendador would be able to grant away any lands I won to whoever pleased him.

The storm was terrible and during the night it tore my ships apart. Each of them was borne off to an extremity, all in different directions, with no hope save of death. Each of them took it for granted that the rest were lost. Was there ever man born – not excepting Job himself – who would not die of despair at being denied refuge, at the hazard of his life and soul and those of his son and brothers and companions, in the very land and harbours which, by God's will and sweating blood, I won for Spain?

And I return to the ships, which, as I say, the storm had dispersed, leaving mine alone. Our Lord restored them to me in His own good time. The ship I had doubts of had thrown everything overboard, even the binnacle, in the effort to escape. The *Gallega* lost her boat, and all lost a good portion of their stores. The one I was in, which was bounced around bewilderingly, was saved by our Lord without damage to so much as a stick. My brother shipped in the one I had doubts of, and, under God, he was its salvation. And pursued by the storm, practically on my hands and knees, I reached Jamaica. There the high sea changed to calm, with a strong current, and carried me as far as the Jardín de la Reina [islands off Cuba to the south-west] without a landfall. Thence, when I could, I sailed for the mainland against a head wind and a terrible adverse current. I struggled against them for sixty days, and at the end of it I had not been able to cover more than seventy leagues.

In all this time I had not entered any port nor could I have done. Nor did the raging of heavens, seas, thunder and lightning leave me for a moment. It seemed like the end of the world. I reached Cape Gracias a Dios and from there our Lord gave me a fair wind and current. That was on 12 September. For eighty-eight days that terrifying storm had not left me, so that I had not seen the sun nor the stars at sea. And my ships were holed; the sails torn; the anchors and rigging lost, with the boats and cables and many provisions; the crew spent, and all full of contrition and of promises to amend their lives; and there was not one who had not sworn a vow to make a penance or pilgrimage. Many times they resorted to making their confessions, one to another.* Other storms there may have been, but never one so lasting or so fearsome. Many were sore dismayed and often enough these were the men whose strength we most relied on.

The sickness of the son I had with me [Fernando] tore at my soul, and all the more for seeing him at so tender an age – thirteen years old – in so much trouble and taking it all so well. Our Lord gave him such strength that he inspired the rest; and he attended to his chores as well as if he had spent eighty years at sea, and he raised my spirits. I had fallen sick and time and enough drew close to death; I commanded the fleet from a little cabin I had built above the deck. My brother [Bartolomé] was in the worst and most perilous of the ships. Great was my grief, and the more so because I had brought him against his own inclination. For, to my sorrow, the twenty years of service I have rendered, with so much hardship and danger, have done me so little good that today in Castile I do not possess so much as a tile for my roof.* If I want to eat or sleep I have nowhere to go save the inn or the tavern, and more often than not I am without the price of a shirt. Another sorrow tore my heart from my breast and that was Don Diego, my son, whom I had left behind in Spain, with no one to look after him, despoiled of the inheritance of my honour and estate, even though I firmly believed that your Highnesses, as just and grateful Princes, would restore all to him with advantage.

I reached the land of Cariay,* where I stopped to repair the ships and replenish the stores and give some respite to the crews, who had fallen very ill. As for me, as I have said, I was often close to death. There I heard of the mines of gold of the province of Ciamba,* which was one of the places I was on the look-out for. Two Indians guided me to Caramburú,* where the people go naked, except for a gold disc hung from the neck, but they are unwilling to sell or barter. They told me the names of many places on the sea coast where, they said, there were gold and mines. The last of these is Veragua, something like twenty-five leagues away. I set off with the intention of trying them all and, when I had got midway, I learned there were mines two days' sail away. I decided to send a party to inspect them. On the eve of St Simon and St Jude, when the party was ready to leave, the wind and sea arose so high that there was no alternative but to run before it, with the Indian who was our guide to the mines still with me.

In all the places I had been to so far, I found that what I had heard was true. This made me feel sure of the truth of what I was told about the province of Ciguare, which, from what they say, is nine days' journey away to the west. There, they say, there is unlimited gold and the people wear necklaces of it around their heads and bracelets on their arms and legs, all of thick gold, and they embellish and decorate their chairs, chests and tables with it. They also said that the women from there wear chains of gold dangling from their heads down their backs. The people of all the places we have visited agree about what I am saying and I would be happy if a tenth of it was true. Also, they all recognised pepper. In Ciguare they trade regularly in markets and fairs. The people here say so, and have shown me the manner and form in which they do business there. Again, they say that the ships from there carry ordnance, bows, arrows, swords and armour, and that the people wear clothes, and that in that country there are horses and they practise war and wear rich apparel and have fair possessions. They also say that the sea goes round to Ciguare and that ten days' journey from there is the River Ganges. It seems that the relationship between these lands is like that of Tortosa to Fuenterrabía or Pisa to Venice.

When I left Caramburú and reached the places I mentioned I found the people were of the same way of life, except that those who had the gold discs were willing to sell them for three hawks' bells, even if they were worth more than ten or fifteen ducats by weight. In all their customs they are like the people of Hispaniola; they gather gold by a variety of different means, though none is efficient by Christian standards.

What I have said so far is hearsay. What I know for certain is that in the year '94 I covered twenty-four degrees of the surface of the sea, sailing west, in the space of nine hours. And there can have been no mistake about it because an eclipse took place. The sun was in Libra and the moon in Aries.* What is more, from my reading I had learned in advance about the things of which I was now being told. Ptolemy thought he had put the calculations of Marinus right, but now we find that the latter's writings were very close to the facts. Ptolemy placed Catigara on the twelfth meridian beyond his limit of the west, which he fixed at two and one-third degrees west at Cape St Vincent in Portugal. Marinus, however, assigned to the portion of the world occupied by land, up to its limits, an extent corresponding to fifteen hours of sun. Marinus made Africa extend more than twenty-four degrees south of the equator and now that the Portuguese sail down there they have found that he was right. Ptolemy claims that the southernmost land is within his first zone and does not extend more than fifteen and one-third degrees.*

This world is small. Land covers six parts of it and only the seventh is covered by water.* Experience has now proved it. And I have written the proof down in other writings of mine, with, in addition, citations from Holy Scripture and the location of the earthly Paradise, as approved by Holy Church. I say the world is not as big as commonly supposed and that one degree measured along the earth's surface at the equator corresponds to fifty-six and two-thirds miles, as sure as I stand here.* Let me put this subject on one side, for it is not my purpose to enlarge on it but rather to give an account of my hard and troublesome voyage – though it may turn out to be my noblest and most profitable.

I have said that on the eve of St Simon and St Jude I ran before the wind wherever it drove me, without being able to resist. I sheltered in a harbour for ten days against the high rage of the sea and the heavens. There I decided that I would not return to the mines but treat them as a gain already made. I left to continue on my voyage. I reached Puerto de Bastimentos* [on 10 November] in heavy rain, where I put in rather unwillingly. The storm and strong current hemmed me in for fourteen days and when I left the weather was still bad. When I had made fifteen leagues, the wind and current forced me back in their fury. As I headed back for the harbour I had just left, I found [on 26 November] that of Retrete* on the way, and struggled in there, through peril and stress in plenty, to my utter exhaustion and that of the ships and men. I stayed there for fifteen days, for such was the will of the cruel weather, and when I thought it was over, I found myself having to start all over again. There I changed my mind about returning to the mines and decided to do something about them while waiting for weather suitable for resuming my voyage by sea.

And when I had made four leagues the tempest returned. And it left me so utterly exhausted that I was barely conscious. Now my old sea-wound began troubling me again. For nine days I wandered, lost, with no hope of coming out of it alive. No eyes ever saw a sea so high and ugly and foaming. The wind would not take us where we wanted to go or give us a chance of running for land of any sort. There I remained, on that sea of blood that boiled like a cauldron on a huge fire. So fearful a sky was never seen. One day it burned all day and night like the fire in a stove and cast such flames, in the form of lightning flashes, that at every moment I had to check to see if the masts and sails had been struck. They flashed so fast and furious that we all believed the ships would sink on me. In all that time the waters of heaven never stopped pouring down. It was not what you would call a rainstorm, rather the coming of a second Flood. The crews were so far ground down by this time, that they longed for death as an escape from so many sufferings. The ships had now lost boats, anchors and cables twice over. They were badly holed and stripped of sails.

When our Lord so pleased, I returned to Puerto Gordo* [17 December], where I made what repairs I could. I turned towards Veragua again. Although I was willing to continue my exploration, the wind and currents were still against me. I had almost got back to where I had been before, when headwinds and adverse currents confronted me once more. I put back into the harbour again, for on a savage coast with battered ships I could not risk facing the weather at a time when Mars and Saturn were in opposition, because more often than not that means tempests or strong winds. It was Christmas Day, and the hour of Mass. Once more I was back to the place it had cost me so much trouble to leave. And after seeing in the new year I resumed the struggle – for although the wind now favoured my chosen route, I had ships that were unfit to sail and my crews were sick and dying.

On the day of Epiphany I reached Veragua, now at the end of my strength. There our Lord showed me a river mouth and safe harbour [Santa María de Belén], though there were only ten palms' draught at the entrance to it. I barely got into it. The day after, it began to blow high again. If I had still been outside the bank would have stopped me getting in. It rained without pause until 14 February, so that there was no opportunity to explore ashore or make repairs of any sort. And on 24 January, when I was feeling safe, the river suddenly rose so strongly that it broke anchor cables and ropes and threatened to sweep away the ships. And, for sure, I never saw them in greater peril. Our Lord came to aid us as He always did. I do not know if any man was ever so martyred.

On 6 February, in heavy rain, I sent seventy men inland and five leagues away they found many mines. The Indians who went with them took them to a very high peak and pointed in every direction as far as the eye could see, saying that there was gold on every side and that to the westward the gold-bearing area stretched for twenty days' journey. And they gave the names of villages and places where it could be found in various amounts. Afterwards I learned that Chief Quibián, who had provided these Indians, had told them to show us the remotest mines and those belonging to another chief who was his adversary; and within his own village a man who so desired could gather in ten days as much gold as a bearer could carry. I am bringing back with me some Indians who are servants of his and witnesses of the same. Our boats can get up-river as far as his village. My brother returned with the party, and they all brought gold which they had gathered in four hours, which was the time they spent there. It is of a conspicuous quality, for none of the men had ever seen a gold mine and most had not seen gold before, and they were seamen for the most part – and most of the rest were ships' boys, [and did not know what to look for].

I had plenty of building materials and supplies. I began to build a settlement and gave many gifts to Quibián, which is what they call the lord of that land. And I fully realised that our good relations were not going to last, with the inhabitants being so uncivilised and our men so demanding; and I was settling in inside their territory. Once the chief saw our buildings erected and our business under way, he resolved to burn them down and put us all to death. Things turned out very differently from the way he had planned: he ended up our prisoner with his wives, children and servants, although his captivity was short-lived. Quibián escaped from the custody of a man of honour, in whose keeping he had been placed under strong guard; and his children escaped from a ship's master to whom they had been entrusted to be kept secure.

That January the mouth of my river anchorage closed up. By April, my ships were all riddled with worm and I could barely keep them afloat. At about that time, the river opened a channel to the sea and, by a tremendous effort, I managed to float out three of the ships, empty of stores. The ships' boats went back to load the salt and water. The sea rose and turned ugly and they could not get back out. Natives appeared in force and attacked the boats but in the end they were killed. My brother and all my other men were aboard a ship that was still inside the estuary, and I was utterly alone outside, on that wild shore, with a high fever upon me. I was utterly drained, dead even to the hope of escape.

That was the state in which I dragged myself up the rigging to the height of the crow's nest. I clamoured and cried aloud in fear, imploring, urgently imploring the captains of your Highnesses' men of war, from every corner of the wind, to come to my help.* But never an answer returned. Still groaning, I lost consciousness. I heard a voice in pious accents saying:

'Oh, foolish man, and slow to serve your God, the God of all!* What more did He accomplish for Moses or for His servant David? From the hour of your birth, He has always had a special care of you. And when He saw that you were of an age that it pleased Him, He made your name resound in all the earth.* The Indies, that are so rich a portion of the world, He gave you for your own. You bestowed them where you pleased, and He empowered you to do so. Of the bonds of the Ocean Sea, which had been bound with such mighty chains, He gave the keys to you.* And you were lord over many lands, and your honour was great among Christian men.

'What more did He do for His people Israel, when He delivered them out of Egypt?* Or for David, when from a shepherd He made him king in Judaea?* Turn to Him and confess your fault. His mercy is everlasting. Old age will not make all great deeds impossible for you. Manifold and great is the inheritance in His gift. Abraham surpassed a hundred years when he begat Isaac. Nor was Sarah a young woman.*

226

'You are calling on God to help you: consider, in your ignorance, who has afflicted you so often and so sorely – God or the world? The privileges and promises that God grants, He does not break. Nor does He say, after service has been done Him, that such was not His meaning and that His words should be otherwise understood. Nor does He bestow a martyr's lot as a means of cloaking compulsion.* He abides by the literal sense of his words. Whatever He promises He bestows with increase. That is His way. As I have told you, so has your creator dealt with you, and thus He deals with all men. And now', the voice told me, 'show Him the resolution you have shown in all your endeavours and dangers in the service of others.'* And, half-dead as I was, I heard all this, but I knew no way to respond to those words of truth, save to weep for my sins. Whoever it was Who spoke, closed with the words, 'Be not afraid, but of good courage. All your afflictions are engraved in letters of marble and there is a purpose behind them all.'*

I arose when I could and at the end of nine days a fair breeze sprang up, but it was not enough to get more ships out of the river. I collected the men who were on shore and all the rest, as I was able to do, because they were too few both to provide a garrison and to man the ships. I would have stayed, with the entire company, to keep the settlement going, if there had been any way of getting the news to your Highnesses. The fear that no ship would ever chance that way determined my decision, and I reckoned that, when a further mission is sent, it will be possible to start again from scratch. I departed in the name of the Most Holy Trinity, on Easter Night, with rotten ships, worm-eaten and holed right through. At the place I called Belén I abandoned one ship, and a great weight of stores. At Belpuerto* I did the same. All I had left were two ships, no better than the others, without boats or victuals, with which to cross seven thousand miles of sea and water, or else to die on the way with my son and my brother and so great a company.

Let us hear what their comments are now – those who are so ready with accusations and quick to find fault, saying from their safe berths there in Spain, 'Why didn't you do this or that when you were over there?' I'd like to see their sort on this adventure. Verily I believe, there's another journey, of quite a different order, for them to make, or all our faith is vain.*

On 13 May, I reached the province of Mangi,* which borders that of Cathay, and from there I set my course for Hispaniola. I sailed with a fair wind for the first two days, but from then on the wind was against me. The route I followed was to avoid certain islands, so as not to founder on the reefs around them. Compelled by high seas, I was forced to put back under bare poles. Driven on to the lee of an island, I lost three anchors all at once, and that night at midnight, with the whole world around me in a state of flux, the cables snapped on the other ship, and she bore down on me. By some miracle, we did not end up smashed to smithereens. It was the anchor – the only one I had left – she it was who kept me alive, under our Lord God.* After six more days, when a favourable wind arose at last, I went on my way again. And so it was, with no tackle left, and the ships eaten away by the worms, more holed than a honeycomb, and the crews in panic and despair, I managed to get a little further than I had got before. Then the wind blew me back again. I stopped at the same island, in a safer anchorage.

At the end of eight days, I put out to sea again and made Jamaica at the end of June, still with adverse winds and the ships in a worse case than ever. With three pumps, buckets and cooking-pots, and all the crew at the work, they still could not bail out the water that was getting into the ship. And for this termite trouble there is no other remedy. I set the course as near as I could to Hispaniola, which was twenty-eight leagues away,* and I wish I had never started. The other ship ran for port as if doomed. I trusted to the open sea again in defiance of the storm. The ship foundered beneath me and our Lord cast me ashore by a miracle.*

Is there anyone who could believe what I am writing here? Let me tell him that I have not committed the hundredth part of it to this letter. Let the men who sailed with me, their Admiral, be my witnesses. If it please your Highnesses to grant me the favour of help in the form of a ship of over sixty-four tons, with two hundred *quintals* of hard-tack and some little provision beside, that will be enough to get me and my men to Spain. From Hispaniola to Jamaica, as I said, there are barely twenty-eight leagues. I would not dream of going to Hispaniola, even if the ships could make it. I have already said that your Highnesses' orders were that I should not go there. Whether this order has done any good, God knows.* I am entrusting this letter to the means and hands of certain Indians. It will be a very wonderful thing if it ever gets to Spain.

I can say of that journey that I had 150 men with me, among whom there were many well qualified to be pilots and others who were great mariners. Not one of them can say for certain where I went nor how I got back. What can be said is straightforward enough. I departed from the area where the port that yields the brazil wood is on Hispaniola. The storm did not allow me to follow the course I wanted. We were forced to go where the wind blew. On that day I fell very ill. No one had ever sailed towards that region. A few days later the wind and the sea fell and the tempest was succeeded by calms and strong currents. I made a landfall at the island known as Las Bocas, and from there to the mainland.*

No one can give an exact account of this, because there is no adequate means of doing so; for it was a matter of drifting with the current for so many days without sight of land. I followed the coast of the mainland: this was managed with the compass and the mariner's craft. There is no one who can say under what part of the heaven or [where on earth we were] when I left the mainland to return to Hispaniola. The pilots thought we were going to end up in the island of San Juan [de Puerto Rico], whereas our point of departure was really in the land of Mangi, four hundred leagues further west than where they said.* Let them say in reply, if they can, where the location of Veragua is. In my submission, they will be able to give no account of it, or method of finding it, except to say that they went to lands where there is a lot of gold; but while they may be sure of that much, they have no idea of how to find the way back there. They would have to set off to discover it again as if from scratch.

There is only one means and account that will suffice: that is, by astronomy, and it is a sure method. Whoever understands it has means enough. It is like the visions of the prophets.*

As for our ships in the Indies, if they only make way with a following wind, that is not because they are badly built or too heavy: the strong currents that flow there, as well as the wind, make everyone unwilling to sail close-hauled, for they could lose in a single day all they might have gained in a week. Nor do I make exception of caravels, even with Portuguese lateen rigging. This is why they sail only with the wind behind them; and they will sometimes spend six or eight months in port waiting for it. Nor is this to be wondered at, for often enough the same thing can happen in Spain.

To judge from the location of this place, and other indications, we have found the people of whom Pope Pius wrote, but not the horses with their reins and harness of gold.* This is not surprising because down on the sea-coast there is no call for any but fishing folk to live.

And I did not wait there because of the need to hurry. In Cariay and the other lands round about there are great sorcerers who are much to be feared. They would have given anything to keep me there for just a single hour. When I arrived, they at once sent out two girls for me, very dolled up. The elder could not have been more than eleven years old and the other about seven, and both were as brazen as any whore. They were carrying hidden pouches of magic powders. As soon as they came aboard I ordered them to be decked out with a few of our things and sent them straight back on shore.

I saw there a burial place on a hill. It was as big as a house and fair to see; and the body inside was exposed and covered in balm. They told me of other artefacts that were even finer. There are plenty of large and small animals of very different kinds from ours. I was given two boar as a present and our Irish hound did not dare abide them. A crossbowman had wounded one creature, which looked like a barbary ape, except that it was much bigger with a face like a man's; his arrow had penetrated the chest and stuck out through the neck, and because the beast was still so dangerous he had to chop an arm and a leg off it. When the boar saw it his bristles stood on end and off he fled. And when I saw it I ordered the 'begare', as they call the creature, to be thrown to him where he was. When the pig got to it it was almost dead, with the arrow still in its body, but it seized the boar's tail in its mouth and held it tightly while grabbing the tufts of his head with its remaining paw, as if struggling with a foe. The novelty of the sight and the good sport made me want to write this down. There were many kinds of animals, but they all die in captivity. I saw plenty of very big fowl with feathers like wool; lions, harts, two kinds of deer, and as many birds.

While I wandered exhausted through that sea, some of the men were taken with the heretical idea that we had been bewitched, and it remains with them to this day. I found another sort of folk who eat people: the ugliness of their faces betrays as much. They say there is a lot of copper in their land: axes are made of it and there were other objects – some wrought, some cast, some soldered – and a forge complete with silversmiths' tools and hearth. There all go clothed and in that province I saw big sheets of embroidered cotton, very deftly adorned, and others skilfully painted in different colours with brushes. They report that inland towards Cathay there are textiles woven with gold. Knowledge is not readily to be had of all these lands and their contents because of the lack of interpreters. The towns are populous but each has a language of its own and the differences are so great that they understand one another no better than between us and folk from Arabia. I believe that this applies only to these savage people on the coasts and not to those inland.

When I discovered the Indies, I stated that it was the richest lordship in the world. I spoke of the gold, pearls, precious stones, spices, the trade and fairs; and because the lot did not emerge all at once I was made an object of scandal. That chastening experience has made me careful this time to declare no more than I have heard from the natives of the land. One thing I dare say, because there are so many witnesses of it, and it is that in a single day in this land of Veragua I saw more samples of gold than in four years on Hispaniola; and the countryside in this region could not be fairer or better tilled, nor the inhabitants more timid; and there is a good harbour with a fair river-mouth which can be defended against all comers. This all means security for Christians who come here and the certainty that we shall be able to establish our rule, with great expectations of the honour and increase of the Christian faith. And the passage here could be as quick as that to Hispaniola if made with a following wind. Your Highnesses are as fully masters of this land as of Jeréz or Toledo. Any ships you send here will be visiting their second home. They will take gold on board here. It will be best to carry it to other lands to buy their products and bring them back; otherwise the ships would return empty and, on shore, their crews would be dependent on the savages for the means of life.

Concerning the other matter to which I have alluded, I explained why I fell silent.* I am not going to repeat now, therefore, or seek to affirm any of what I have said or written in the past, even though I am now drinking in the proof of it at the source.

The Genoese and Venetians and everyone who has pearls and precious gems and other things of value carry them to the ends of the earth to trade and turn them into gold. Gold is very excellent. Of gold treasure is made, and he who possesses it can do with it what he likes in this world. And it can even boost the flight of souls to Paradise.* The lords of those lands around Veragua have so much of it that it is said they bury it with them. Every year by way of trade were borne 666 *quintals* of gold to King Solomon, apart from what was disbursed on the way in Arabia. From that gold he made 200 lances and 300 shields and he made the elaborate throne which must have been cast in gold and gold baubles and many vessels of great size set with precious stones. So Josephus writes in his chronicle, *De Antiquitatibus*.* In the *Paralipomenon* and the Book of Kings, this is reported.* Josephus wished to locate the source of this gold in the land of Aurea. If that were so, I say, then those mines of Aurea must be one and the same as these of Veragua, which, as I said, stretch for twenty days' journey to the westward and are equally far from the equator and the pole. Solomon had to buy all that gold and store of gems and silver; and your Highnesses can order it to be gathered at your pleasure. David in his will left 3,000 *quintals* of the gold of the Indies to Solomon to help with the building of the Temple and, according to Josephus, it came from these same lands.

Jerusalem and Mount Zion shall be restored by the hand of a Christian. What sort of man this shall be, God declares through the mouth of His prophet and in the XIVth [XVth] Psalm. Abbot Joachim said that he would surely come from Spain.* St Jerome showed the way thereto to that saintly woman.* A while ago, the Emperor of Cathay asked for wise men to teach him the faith of Christ.* Who shall it be who shall put himself forward for this task?

If our Lord returns me to Spain, I swear to bring to safety in God's name all these men who sailed here with me. They have undergone incredible perils and sufferings. As they are poor men, I beseech your Highnesses to order them to be paid promptly and to grant favours to each according to the quality of his estate, for I assure you that, in my estimation, they shall be bringing to Spain the best news that ever was heard there.

It does not seem right to me, nor serviceable to your Highnesses, that the gold owned by Quibián in Veragua and the other chiefs in the country round about, however much there may be, according to reports, should be seized from them by violent means. With good order, scandal and ill rumour shall be avoided and as a result all the gold will be secured for your treasury, without a grain remaining. With just one month of fair weather I could have completed my explorations. For want of sound ships I could not risk waiting for good enough weather to resume. For everything that conduces to your Highnesses' service, my hope is in Him Who made me; and I shall be made whole. . . . I believe your Highness [*sic*] will recall that I wanted to build the ships from scratch according to a new design. The shortage of time prevented it, and surely I stumbled on what was needed.

I attach greater importance to the business now in hand, and to the mines in the most recently discovered coast and realm, than to everything else that has been found in the Indies. This is not the sort of infant whom it would be proper to hand over to a foster-parent. I cannot think of Hispaniola and Paria and the other lands without weeping. I hoped that they would establish useful precedents for these other lands. On the contrary, they are practically at their last gasp: if they are not actually moribund, their infirmities are incurable or, at best, long-term. Let those responsible for bringing them to this pass now produce the remedy, if they can. It is easy enough to be good at wrecking a thing.

Formerly, it was always customary to grant favours and fortune to those who risked their lives in royal service. There is no reason why these should be enjoyed by someone who has been so opposed to this enterprise, nor by his heirs. Men who fled the Indies, escaping from their responsibilities and complaining of the discoveries and of me, were restored to their jobs. If the same sort of rule were now applied in Veragua, it would be an evil example, without profit for the business or justice for the world.

It was fear of this, inspired by plenty of similar cases, which I was well aware of, that made me petition your Highnesses, before I first set out to discover these islands and mainland, to allow me to be the Governor of them in your royal name. It so pleased you. By a charter of privilege and agreement sworn and sealed, you granted me the title of Viceroy and Admiral and Governor-General of all of them, and assigned limits which were to be fixed a hundred leagues beyond the islands of the Azores and of Cape Verde, along a line running from pole to pole, and which were to include everything that ever should be discovered therein. And you granted me extensive powers. My commission states all this at greater length in writing.

The other – and most highly celebrated – undertaking now beckons us with open arms. Till now I have been accounted a foreigner. I spent seven years in your royal court when all who heard of this enterprise treated it as a joke.* Today, everyone down to the jobbing tailors is clamouring to go and make discoveries. If only they were coming to ply their trades! And yet permission is granted to them, to the prejudice of my estate and the undoing of this great work.

It is right to render to God the things which are God's and to give Caesar his due.* That is a just commandment, from a righteous source. The lands which are here at your Highnesses' command are bigger than all other Christian lands put together, as well as being rich. No sooner had I, by God's will, placed them beneath your high and royal sceptre, with every prospect of yielding immense revenues, at a time when I was awaiting ships which would return to your lofty presence with great news of victory and of gold, than I suddenly found myself arrested. With two of my brothers I was flung on to a ship, loaded with chains, stripped to my skin and very ill treated – all without being summoned or subjected to trial. Can any man believe that a poor foreigner like me would dare to start a rebellion in a place like that, without any reason and without help from any other prince, while surrounded by your vassals and native subjects and with my own sons in your royal court?*

My service began when I was about twenty-eight years old and now there is not a hair on my body that is not white. My health is broken. The years that remained to me I have spent. And I and my brothers have been deprived of all we had, down to the last garment, and it has all been sold off without a trial or even an audience, to my deep dishonour. I have to believe that none of this was done by your royal command. To restore my honour and to punish those responsible would make your royal and noble name resound anew; so would the punishment of him who robbed me of the pearls, and those who have deprived me of my rights in the office of Admiral. If this were done, it would be an exemplary act, of the greatest virtue, and famous. And your Highnesses would be commemorated in Spain as grateful and just Princes. However I might strive to stay silent, my spirit refuses to be quelled before the combination of the very wholesome intent with which I have always served your Highnesses and my unmerited injury. I beg your Highnesses' indulgence.

My plight is as I have described it. So far, I have wept my own tears. Now let the skies pity me and the earth weep for me! Of worldly goods, I have not so much as a mite for the offertory. Of spiritual comforts, here I am in the Indies, bereft as has been said. I am marooned amid this terrible sorrow; sick; waiting day by day for death; surrounded by a million savages, who seethe with cruelty and hostility towards us; and I am so cut off from the holy sacraments of Holy Church, that my soul shall be forgotten if it leaves my body in this place. I implore the tears of all wh love charity, truth, and justice.

I did not undertake this voyage to win status or wealth – that much is certain, for by then all hope of such was dead. I appeared before your Highnesses with a wholesome intention and a goodly zeal. I

234

humbly beseech your Highnesses, if it please God to take me from this place, to grant me leave to make my pilgrimage to Rome and other places. May the Holy Trinity preserve and increase your lives and high estate.

Given in the Indies, on the island of Jamaica, on 7 July 1503.

For the time being, Columbus had to make what arrangements he could for his men's survival and rescue from their closely beached ships on the Jamaican shore. They were dependent for supplies on what they could get from the natives by barter and were restricted to a dyspeptic diet of rodents' flesh and cassava bread. When the natives became truculent and stopped the trade, Columbus showed all his own resourcefulness and ingenuity. A partial eclipse of the moon was imminent – it occurred on 29 February – and he prefigured one of Rider Haggard's heroes by using it to intimidate the Indians into renewing supplies.*

His abilities were again called forth by a rebellion among a group of his own men. The Porras brothers, Francisco and Diego, had been nominated by the royal treasurer, Alonso de Morales, to commands with the expedition; Columbus had shipped them reluctantly and they had never got on. They conceived a plan to return to Hispaniola by canoe with other malcontents, but foundered and were reduced to living by terrorising the Indians. The consequences might have been disastrous for Columbus had he not finally been able to defeat the rebels in a pitched battle by the beach-head. In the meantime, Columbus had taken steps to procure the expedition's salvation. His loyal subordinate, Diego Méndez de Salcedo, was one of the most daring adventurers of the expedition. He had given good service in negotiations and action with the Indians on the mainland and on Jamaica. His new task was to reach Hispaniola by canoe with native oarsmen, accompanied by a second canoe with the Genoese officer, Bartolomeo Fieschi, aboard. The distance was modest judged by present-day standards of seamanship and endurance in small craft, but at that time the Spaniards had no experience of canoes and to undertake the expedition was a great feat of daring. The canoes laboured against the current; the fresh water gave out; the oarsmen began to die of thirst and Méndez fell sick. At last, after five days' toiling at the paddles, both canoes reached Hispaniola safely, though at a point far distant from Santo Domingo.

Despite the enthusiasm evinced by Columbus in the following

letters to Ovando, their reception on Hispaniola gave little grounds for gratitude. Ovando was predictably unsympathetic to Columbus's plight. He refused to release ships for an immediate rescue, but obliged Méndez to await the next fleet from Spain and hire vessels on his own account. In the meantime, Ovando sent Diego de Escobar to verify Columbus's plight: this was an inauspicious choice of emissary, for Escobar was a veteran mutineer who had joined Roldán's rebellion on Hispaniola in 1499. By then, however, even the sight of an enemy was welcome to Columbus, for it showed that Méndez had got through and that help would eventually materialise. A year was spent on the rebellious and incommodious island before relief arrived. Though the warmth with which Columbus expresses his thanks to Ovando in the following two letters might be diplomatic, his elation at his escape seems genuine enough.

Las Casas parades these fragments as models of epistolary simplicity and of Columbus's artless character: they may, however, like his similar correspondence with Roldán after the third voyage, be disingenuous.* The text includes a paraphrase by Las Casas of a lost part of the original letter.

Fragments of a letter to Nicolás de Ovando, Jamaica, March 1504*

Very noble Sir, I have received your letter this very moment. I read the whole of it with great joy. Paper and pens could not serve to express the relief and strength that I and all my men derived from it. My lord, if I only sent a brief letter with Diego Méndez de Segura, it was in the hope of supplying a longer account in person. I can safely say that a thousand sheets of paper would not suffice to recount the gruelling time I have had from the storms and impediments encountered.

[Here he tells him many things concerning the whole of his voyage and the wealth of the lands which he had discovered, and how, on his arrival in Jamaica, the men he had with him swore to obey him even to death, and how they then rebelled, etc.]

When I left Castile, it was with every satisfaction from their Highnesses and with great promises from them. In particular, they would restore to me all that belonged to me and would augment my honour. This was vouchsafed by word of mouth and in writing. My lord, I am sending you there an extract from their letter in which this

236

Facsimile of Columbus's letter
to the Bank of San Giorgio, Genoa

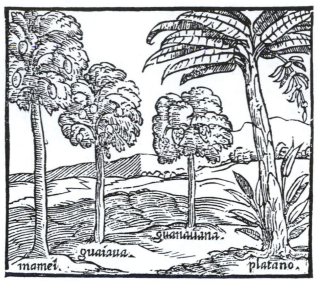

Fruit trees on Hispaniola: 'Its lands are lofty and
there are many ranges and high mountains . . .
all furnished with trees of a thousand kinds'

The fort at Navidad: 'I took possession of a great
town to which I gave the name of Villa de Navidad.
There I have built a stronghold and fortress'

subject appears. But, with or without such favours, I have thought of nothing but serving them, ever since I began to do so. I beg you, my lord, to be assured of this, as a favour to me. If I mention it, it is so that you will be aware that I shall perform and follow your commands without overlooking a single point. Escobar tells me, my lord, how well my affairs have been looked after and how my revenues have mounted up. My lord, I take it all as a great favour and now I think only of how I shall be able to repay it. If I ever spoke a true word, such is what I am about to say: that from the time I met you, my heart has always been satisfied with whatever you have done for me, there in Hispaniola or wherever the occasion has arisen. For that reason, I have always felt reassured while I have been here, and firm in the hope of help, provided news of the need and peril in which I found myself, and find myself still, should reach your ears. I have neither the wit nor strength to express how convinced I am of it. Let me only say, my lord, that my hope has been and is that you will not spare yourself to save me, and I am certain of it, for so all my senses inform me. I am not extravagant with compliments. On the contrary, I am said to be rather curt. If the occasion affords, deeds will speak loudly enough.

I beg you once more, my lord, for a favour, that you be satisfied with my conduct and aware of my loyalty. I also ask you as a favour to receive Diego Méndez de Segura with every recommendation, and Fieschi, too, who belongs to one of the best families of his land, who are, moreover, closely related to me. And believe that they did not go there, nor were they sent, with any ulterior motive, but only to inform you, my lord, of the grave danger I was in and in which I remain to this day. I am still lodged aboard the ships I have beached here, hoping for help from God and yourself, for which my descendants shall ever be beholden.

Letter to Nicolás de Ovando, La Beata, an islet between Jamaica and Hispaniola, 3 August 1504*

Diego de Salcedo arrived with succour for me in the form of the ships which your Grace sent me. It gave me life and life to all who were with me. It can never be repaid at any price. I am so happy that ever since I saw him I cannot sleep for happiness – not that I am afraid of dying, but I think rather of what this means for the glory of our lord King and lady Queen.

The Porras brothers returned to Jamaica and sent to me demanding that I should hand over all my supplies, or else they would come and get them and it would cost me dear, and my son and brothers and all the others who were with me. And as I did not accept this demand they – to their undoing – set in motion the execution of their threat. There were many dead and wounded enough; and in the end our Lord, who hates pride and ingratitude, delivered the whole pack of them into our hands. I pardoned them and, at their plea, restored them to their commissions. I am taking Captain Porras to their Highnesses so that they shall know the truth of it all.

Every effort has been made to dispel suspicion of me but it is hard a-dying. Diego de Salcedo is still troubled at heart about it. I know there can have been no reason for it, either seen or felt, for my intent is entirely wholesome and that is why I am so shocked.

It gave me as much pleasure to see the new title with which you signed your last letter as if it had been from Don Diego or Don Fernando. May it bring you much honour and good fortune, my lord; and I hope soon to see you sign with the title of Grand Master of the Order.*

May our Lord keep your house and noble person. From La Beata, where the wind forcibly detains me. This day, Saturday, 3 August. At your lordship's command,

.S.

.S.A.S.

X M Y

Xpo Ferens

Columbus has left an account of the aftermath of the affair of the brothers Porras in the following autograph letter to his son.* It is remarkable that the explorer remains without overt hostility towards Ovando: at most, a measure of irony can be detected in the references to his courtly habits, which apparently impeded his ability to discharge justice. The letter alludes to a number of individuals who were important in Columbus's world, especially towards the end of his life. His elder son and heir, Diego, was now, with hope spent of a recovery of Columbus's own fortunes, the main focus of his ambitions. He was also increasingly undertaking the management of his father's affairs, especially at court, where he seems to have been well regarded.

The main primary source for the last couple of years of Columbus's life is a sheaf of the explorer's letters to Diego, from which the next and subsequent items are drawn. A theme of the correspondence is the need to exploit the patronage of Diego Deza, Bishop of Palencia, former tutor to Prince Juan and, according to his fellow-Dominican, Las Casas, a constant protector of Columbus: in another letter of this period, Columbus couples him with Luis de Santángel as chiefly responsible for the monarchs' decision to back the enterprise of the Indies in 1492. A further link with the Prince's household is suggested by the mention of 'the secretary' in the postscript – probably an allusion to Gaspar Gricio, who, having formerly served the Prince, became a royal secretary in 1504. Other names introduced in the letter are those of Dr Angulo and the Licentiate Zapata, of the Council of Castile; Juan López de Lazárranga, a royal secretary; and Alonso Sánchez de Carbajal and Jerónimo de Agüero, loyal servants of the Columbus family.

Letter to his son, Diego, Seville, 21 November 1504

My very dear Son, Your letter arrived with the post. You were right to stay where you are and try to get something done and to attend to our affairs.

The lord Bishop of Palencia has always favoured me and sought my welfare ever since I came to Castile. Now we must beg him to find ways of redressing all my wrongs and seeing that the commission and charters of privileges granted to me by their Highnesses are honoured and all my injuries compensated. And he must be made aware that if their Highnesses do this their revenues and greatness will be increased to an incredible degree. And let him not think that 40,000 *pesos* of gold is more than a sample; for there could have been a much greater amount if Satan had not interfered to frustrate my purpose: indeed, when I was removed from the Indies I was well on the way to providing a sum of gold incomparably greater than 40,000 *pesos*.

I take my oath – and let this be for your eyes only – that the losses owed to me from the revenues promised by their Highnesses amount to ten million a year and can never be recouped. You can see what their Highnesses' portion is or could be, and they are not getting a hint of it.

I am writing to his Grace and I shall do my best to set off for the court. Whether I get there – and everything else – is in the hands of our Lord. His mercy is infinite. All that happens and is yet to happen, says St Augustine, was already ordained before the world began. *

I am also writing to the other members of the Council giving them the gist of Diego Méndez's letter. Commend me to his Grace with the news of my departure, as I mentioned: I am certainly very uneasy about it because this cold weather is so bad for this illness of mine that I shall probably fall by the wayside.

I was greatly pleased to read your letter and the words of our lord King, for which kiss his royal hands. If one thing is certain, it is that I have put more effort and dedication into their Highnesses' service than into my own soul's salvation. And if there have been failures of any sort, they have been because of the impossible odds and because my wisdom and strength could stretch no further. In circumstances like these, our Lord God asks no more of a man than a willing spirit.

From here in Seville, I took two brothers called Porras by name, at the behest of Treasurer Morales. One went as a captain, the other as purser, and neither with any aptitude for such tasks. It was with foreboding that I asked to enlist them, and only for the sake of him who sent them to me. When we got over there to the Indies they turned out to be even more feckless than they had seemed. I paid them many courtesies, such as I should hardly show to a member of our own family, and their behaviour was such as to deserve something much stronger than a mere reprimand. In the end, their behaviour got to such a point that, however much I might have wished, I could no longer excuse their excesses. The official inquiries will bear me out if my word is not enough. They started an uprising on the island of Jamaica, which caused me more surprise than if the sun had cast rays of darkness. I was at death's door and for five months they tormented me, so cruelly and without cause. In the end I took the lot of them prisoner and then gave them their freedom again, except for the captain, whom I brought in custody to their Highnesses. A petition, which they swore and addressed to me and which I am sending to you enclosed, will inform you more fully about this pending the inquiry. Inquiries take a long time, what with all the talking, and day by day I wait for the outcome, which is coming with a scribe in another ship.

In Santo Domingo, the Governor took custody of my prisoner. He felt obliged to do so by habits learned at court. My orders contained a clause in which their Highnesses ordered that I should be obeyed by all and should exercise civil and criminal jurisdiction over all those who made the voyage with me. But the Governor was not impressed by it. He said it did not apply inside his territory. He sent him here to appear before my lords of the Council without any investigation or preliminary hearing or written account. They turned him away and the culprits have gone free. I shall not be surprised if our Lord punishes them for it. The delinquents turned up at court brazen-faced. Such effrontery, such wicked treachery was never heard of before. I wrote to their Highnesses about this in my other letter and said that it was not right that they should permit such an affront. I also wrote to my Lord Treasurer asking him as a favour not to make up his mind on the basis of what those men might say without hearing me. It will be as well if you remind him of it now. I cannot understand how they have the nerve to look him in the face after what they got up to. I am going to write to him again and send him a copy of the same sworn petition as I am sending to you; and I shall do the same for Dr Angulo and the Licentiate Zapata. Commend me to them all and let them know that I shall soon be setting off.

It would relieve me greatly to see a letter from their Highnesses and to know their commands. You must see if you can do anything about it. Also remember to commend me to my lord Bishop and Juan López and remind them of my sickness and of the reward due for my services. Do not neglect to read the letters enclosed and become familiar with their contents. I thank Diego Méndez for his letter. I have not written to him because he will get all the news from you, and because of my illness which has left me weak. It would be well if Carbajal and Jerónimo could be at court at a time like this and talk of our affairs to the members of the Council and the secretary. Written in Seville on 21 November. Your father who loves you more than himself,

.S.
.S.A.S.
X M Y
Xpo Ferens

I have written to their Highnesses again, beseeching them to order the verification of the wages to be paid to the men who made the voyage with me, because they are poor and it is going on three years since they left their homes. The news they bring is more than great. They have been through untold dangers and hardships. I did not want the country to be despoiled because the right thing is for it to be settled: after that, all the gold will be to hand without any scandal. Talk about it to the secretary and my lord Bishop and Juan López and anyone who you think would be useful.

From Columbus's other letters to Diego a picture emerges of the Admiral as he was for the remaining fifteen months of his life. Sick, tired of controversies, complaining of loneliness and cold, he projects the image of extreme old age though he was only in his early fifties. He claims in letters to patrons still to have a long career before him, but his letters to his son are implicitly resigned to a more or less early end, written under the shadow of death: one of the major concerns is to ensure the smooth transition to Diego of Columbus's inheritance and to equip the young man to continue Columbus's suit to the crown.

In the first of the following letters Columbus summarises his disappointed financial claims: in the translation below, his allusions are slightly expanded to make them intelligible. The claims were based on the 'capitulations' or terms of commission – often referred to by Columbus as his 'contract' – issued by Ferdinand and Isabella before Columbus's departure on his first ocean crossing; they seem to have been based on Columbus's own petition and issued without much reflection on the monarchs' part. With other documents connected with the vindication of his claims and the transmission of his estate, Columbus had them compiled in the document he called his 'Libro de Privilegios' or 'Book of Charters', and distributed, in multiple copies, to interested and influential parties.* The financial clauses seem to justify Columbus's generous interpretation of his right to a tenth of the yield of the Indies; the monarchs, however, were willing to acknowledge his title only to a tenth of their own dues, amounting to two per cent, rather than ten per cent, of the total.

Letter to Diego Colón, Seville, 1 December 1504*

My very dear Son, Since receiving your letter of 15 November, I have heard nothing more from you. I could wish that you might write to me very frequently. Hour by hour, my hope is to see a letter from you.

You can guess for yourself that I am now left with no other source of solace. Copious post arrives every day. And the news here is of such a sort that my hair stands on end to learn how everything turns out – always the opposite of the hopes of my heart.

May it please the Holy Trinity to grant better health to our lady Queen, so that what is now in hand can be authorised by her.

I sent you another message a week ago last Thursday. By now I suppose your reply must be on its way. In it, I told you that my departure was assured, but my hopes of arriving – to judge from experience – very much the opposite. For this trouble of mine is so painful, and the cold aggravates it so, that I shall be unlikely to avoid ending up in some inn. The litter and everything were ready. But the weather was so disagreeable that everybody agreed that it would be unthinkable to set off in the circumstances, and that it would be better to attend to my health and try to get better before putting my life to such an obvious risk. With the letter I sent I told you what I am telling you now: that it was a good idea to stay where you are for the present and right to begin to look after our affairs.

It seems to me that a copy in a fair hand ought to be made of the passage in that letter which their Highnesses wrote to me [on 14 March 1502] in which they say that they will keep their bargain with me and will put the whole of it in your hands. Give it to them with another petition explaining that I am sick and that it is impossible at present for me to go to kiss their royal hands; and that the Indies are going to ruin and are exposed to fire on a thousand sides; and how I have not received and do not receive anything from the income I have there, nor will anyone dare to demand or obtain anything for me there, and that I am living on credit. Some of the money I had I spent there, bringing the men who went there with me back home, because it would have weighed very heavily on my conscience to leave them there, abandoned. A copy should be given to the lord Bishop of Palencia, with an expression of the great trust I have in his grace, and another to the Lord Chamberlain.

I hoped that Carbajal and Jerónimo would be there by now. He who is there in any case is our Lord, who will ordain matters as He knows will be for our good. Carbajal arrived here yesterday. I wanted to send him off at once with these instructions. He begged profusely to be excused, explaining that his wife was near to death. I shall arrange for him to go, because he knows a lot about this sort of business. I shall also try to arrange for your brother [Fernando] and your uncle [Bartolomé] to go to kiss hands to their Highnesses and give them an account of the journey, if my letters do not suffice. Take good heed of your brother. He has great gifts and is now no longer a child. Ten brothers would not be too much for you. I never found a better friend than my own brothers in good times and bad.

The things to work for are first to obtain the office of Governor of the Indies and secondly to arrange for the despatch of the income. I have left a memorandum for you at court of everything that belongs to me from the Indies. What they sent to Carbajal was nothing and nothing has been left from it. Anyone who wishes can ship goods, so that my right to invest and recoup an eighth share of all such ventures amounts to nothing; for without making any such contribution I can engage in the trade on my own account without anyone else as a partner. I have explained this time and again in the past: my right to this eighth would never count for anything. This eighth, and all the rest, belongs to me by virtue of the grant which their Highnesses made to me, as I had clearly explained in the book of my charters, a copy of which I have left for you; the same applies to my rights to a third and a tenth. Of the said tenth, all I get is a tenth of what their Highnesses receive, whereas it ought to be calculated on the basis of the entire output of gold and other products found and obtained, by whatever means, within my jurisdiction as Admiral, with a tenth besides of the value of all the goods imported and exported, after deduction of costs. I have already said that this and everything else is fully explained, with the reasons for it, in the book of my charters, as is [*my claim to a share of the profits*] of justice administered by the Board of Trade of the Indies here in Seville. You must try to get their Highnesses to reply to my letter and to order my people to be paid. It must be four days ago that I sent Martín de Bamboa with another letter to them; and you will see my letter to Juan López enclosed with your own.

It is being said here that three or four bishops are being ordained for a mission to the Indies, and that this business has been confided to the lord Bishop of Palencia. After commending me to his Grace, tell him that I believe it would be to their Highnesses' advantage if I had an opportunity to be heard before this matter was finalised.

Give my respects to Diego Méndez and let him see this letter. My sickness does not allow me to write except at night for during the daytime it robs me of the strength of my hands. I expect this letter will be taken by one of Francesco Pinelli's sons.* Receive him warmly, for he does all he can for me with great affection and a generous enthusiasm.

The caravel which lost a mast on leaving Santo Domingo has arrived in the Algarve. It is carrying the results of the investigation into the affair of the Porras brothers. Such ugly deeds, with such brazen cruelty, were never seen before. If their Highnesses do not punish them, I know not who will dare again to go abroad in command of men in their service.

Today is Monday. I shall try to see to it that your uncle and brother leave for court in the morning. Remember to write to me very often – and remind Diego Méndez to do so – and in plenty of detail. Post arrives here from court every day. May our Lord preserve you in His holy keeping. Given in Seville on 1 December. Your father who loves you as himself.

.S.
.S.A.S.
X M Y
Xpo Ferens

When Columbus wrote this letter, with its entreaties to God for the health of the Queen, Isabella had been dead for four days. By the time of the document which follows,* Columbus had heard the news, and opens his memorandum with appropriate sentiments. He does not appear apprehensive about dealing with the King alone, and recalls the terms, suggestive of the image of the Last World Empire, in which he had been envisaged by the explorer, in prophetic mood, as 'head of Christendom'. The document must have been written before 6 December, when Fernando and Bartolomé finally set off for court; the surviving version breaks off abruptly and more was evidently intended to be included. The contents overlap with those of the previous letter, but far more space is devoted to affairs on Hispaniola, of which Columbus was apparently going to say more at the point where the document ends. This implies that Columbus's suggestion that he could be sent back to resume his gubernatorial duties was not mere bravado: he was still thinking actively about the problems of the colony. It is a pity that he confined his thoughts on the appointment of bishops to the realm of word of mouth. The new sees for Hispaniola were created in Rome, at the request of Ferdinand and Isabella, on 15 November and bishops nominated at once. They did not, however, leave for the island until 1511, by which time the dioceses had been redrawn.

Memorandum for Diego Colón, Seville, December 1504

Memorandum to you, my dear son, Don Diego, of matters which require present attention. First and foremost, to pray earnestly and devoutly for the soul of our lady Queen. Her life was ever Catholic and saintly and she was exacting in all that pertained to God's holy service: therefore we can be confident that she has gone to glory and is free of all the concerns of this harsh and wearisome world. The next thing is to be vigilant and diligent, in all and for all, in the service of our lord King and to strive to spare him from adversity. His Highness is the head of Christendom. You know the old saying: when the head sickens, so do all the members. That is why all good Christians should pray for his life and health, and those of us who are committed to his service should contribute with all diligence and zeal.

The same reason has moved me to write to you now, despite my grave sickness, so that his Highness should be in a position to decide as may best please him. And for greater assurance I am sending your brother to court, for while he may be a child in years, he is mature in understanding. And I am sending your uncle and Carbajal because if this letter of mine does not suffice, all of you by word of mouth can intervene to see that his Highness is well served.

As far as I can see, there is nothing that requires more urgent attention and correction than the Indies. There must be something like 40–60,000 *pesos* of gold there by now for his Highness. When I was there, I realised that the Governor was none too keen to send them over. In addition, it is believed that other people will have accumulated about 150,000 *pesos* by now and that the mines are fully into the swing of production.

Most of the men who are out there are low class, of little learning and little sense of the value of things. The Governor is very poorly regarded all round. My fear is that the men may attempt some sort of upheaval. If this should happen – which God forbid – it will be hard to patch things up afterwards. It would be just as bad if, with all the great news about the gold, those in authority here or elsewhere started to impose unjust taxes on the men. In my opinion, his

246

Highness ought to do something about this quickly, and send out someone on whose sympathies he can rely, with 150 or 200 well equipped men, until the situation is thoroughly under control. This could be achieved within two or three months. And he should see to it that two or three forts are built there. There is a big risk attached to all the gold there, precisely because it is so easy to control with so few men. I could quote the old saying which is current here: 'All prey is tempting to a greedy eye.' In this matter, as in all else, I am ready to serve his Highness with a good will, until my spirit leaves this body.

I said above that his Highness is the leader of Christendom, and it is needful for him to take charge of the business of defending Christian people and extending their boundaries. This, men say, is the reason why he is unable to provide for the good government of all the vast Indies, and why, therefore, they are going to waste without yielding the benefits that are rightfully expected and without being properly husbanded. In my view, his service requires that something be done to settle these misgivings, by someone whose sympathies are aroused by the way the discoveries have been abused.

At the time of my arrival, I wrote a very long letter to their Highnesses, full of problems which required urgent attention with a firm hand. I have had no reply and am not aware that any action has been taken. There are some ships in Sanlúcar which have been held back by the wind. I have told my lords, the members of the Board of Trade of the Indies, that they must order them to be detained in port until our lord King makes some provision in this matter, either in writing or by appointing someone and sending him with men.

Something of this sort is very necessary and I know what I am talking about. And it is essential to order a careful watch to be kept in all ports to stop anyone from going out there without permission. As I have explained, there is a lot of gold gathered in unfortified huts of straw, and plenty of disaffected men in the country, while hostility surrounds the man in the Governor's job, exacerbated by the inadequate punishment of those who were guilty of previous conspiracies and emerged with rewards for their treason. If his Highness decides to take action, it must then be done at once so that the waiting ships suffer no loss through spoilage.

I have heard that three bishops are about to be appointed for

Hispaniola. If it should please his Highness to hear my views before making a final choice, I shall be able to suggest how our Lord could best be served and his Highness best be pleased.

I have been held up here, making arrangements for Hispaniola.

Las Casas has preserved only one small fragment of Columbus's correspondence with Fray Diego de Deza, whom he used himself and recommended to his son as a mediator of his suits at court.* Columbus's relationship with this Dominican friar was of the highest importance both because of the powerful positions of influence which Deza occupied and because of the apparent intimacy and confidence which existed between them.

As a member of the community of San Estéban, Deza had occupied the prime chair of theology at the University of Salamanca and may therefore have been able to influence erudite opinion on Columbus's plans. In 1485 or 1486 he became tutor to Prince Juan, where he was at the heart of a circle of Columbus's friends at court, who included Juana de Torres, the Prince's nurse, Antonio de Torres, her brother, and Juan de Cabrera, treasurer of the Prince's household. As Bishop of Palencia and, from January 1505, Archbishop of Seville, he continued to have privileged access to the monarchs. Columbus alluded at different times to the 'brotherly love' between Deza and himself; he lodged, or normally expected to lodge, with him at court, and at least twice singled out his advocacy as 'the reason why I remained in Castile' or 'the reason why the Indies belong to your Highnesses'.* The Dominican's efforts in the last period of Columbus's life, however, did not satisfy the explorer. The fragment preserved by Las Casas shows that Deza was unsuccessful in getting satisfaction from the King, and that Columbus was prepared to exploit his intimacy with this correspondent to accuse the King explicitly of bad faith. That was a liberty he had not quite taken even in his letters to his son:

And since it seems that his Highness is not willing to comply with what he has promised with his word and in writing jointly with the Queen – God rest her soul – I feel that for a simple ploughman like me to battle on with him against me would be like beating the wind. And it will be for the best. For I have done what I can; and now let it be left to the Lord our God to do it, whom I have always found very favourable and a present help in my troubles.

248

The following further letter to Diego,* written from Seville on 5 February 1505, is chiefly remarkable for its eulogy of Amerigo Vespucci, which suggests that Columbus's judgement of men was as aberrant as ever and that he was still characteristically inclined to bestow trust on secret adversaries. Vespucci, apparently unknown to Columbus, had already profited at the Admiral's expense by joining Alonso de Hojeda's voyage of 1499 to the pearl fisheries of Paria. After worming his way into Columbus's confidence, he published his claim to have been the first discoverer of the American continent; and although his subsequent career justifies his claim to recognition as a notable explorer and navigator, it is ironic that Columbus should have befriended so generously the individual who was to do most to usurp his reputation.

Letter to Diego Colón, Seville, 5 February 1505

My very dear Son, Diego Méndez departed from here on Monday, the 3rd of this month. After he left, I had some talk with Amerigo Vespucci, the bearer of this letter, who is off to court on a mission concerned with navigational matters. It was always his wish to follow my orders. He is very much a man of good family. Fortune has been adverse for him, as for so many others. His labours have not brought him the benefits they rightly deserved. He leaves here devoted to me and very much in hope of doing something that may redound to my good, if it is in his power.

I cannot tell from here what service it would be best to ask of him on my behalf, because I do not know what they want him there for. He is going with every determination to do all he can for me. Look into what can be done for the best and work towards it, for he will handle everything and do the talking and put the matter into effect; and see that all is done secretly, so that no one should suspect him. I have told and informed him as much as I can about the payments that have been made and are being made to me. Show this letter to the lord Adelantado [Bartolomé Colón] too, so that he can see what can be done for the best and advise Vespucci accordingly.

Give his Highness to understand that his ships have been to the best and richest part of the Indies. And if anything remains to be disclosed, apart from what has already been said, I shall come to court and satisfy him by word of mouth, because it is impossible to put it in writing. Our Lord guard you in His holy keeping. Dated in Seville on 5 February. Your father who loves you more than himself.

.S.
.S.A.S.
X M Y
Xpo Ferens

On 25 August 1505, Columbus added a pensive retrospect and codicil to his will:*

When I sailed from Spain in the year 1502, I drew up a disposition and entail of my estate and of all that then belonged to me, for the good of my soul and the service of the eternal God and for my honour and that of my successors.* I left the said writing in the monastery of Las Cuevas in Seville, in the keeping of Brother Don Gaspar with other writings of mine and my letters of privilege and charters which I have from the King and Queen, our lord and lady. The said disposition I hereby approve and confirm, by these presents which I am setting down for the better fulfilment and clarification of my intent and I command that it be executed just as I here declare it. And it is understood that whatever is done in fulfilment of these presents shall not be done again to comply with my former disposition, to avoid repetition. I designated my dear son Don Diego to be my heir of all my goods and offices which I hold by hereditary right, and of which I made an entail in his person; and in case he should have no male heir, I ordained that my son Don Fernando should inherit in the same wise, and in case he should have no male heir, that my brother Don Bartolomé should inherit in the same wise; and in the same wise, if he should have no male heir, that another brother of mine should inherit. Let it be understood that this shall apply in the same way to each relative most closely allied to my line in turn for ever. And let no female inherit, unless it be that no male can be found; and if this should befall, let it be the female closest to my line. And I command the said Don Diego, my son, or whoever shall inherit, not to think or presume to diminish the entailed estate, but rather to increase it and apply it – apply, that is, the income he shall have from it – in serving the King and Queen, our lord and lady, with his person and estate, for the increase of the Christian religion.

250

The King and Queen, our lord and lady, when I served them in the Indies – I say 'served' but it would be truer to say that by the grace of the Lord our God I gave them the Indies as if, I might say, they were a possession of my own, for I urged their Highnesses to seek them at a time when they were unknown and the way to them hidden to all who spoke to them. Apart from granting their permission and adventuring my person, their Highnesses were unwilling to spend more than a million *maravedis* to go and discover them – I had to raise the rest – and it so pleased their Highnesses that I should have for myself a share in the said Indies, islands and mainland, which lie to the west of a line which they ordered to be drawn from pole to pole one hundred leagues beyond the island of the Azores and of Cape Verde; and the share I should have was a third and an eighth of the whole, plus one tenth of whatever they contained, as is shown at greater length in my said letters of privilege and charters. Because hitherto no profit has been got from the said Indies from which I might be able to distribute the bequests that I shall hereinafter declare, and it is hoped in our Lord's mercy that such profits will be had in great quantity, my intention should be and is that my son, Don Fernando, shall have a million and a half out of it every year, and my brother, Don Bartolomé, 150,000 *maravedis*, and my brother, Don Diego, a hundred thousand *maravedis*, because he is of the clergy. But this I cannot ordain for certain because until now there is not and has not been any known profit, as has been said.

I declare, for the better understanding of the aforesaid, that the said Don Diego, my son, shall have the said entail with all my possessions and offices, in the same wise as aforesaid and as I myself hold them. And I declare that all the income he shall have by virtue of the said inheritance he shall divide every year into ten portions and that he shall distribute one of the said ten portions among our kin to those who appear most in need and to needy folk and in other good works. And thereafter of the remaining nine parts he should take two and divide them into thirty-five portions, and of these my son, Don Fernando, shall have twenty-seven and Don Bartolomé shall have five and my brother, Don Diego, shall have three. And because, as I said above, my wish would be that my son, Don Fernando, should have a million and a half, and Don Bartolomé 150,000 *maravedis* and Don Diego one hundred, and I do not know how this may be in practice because hitherto the said income from the said entail is not known and has no certain value, I declare that the method I described above shall be applied until it shall please our Lord that the said two parts of the said nine shall suffice and shall grow to such a point that there shall be found within them the said million and a half for Don Fernando and 150,000 *maravedis* for Don Bartolomé and 100,000 for Don Diego. And when it shall please God that this shall come to pass, or that the said two parts – that is, of the aforesaid nine – shall amount to 1,750,000 *maravedis*, all that remains shall be for, and shall be had by, Don Diego, my son, or his heir. And I declare and beseech the said Don Diego, my son, or his heir, that if the income from this said entail should increase greatly, that it would please me if the portions of Don Fernando and of my brothers were to be increased beyond what is stipulated herein.

I declare that of this portion which I command to be given to my son, Don Fernando, I make an entail in his line, and that his elder son shall succeed him therein, and so on from one generation to the next forever, so that it shall not be sold or exchanged or given or alienated in any way and shall be after the same manner and in the same wise as has been declared in the case of the other entail which I have created for my son, Don Diego.

To Don Diego, my son, I declare and command that at such time as he shall receive from the said entail and inheritance sufficient income to maintain a chapel, he shall endow three livings for chaplains who shall say three masses every day, one in honour of the Holy Trinity, and another in honour of the Conception of Our Lady, and the other for the souls of all the faithful departed and for my soul and those of my father and mother and my wife. And if his means shall be sufficient, he shall endow the said chapel honourably and increase the prayers and orations offered in honour of the Holy Trinity. And if it may be that this shall be in the island of Hispaniola, which God gave me by a miracle, it would please me if it were in that place where I called upon His name, that is in the plain which is called Vega de la Concepción.*

To Don Diego my son or his heir I declare and enjoin that he pay all the debts which I leave herewith listed in a memorandum, in the manner which there appears, and all other debts which it shall justly appear that I owe. And I enjoin him to take Beatriz Enriquez in his keeping, the mother of Don Fernando, my son, that he provide for her to live decently, as a person to whom I am very greatly obliged. And let this be accomplished for the discharge of my conscience, for it weighs heavily upon my soul.* The reason for it is not proper to be written here. Dated 25 August 1505. Signed Christo Ferens.

After the list of witnesses follows the memorandum of outstanding debts, all – with perhaps one exception which might have remained from Columbus's early life or family obligations in Genoa – dating from his time in Lisbon: of these, all but one 'to a Jew who lived by the gate of the Jewry' are to Genoese merchants.

Two letters to royal correspondents reveal the state of Columbus's mind as his life drew to a close. The first appears to belong to a series of letters written to Ferdinand in 1505, in an attempt to secure the objective Columbus had already declared in letters to his son: to ensure that Diego should succeed him in his titles and, particularly, in the office of Governor of Hispaniola, of which Columbus felt himself unfairly deprived.

Las Casas sketches in a broader context:* from mid-1505 Columbus was with the court at Segovia, after a painful mule-back ride from Seville, petitioning the King in a series of interviews which seem to have covered the whole of the explorer's claims against the crown. In particular, if Las Casas's testimony is anything to go by, Columbus seems to have conceived the notion that the King was hostile to him and bent on depriving Diego of his inheritance. If we are right in thinking that dynastic ambition had been the motor of Columbus's life, it is understandable that fears of this sort should have weighed heavily with the dying Admiral. Though the King was in no hurry to satisfy Columbus – delay was the crown's constant resource in dealing with petitioners – he seems in reality to have been remarkably friendly to the interests of the Columbus family. For example, he saw to it that Diego received a pension of 50,000 *maravedis* a year; he used royal clout in the marriage market to bring the boy a brilliant match with Doña María de Toledo; and after the explorer's death he did indeed eventually restore Diego in the office of Governor. On the matter of Columbus's pecuniary rewards he was, however, unyielding. Las Casas depicts an interview in the early summer of 1505 at which Columbus declared he would return his letters of privilege to the King and retire to some sequestered place in which he might have rest. The King replied with his usual reassurances: he would give Columbus his due and more besides; the discoverer then withdrew, somewhat consoled, explaining to himself that the King would be unable to settle the affair definitely while the heirs to the throne of Castile, King Felipe and Queen Juana, were absent from the kingdom.

The tone of encounters of this sort seems to be faithfully captured in the following letter.* Columbus's insistence on his personal divine election may have seemed irksome in the circumstances; his recollection of his opportunities to serve other princes may have struck the King as an implied threat. His promise to render more glorious service than ever can hardly have been credible. These features, with the renewed proclamation of his conviction that his identification of his discoveries had been right all along, conjure up the mental world into which Columbus had withdrawn: impenetrably self-righteous, inaccessible to reason. The surviving copy, made by Las Casas, omits the subscription.

Letter to King Ferdinand, undated

Very exalted King, It was by a miracle that our Lord God sent me here to serve your Highness. I have called it a miracle, because I first went to seek support in Portugal, where the King of that country took personal responsibility for matters connected with exploration, rather than delegating them to anyone else. God closed his eyes and ears and muffled all his senses, for I could not make him understand what I was saying, not in all those fourteen years. Again I have called it a miracle, for I had letters summoning me to the courts of three other Princes, which were seen by the Queen – God rest her soul – and which were read to her by Dr Villalón.*

Once your Highness was aware of my project, you honoured me and granted me titles of honour. Today, my enterprise has created new possibilities, and men are saying that it is, and will prove to be, what I have always claimed. Your Highness is a very Christian prince. I, with all who are aware of my deeds in Spain and all the world, am bound to believe that your Highness will restore with increase the favours which you granted me, and which you guaranteed by word of mouth and in writing and with your signature. For you honoured me when you had nothing to go on but my promises and now you can see the effect of the deed. And if I am restored to favour, you may be sure that I shall serve you for these few remaining days that our Lord shall grant to me to live; and that I hope in Him, as I feel in my heart and seem to know for certain, that I shall make that service which I have still to perform resound a hundred times more loudly than that which I have done.

On Isabella's death, she had been succeeded by her daughter and son-in-law, Juana and Felipe, while Ferdinand remained in Castile as regent. The royal couple were in their Burgundian lordships, and were expected to sail from the Low Countries to Spain. According to Las Casas, Columbus took some comfort from the hope of their arrival, perhaps because he was dissatisfied with Ferdinand's posture, perhaps because he felt that the conclusion of his case was bound to be suspended during the absence of the heirs. By the time they arrived, however, on 26 April 1506, he was in the grip of his last illness, barely a month from death. The last document from his hand, apart from the final ratification of his will and a codicil added to it, is the following pathetic letter in which he excuses himself from welcoming the monarchs ashore at Laredo.* When Ferdinand and the rest of the court set off, Columbus remained in Valladolid on his death-bed, pitying himself and still dreaming of the terms of his 'contracts'.

Letter to King Felipe and Queen Juana, Valladolid, late April 1506?

More Serene and very high and mighty Princes, our lord King and lady Queen, I trust your Highnesses will believe me when I say that I never hoped so earnestly for my body's health as when I heard that your Highnesses were to come here across the sea, so that I should be able to come to you to place myself at your service and so that you should see the knowledge and experience I have in navigation. But our Lord has ordained otherwise.

I therefore very humbly beseech your Highnesses to reckon me among the number of your royal vassals and servants and to take it as certain that, although this sickness now tries me without mercy, I shall yet be able to serve you with such service as the like of it has never before been seen.

The untoward circumstances into which I have been plunged, contrary to all rational expectation, and other adversities, have left me in dire extremity. For this reason I have not gone to meet your Highnesses, nor has my son. I very humbly beseech you to accept my purpose and intent, instead of my presence, as from one who hopes to be restored to his honour and estate, as is promised in writing in the terms of my commissions.

May the Holy Trinity keep and increase the high and royal estate of your Highnesses.

NOTES

page

11   *The first:* J. Pérez de Tudela Bueso, *Mirabilis in Altis: estudio crítico sobre el origen y significado del proyeto descubridor de Cristóbal Colón* (Madrid, 1983).

     second study: P. M. Watts, 'Prophecy and Discovery: on the Spiritual Origins of Christopher Columbus's "Enterprise of the Indies"', *American Historical Review*, xc (1985), 73–102.

13   *the texts:* A. Čioranescu, ed. and trans., *Oeuvres de Christophe Colomb* (Paris, 1961).

14   *S. E. Morison:* ed., *Journals and Other Documents on the Life and Voyages of Christopher Columbus* (New York, 1963).

18   *world:* Le Historie della vita e dei fatti di Cristoforo Colombo per don Fernando Colombo suo figlio, ed. R. Caddeo, 2 vols (Milan, 1930), i, 43–55.
     my line: Ibid., p. 55.
     patronage: Raccolta di documenti, e studi pubblicati della Reale Commissione Colombiana, part II, i, ed. L. Belgrano and M. Staglieno (Rome 1896), 167.

     'creature': below, p. 189; C. Varela, *Cristóbal Colón: textos y documentos completos* (Madrid, 1984), p. 271.

19   *early age:* below, p. 202

     January 1495: B. de Las Casas, *Historia de las Indias*, ed. A. Millares Carló, 3 vols (Mexico, 1951), i, 32–3; *Le Historie*, i, 57-9; *Raccolta*, part I, ii, ed. C. De Lollis (Rome, 1894), 289. The text translated here is from Varela, *Cristóbal Colón*, pp. 166–7. I have added numbers to the paragraphs.

20   *the Lion:* 'Gulf of Lyon' is a late corruption. The original name captures the sea's terrible reputation with sailors. J. H. Pryor, *Geography, Technology and War* (Cambridge, 1988), p. 19.

     his life: Raccolta, part I, ii, 225; Varela, *Cristóbal Colón*, p. 306.

21   *further west:* The reference to Ptolemy's limit of the west commands attention, because it raises the problem of how and when Columbus first conceived an interest in exploring a possible westward route to the Orient. Writing in 1495, he was at liberty to ascribe to observations made in the late 1470s significance which might have eluded him at the time; but the implication of his remark is that Columbus considered himself to have been in a region which was in some sense oriental, as soon as Ptolemy's dividing line (located on Cape St Vincent – see below, pp. 158–9) was passed. It was technically possible for Columbus to make an observation based on Ptolemy in 1478: he possessed a copy of the Alexandrian sage's *Geography* published in that year. His use of the text at first hand, however, was always very limited, and almost all his references to Ptolemy were mediated at second hand,

mostly through the writings of the early fifteenth-century cosmographer, Pierre d'Ailly. His first perusal of d'Ailly is hard to date precisely, and he seems to have read and reread him over a long period of time; the earliest edition in his library was of 1480 or later (though that does not necessarily mean that he can have had no access to d'Ailly's writings before that date); the only two dated marginal annotations by Columbus are of 1488 and 1491 respectively and all the other evidence of Columbus's literacy – the dates of publication of most of his books, the probable dates of his annotations – belong to the 1480s and later. While these facts may not appear very impressive in themselves, the absence of positive evidence of bookish culture on Columbus's part before the 1480s should make us wary of seeing him as a cosmographical theoretician in any but the most shadowy potentiality at the time of the Iceland voyage of G. Caraci, 'Quando cominció Colombo a scrivere le sue "postille"?', *Scritti geografici in onore di Carmelo Calamonico* (Naples, 1963), pp. 61–84, and I. Luzzana Caraci, 'La Postilla B858c e il suo significato cronologico', *Atti del II Convegno Internazionale di Studi Colombiani* (Genoa, 1977), pp. 197–223. Columbus's own copy of d'Ailly's *Imago Mundi* and other works, with the annotations, is reprinted in E. Buron, *Ymago Mundi de Pierre d'Ailly*, 3 vols (Paris, 1930).

22 *Las Casas: Historia*, i, 35–6; *Le Historie*, i, 62.

23 *their heirs: Raccolta*, part I, ii, 266; Varela, *Cristóbal Colón*, p. 363.

   the story: Las Casas, *Historia*, i, 34–5; *Le Historie*, i, 59–61; P. E. Taviani, *Cristoforo Colombo: la genesi della grande scoperta* (Novara, 1982), pp. 265–71.

24 *Ireland: Raccolta*, part I, ii, 292; Varela, *Cristóbal Colón*, p. 9.

   Azores: Le Historie, i, 74.

25 *seen: Raccolta*, part I, ii, 375; Varela, *Cristóbal Colón*, p. 10.

26 *Guinea: Raccolta*, part I, ii, 390.

   at the time: Ymago Mundi, i, 223; ii, 522; A. de Altolaguirre y Duvale, *Cristóbal Colón y Pablo del Pozzo Toscanelli* (Madrid, 1903), pp. 42–3, 375; G. E. Nunn, *The Geographical Conceptions of Columbus* (New York, 1924), pp. 1–30.

   Asia: A. de Bernáldez, *Historia de los Reyes Católicos*, ed. J. de Mata Carriazo (Madrid, 1943), p. 292.

27 *fashion:* P. Adam, 'Navigation primitive et navigation astronomique', *VIe Colloque International d'Histoire Maritime* (Paris, 1966), pp. 99–110.

   he had: F. Laguarda Trías, *El enigma de las latitudes de Colón* (Valladolid, 1974), pp. 13, 15–16, 35; *Ymago Mundi*, i, 159–63.

28 *royal backing:* Laguarda Trías, *El enigma*, pp. 30, 37, 53–4.

29 *coast of China:* F. Fernández-Armesto, *Before Columbus* (London and Philadelphia, 1987), pp. 248–52; W. S. L. Randles, 'Le nouveau monde, l'autre monde et la pluralité des mondes', *Actas do Congresso Internacional da História dos Descobrimentos*, iv (Braga, 1961), 347–82; Las Casas, *Historia*, i, 149–50; *Le Historie*, i, 77, 85.

   verdict: J. Manzano Manzano, *Cristóbal Colón: siete años decisivos de su vida* (Madrid, 1964), pp. 105, 257–8.

30 *supporting him:* Las Casas, *Historia*, i, 149–50. Resentment of snobbish mockery seems implicit in comparisons he made of himself with the lowly born David: below, p. 226.

   a diary: The text used in this and the next chapter is from the facsimiles published by C. Sanz, *Diario de Colón: Libro de la primera navegación y descubrimiento*, 2 vols

(Madrid, 1962) and M. Alvar, *Diario del descubrimiento* (Las Palmas, 1976). I have adopted some readings from Varela, *Cristóbal Colón*, pp. 15–158, and others of my own, in doubtful passages.

31 *another source:* M. Fernández de Navarrete, *Obras*, ed. C. Seco Serrano, 3 vols (Madrid, 1954), i, 363.

33 *Jerusalem:* below, p. 92.

    Atlantic exploration: Fernández-Armesto, *Before Columbus*, pp. 203–7.

34 *Extremadura:* M. Andrés Martín, *El dinero de los Reyes Católicos para el descubrimiento de América* (Madrid, 1987); F. Fernández-Armesto, 'La financiación de la conquista de Canarias durante el reinado de los Reyes Católicos', *Anuario de estudios atlánticos*, xxviii (1982), 343–78.

    provenance: below, p. 178.

    awareness of it: The most influential works are S. de Madariaga, *Vida del muy magnífico señor don Cristóbal Colón* (Madrid, 1975) and S. Wiesenthal, *The Secret Mission of Christopher Columbus* (New York, 1979).

35 *Italian:* V. I. Milani, *The Written Language of Christopher Columbus* (Special Supplement to *Forum Italicum*) (Buffalo, 1973); J. Gil, 'Ortografía y fonética' and 'La ambigüedad lingüística' in Varela, *Cristóbal Colón*, pp. xliv–lvi.

    access: A. Milhou, *Cristóbal Colón y su mentalidad mesiánica en el ambiente franciscanista español* (Valladolid, 1983).

    unimpressed by it: Information of Dr Ron Barkai.

    influence: The foundation of this school is represented by A. Castro, *La realidad histórica de España* (Mexico, 1954); see J. L. Gómez-Martínez, *Américo Castro y el origen de los españoles* (Madrid, 1975).

    romance: I follow the arguments of A. Rumeu de Armas, *La Rábida y el descubrimiento de América* (Madrid, 1968), pp. 33–41.

    discoveries: J. M. Martínez Hidalgo, *Las naves de Colón* (Barcelona, 1969); S. E. Morison, *Admiral of the Ocean Sea* (Boston, Mass., 1942), pp. 109–31; A. B. Gould, 'Nueva lista de los tripulantes de Colón', *Boletín de la Real Academia de la Historia*, lxxxviii (1926), 721–84.

36 *contemplated: Libro de los privilegios del almirante don Cristóbal Colón (1498)* ed. C. Pérez Bustamante (Madrid, 1951), pp. 41–4.

    China: Pius II, for instance, who shunned the use of Marco Polo, used the same anachronistic title in referring to the Chinese emperor in 1461. *Raccolta*, part I, ii, 303.

    rash inferences: Taviani, *Cristoforo Colombo*, p. 369; cf. below, p. 46, and on the relationship between the Toscanelli letter and the preface to 'The First Voyage', A. Rumeu de Armas, *Hernando Colón, historiador del descubrimiento de América* (Madrid, 1973), p. 269. If the whole of the Toscanelli correspondence is genuine, Columbus must have been contemplating a westward crossing to Asia by 1482, the date of Toscanelli's death – which seems early; if all or part of it is false (H. Vignaud, *Toscanelli and Columbus*, London, 1902) it must be a Portuguese fabrication, as no other possible culprits can have had a rational motive. A Čioranescu, 'Portugal y las cartas de Toscanelli', *Estudios americanos*, xiv (1957), 1–17. On the mysterious oriental traveller see D. L. Molinari, 'La empesa colombina y el descubrimento' in R. Levene, ed., *Historia de la nación argentina*, ii (Buenos Aires, 1939), pp. 302–5.

40 *New World:* The best statement of the case on behalf of the unknown pilot is now
    J. Manzano Manzano, *Colón y su secreto* (Madrid, 1976). The state of the debate is
    summarised by J. Larner, 'The Certainty of Columbus: some Recent Studies',
    History, lxxiii (1988), 9–15, 22.

41 *well documented:* Especially by E. Benito Ruano, *San Borondón: octava isla canaria*
    (Valladolid, 1978).

    substantial: F. Fernández-Armesto, 'Atlantic Exploration before Columbus: the
    evidence of maps', *Renaissance and Modern Studies,* xxx (1986), 12–34.

    Sargasso Sea: Las Casas, *Historia,* i, 68–9; *Le Historie,* i, 76–7.

43 *'very temperate':* Raccolta, part I, ii, 390.

44 *heron:* Columbus's word is *alcatraz,* later applied to the American pelican, but too
    rare in medieval Spanish for its meaning to be clear, except that it appears to have
    denoted an aquatic, fish-eating bird, which, in his next reference, Columbus appears
    to associate with rivers. I therefore favour 'heron' (commonly *garza*) in preference to
    'pelican' *(pelícano)* or 'tern' *(golondrina de mar).* The albatross *(albatros),* which
    Columbus may have known from his voyage or voyages in the African Atlantic,
    cannot be ruled out either, especially as the name may derive from *alcatraz* or
    Catalan *alcatras.* See J. Coromines, *Diccionari etimologic i complementari de la
    llengua catalana* (Barcelona, 1980), i, 161, s.v. 'alcatras'.

46 *own hand:* Above, p. 36.

    Portugal: Las Casas, *Historia,* i, 63–5; *Le Historie,* i, 68–73.

47 *latitude:* Above, p. 27. Laguarda Trías, *El enigma,* pp. 13–17, 27–8, shows how this
    method caused Columbus's notorious misreadings of latitude.

    grid system: Above, p. 36; G. Uzielli, *La vita ed i tempi di Paolo dal Pozzo
    Toscanelli (Raccolta,* V, i) (Rome, 1892), pp. 558–9, 577–80.

    bizarre results: Below, pp. 206, 210, 271 (223 notes).

49 *his crew:* A. Magnaghi, 'Incertezze e contrasti delle fonti tradizionali sulle
    osservazioni attribute a Cristoforo Colombo intorno ai fenomeni della declinazione
    magnetica', *Bollettino della Società Geografica Italiana,* lxix (1937), 595–641;
    Laguarda Trías, *El enigma,* pp. 24–7.

    south-west: Las Casas, *Historia,* i, 195.

    landfall: O. Dunn, 'Columbus's First Landing-Place: the Evidence of the Journal',
    Terrae Incognitae, xv (1983), 35–50.

50 *nakedness:* Milhou, *Colón y su mentalidad mesiánica,* pp. 102–11; Fernández-
    Armesto, *Before Columbus,* pp. 223–45.

52 *West African terms:* J. Gil in Varela, *Cristóbal Colón,* pp. xxxvi–xxxviii.

    'San Salvador': The dateline here and in subsequent fragments represents my
    attempt to work out from the complete text of the 'First Voyage' the location in
    which Columbus wrote the entry; locations in inverted commas are in Columbus's
    nomenclature and modern names are not added except where we can be reasonably
    certain of them. Readers who attempt to follow Columbus's progress in Morison,
    Admiral of the Ocean Sea, pp. 222–352 should not be alarmed by the discrepancies.
    The places described in the entries are often different from those in which they were
    written.

54 *cotton in them:* Values in Spain were expressed in terms of a unit of account, the
    maravedi. Values of coin varied from place to place and time to time according to

the date of issue and intrinsic value. J. Lluis y Navas Brusi, *La amonedación española bajo los Reyes Católicos*, 2 vols (Madrid, 1960), i, 39–55; M. Ladero Quesada, *La hacienda real en el siglo XV* (La Laguna, 1973), p. 42. Not until 1497 were fixed values introduced. The *arroba* as a measure of weight was also variable but equivalent to about a quarter of a hundredweight, though Columbus may have intended it here as a measure of capacity. Again, fixed values were not introduced until 1496. Columbus is not attempting to assign a precise value to the cotton, only to suggest in a general way that a large amount could be acquired cheaply.

68 *set out:* E. Jos, 'El plan colombino del descubrimiento', *Reseñas y trabajos científicos del XXVI Congreso Internacional de Americanistas* (Seville, 1935), pp. 154–67.

69 *century:* I. de Rachewitz, *Papal Envoys to the Great Khan* (London, 1971); R. de Clavijo, *Embassy to Tamerlane*, ed. G. Le Strange (London, 1928). Confusion with the oriental traveller to the court of Eugenius IV may have helped to arouse Columbus's expectations, as they did those of Toscanelli. Above, p. 36.

   presumption: Above, pp. 46–7.

   made later: E. G. Ravenstein, *Martin Behaim: His Life and Globe* (London, 1908), plate II; A. O. Vietor, 'A pre-Columbian Map of the World, circa 1489', *Yale University Library Gazette*, xxxvii (1963), 10–11.

72 *next century:* G. Baudot, *Utopie et histoire en Mexique* (Toulouse, 1977); Milhou, *Colón y su mentalidad mesiánica*, pp. 145–53; L. I. Sweet, 'Christopher Columbus and the Millennial Vision of the New World', *Catholic Historical Review*, lxxii (1986), 369–82.

73 *Gibara:* Morison, *Admiral of the Ocean Sea*, p. 256; *The European Discovery of America: the Southern Voyages* (Oxford, 1974), p. 74.

74 *Sanía Bay:* Morison, *Admiral of the Ocean Sea*, p. 262.

   Pliny describes: Historia Naturalis, chs 13, 23.

76 *Baracoa:* Morison, *Admiral of the Ocean Sea*, p. 274. The first fragment preserved under this date is not preserved in 'The First Voyage' except in paraphrase but does occur in *Le Historie*, i, 129, in what purports to be an Italian translation of Columbus's own words. In translating this and other passages from the same source I have been helped by the version of B. Keen, *Ferdinand Columbus: the Life of the Admiral* (Folio Society edn, London, 1960).

   words here: The text of 'The First Voyage' is resumed from this point.

79 *of gold:* M. W. Helms, 'The Indians of the Caribbean and Circum-Caribbean at the end of the Fifteenth Century' in L. Bethell, ed., *The Cambridge History of Latin America* (Cambridge, 1954), pp. 50–2.

88 *24 December: Le Historie*, i, 135.

92 *empire:* Fernández-Armesto, *Before Columbus*, pp. 128–30.

   world: Milhou, *Colón y su mentalidad mesiánica*, pp. 361–400.

   Holy Sepulchre: Ibid., pp. 391–2.

   'grand design': The phrase was invented, as far as I know, by J. B. Thacher, *Christopher Columbus: His Life, His Work, His Remains*, 3 vols (New York, 1903–4).

93 *Atlantic:* P. M. Watts, 'Prophecy and Discovery: on the Spiritual Origins of Christopher Columbus's "Enterprise of the Indies"', *American Historical Review*, xc (1985), 73–102.

96 *mother:* The younger boy's mother, Beatriz Enríquez de Harana, was still alive, but, as she was only a concubine of low birth with no place at court, Columbus may have felt she did not count in a context in which he was thinking of the boys' protection in their courtly careers; or perhaps the phrase is merely a rhetorical exaggeration. On the problems of the status of Beatriz, see J. Manzano Manzano, *Cristóbal Colón: siete años decisivos de su vida* (Madrid, 1964), pp. 115–35.

   Le Historie: i, 146.

99 *Le Historie:* i, 148.

101 *the press:* C. Sanz, ed., *La carta de Colón* (Madrid, 1956), includes a facsimile of the Barcelona printing, which I have used for the present translation. D. Ramos, *La carta de Colón sobre el descubrimiento* (Valladolid, 1983), includes a facsimile of the manuscript, which helps with some doubtful readings.

102 *deny him:* C. Sanz, *El gran secreto de la carta de Colón* (Madrid, 1959), p. 193.

   discovered: Ramos, *La carta*, no pagination.

   'Corunna': *Raccolta*, part I, ii, p. 95.

103 *understand why:* Cf. A. Remeu de Armas, *La política indigenista de Isabel la Católica* (Valladolid, 1969); Fernández-Armesto, *Before Columbus*, pp. 237–9.

111 *exploration:* Navarrete, *Obras*, i, 363.

   30 January 1494: Text from Varela, *Cristóbal Colón*, p. 189.

112 *begun:* The best account of the voyage is that of Morison, *Admiral of the Ocean Sea*, pp. 389–502.

115 *'just':* Navarrete, *Obras*, i, 152.

127 *Xpo Ferens:* This is the earliest document of undoubted authenticity to bear Columbus's cryptic signature, on which see below, p. 131.

129 *February 1498:* Text from Varela, *Cristóbal Colón*, p. 189.

131 *world:* Milhou, *Colón y su mentalidad mesiánica*, p. 69.

   levels: F. Streicher proposed an entirely secular reading: Subscripsi Xpophorus Almirante Mayor de las Yndias – 'Signed Christopher, High Admiral of the Indies'. 'Die Kolumbus-Originale: eine Paläographische Studie', *Spanische Forschungen der Görresgesellschaft*, i (Münster, 1928), 196–202, which I have not seen, is reported by R. Caddeo in App. M to *Le Historie*, ii, 206 and Taviani, *Cristoforo Colombo*, p. 231.

132 *22 February 1498:* Text from Varela, *Cristóbal Colón*, p. 190.

141 *Oran:* An expedition to Oran was often contemplated, but not effected until 1509, by a force organised by Cardinal Cisneros.

144 *The letter:* Text from Varela, *Cristóbal Colón*, p. 202.

146 *from Spain:* Columbus elsewhere attributed a similar prophecy, equally erroneously, to Joachim of Fiore (below, pp. 206–32). He may have picked the idea up from Messianic propaganda in praise of Ferdinand (above, p. 35). Cf. Milhou, *Colón y su mentalidad mesiánica*, p. 250. The texts he is thinking of here could be, in particular, Isaiah 60:9, which reads in the Jerusalem version, 'Why, the coasts and islands put their hopes in me/ and the vessels of Tarshish take the lead/ in bringing your children from far away/ and their silver and gold with them/ for the sake of the name of Yahweh your God,/ of the Holy One of Israel who had made you glorious.' Tarshish was commonly and plausibly identified as Spain. Las Casas (*Historia*, i, 486) endorsed Columbus's view that Isaiah had foretold 'that from Spain would come the

first men to convert these peoples' but regarded it as presumptuous to try to single out particular texts. Columbus's self-image as a derided prophet suggests Jeremiah 20:17–13. Cf. below, pp. 226, 233, 254.

147 *scarce:* The story of Alexander and the Isle of Taprobana could have been known to Columbus from a classical source, such as Pliny, *Historia Naturalis*, VI, 22, but was commonly included in medieval versions of the Alexander Romance. Columbus's source for the Nero legend was Pius II's *Historia Rerum*, as shown by an annotation in his own copy. *Raccolta*, part I, ii, ed. C. De Lollis (Rome, 1894), 294. Taprobana is mentioned in the same chapter of Pius's work, which was of particular interest to Columbus because of the pope's argument that equatorial regions were not uninhabitable. Cf. above, p. 25.

148 *West Africa:* Navarrete, *Obras*, i, 362.

150 *Erin Bay:* Morison, *Admiral of the Ocean Sea*, p. 533; *The European Discovery of America: the Southern Voyages* (Oxford, 1974), p. 147.

152 *candidate:* Morison, *Admiral of the Ocean Sea*, p. 541; *European Discovery*, p. 147.

153 *River Guiria:* Ibid., p. 151; *Admiral of the Ocean Sea*, p. 542.

154 *mainland:* The reference is to the exploration of Cuba on his second voyage: see Morison, *Admiral of the Ocean Sea*, pp. 443–68.

156 *healthy:* above, p. 43.

magnetic variation: See above, p. 48. There can be no doubt that on this occasion Columbus recognised the phenomenon for what it was.

uphill: Encouraged, no doubt, by his reading of Pierre d'Ailly, who discussed the possibility of an extrusion of the world's surface. *Ymago Mundi*, i, 184.

'*Orient*': Columbus's annotations to the *Historia Rerum* of Pius II reveal what may be an early interest in the location of the earthly Paradise. *Raccolta*, part I, ii, 294. Most of the authorities cited in this letter, however, seem to have been drawn to his attention by Pierre d'Ailly.

158 *distance:* As I understand the text, Columbus's point is that the variation in the relationship between the North Star and the Guards suggests of itself that he is sailing uphill; but that, over a period of days, the readings he made in an attempt to verify his observations recorded a fall in the star's apparent angle of elevation, at the same latitude and at the same time of day: this observation decisively confirmed, for him, the notion that the ships were gaining height. He goes on to suggest that the same phenomenon also accounts for magnetic variation (though his reasoning here seems impossible to follow) and the apparent movement of the Pole Star in relation to the Guards. The last point is easily understood: from a relatively high vantage point, the star would appear to describe a wider radius around the pole than from a low one.

Arin: Columbus's source for the central position of this place was probably again Pierre d'Ailly, who discusses it in an attempt to show that the 'central place' of Jerusalem in the world should not be understood literally.

159 *Catigara:* The easternmost point of China. Below, p. 223.

160 *to heaven:* A point made by Pierre d'Ailly and noted by Columbus in a marginal annotation to the text. *Ymago Mundi*, i, 6; *Raccolta*, part I, ii, 375.

161 *Alexandria:* Columbus seems to misremember Genesis 2:9–14.

rose above, etc: This sentence is broadly based on Pius II's discussion of the habitability of the tropics. Above, p. 147.

Canary Islands, etc: Texts of this sort are collected in A. O. Lovejoy and G. Boas, *Primitivism and Related Ideas in Antiquity* (Baltimore, 1935), pp. 280–303, and discussed in L. A. Vigneras, *La búsqueda del Paraíso y las legendarias islas del Atlántico* (Valladolid, 1976).

Orient, etc: In Las Casas's summary of Columbus's journal, this observation is first made on 17 August. The authorities Columbus cites are discussed by Las Casas, *Historia*, ii, 44–58. What is essential and distinctive about Columbus's thinking at this point is not that the Paradise is at the end of the orient, which was a commonplace almost universally accepted, but that it was at the end of the equator. Las Casas (ibid., pp. 51–5) finds it hard to track down specific authority for this view. Columbus could have got the idea from the fifth chapter of Pius II's *Historia Rerum* (which, in addition to Pierre d'Ailly, seems to be an important influence on the geography underlying this letter as a whole), although the Pope's own opinion inclined against it: it would be consistent with Columbus's usual dogmatic empiricism to claim to have vindicated by experience an opinion rejected by authority.

163   *the opposite: Ymago Mundi*, i, 207–15; Aristotle, *De Caelo*, ed. W. K. Guthrie (London, 1939), p. 253.

   around it: Historia Naturalis, II, 66–7.

164   *little space:* Petrus Comestor, 'Historia scholastica: Historia Libri Genesis' in J. P. Migne, ed., *Patrologiae cursus completus ... series Latina*, cxcviii, col. 1059.

   in this: Glosa Ordinaria: Genesis, 1:2.

   their people: Ymago Mundi, i, 164–9, 197, 207–15. *Raccolta*, part I, ii, 366–406.

   Mairones: All this material derives, in garbled form, from Pierre d'Ailly. The text of Esdras is not in the third book, but IV, 6, which is excluded from St Augustine's defence of the prophet's canonical status (*De Civitate Dei*, XVIII, 36, though Columbus also cites XVII, 24) and the text of St Ambrose is not from the *Hexameron* but the *De Bono Mortis*, ch. 10 (Las Casas, *Historia*, ii, 34–5). Mairones's thirteenth-century commentary may have been consulted independently by Columbus, though it is alluded to by d'Ailly.

167   *Las Casas:* Text from the facsimile edition of C. Sanz, *Descubrimiento del continente americano* (Madrid, 1962).

171   *Mairones:* Above, p. 164.

173   *20 October 1498:* Text from Varela, *Cristóbal Colón*, p. 247.

174   *May 1499:* Text from ibid., p. 255.

180   *Historie: Le Historie*, ii, 71.

   possible: Las Casas, *Historia*, ii, 82–92. Text from Varela, *Cristóbal Colón*, pp. 244–7.

181   *as arms: Don Quixote*, II, 52.

   interference: See above, p. 98, below, p. 212.

186   *November 1500:* Las Casas, *Historia*, ii, 191.

   his case: Text from Varela, *Cristóbal Colón*, p. 263, with modifications based on Bustamante, ed., *Libro de los privilegios*.

187   *Columbus:* J. Villamil y Castro, 'Cristóbal Colón y los franciscanos', *Boletín histórico*, i (1880), 43–6; *The Voyages of Discovery in the Bratislava MS Lyc 515/8*, ed. M. Krása, J. Polišensky and P. Ratkoš (Prague, 1986), p. 111.

188   *Isaiah:* 65:17; Revelation, 21:1.

189   *vilifying me:* Job 30:1.

    hidden: Prince Juan had died in October 1497 and the Infanta Isabel in August of the same year.

192   *young men:* Daniel 3:24, 6:22.

195   *kingdoms:* Las Casas peppered the margins of this document with sententious comments, including, at this point, 'Thanks to these gains, unjust and ill gotten, she will turn into the world's poorest.'

196   *La Mejorada:* Columbus was in La Mejorada in the summer of 1497, perhaps composing a memoir for the monarchs on the problem of defining the limits of the Castilian and Portuguese zones of navigation in the east. A. Rumeu de Armas, *Un escrito desconocido de Cristóbal Colón: el Memorial de La Mejorada* (Madrid, 1972). This would provide a suitable context for the formulation of a plan to attack Islam from the east and, perhaps, bring about a conjunction – the overthrow of Islam and the reconquest of Jerusalem – of chiliastic significance. Early in the next century, the same plan was revived and partly implemented by Afonso de Albuquerque. The source of the idea for the expedition could have been a text of Roger Bacon's, cited by Columbus from Pierre d'Ailly, prophesying the downfall of Islam. *Raccolta*, part I, ii, 107.

197   *late 1500?:* Text from Varela, *Cristóbal Colón*, p. 271.

198   *royal archives:* A. Rumeu de Armas, 'Colón en Barcelona', *Anuario de estudios americanos*, i (1944), 523–4. Text from Varela, *Cristóbal Colón*, p. 303.

200   *project:* Text from Varela, *Cristóbal Colón*, p. 277.

201   *Jerusalem: Raccolta*, part I, ii, 434.

    Roger Bacon: Ibid., pp. 107, 410.

    of the time: Milhou, *Cristóbal Colón y su mentalidad mesiánica*, pp. 349–400; A. Čioranescu, *Oeuvres de Christophe Colomb* (Paris, 1961), p. 495, n. 14.

203   *'learning':* Matthew 11:25, 21:15–16; John 1:1.

204   *world:* Columbus shows himself to be a follower of Pierre d'Ailly's doctrine that astrology is compatible with Christianity, and goes further to include other forms of divination, such as augury, as valid, along with scriptural and astrological methods. In the *Book of Prophecies*, he cited a text of St Isidore's (*Etymologiae*, VII, 8) which partly justified this approach, specifying seven types of prophetic revelation: ecstasy, vision, dream, voices from heaven, cryptic utterances, and the direct communication of the Paraclete. Columbus's broad-minded admission that non-Christians could receive the communications of the Spirit was necessary, perhaps, because he had made use of the computations of al-Farghani to justify his plans for an Atlantic crossing, and had obtained some, at least, of his material on the calculation of latitude and on the imminence of the end of the world from Abraham Zacut.

    chapter: Of the *Vigintiloquium de concordantia astronomicae veritatis cum theologia et cum historica narratione*, which was bound with his copy of *Imago Mundi*, and which supplied him with the reference to St Augustine, *De Civitate Dei*, XXII, 30. See below, p. 206n.

    chapter X: Raccolta, part I, ii, 107. Columbus is still referring to the *Vigintiloquium*. He was or became aware also of a computation by Abraham Zacut which dated the Incarnation in the 5,242nd year of creation. Ibid., p. 368.

205   *unto you:* Matthew 7:7, 14:29–30, 17:20; I Corinthians 13:2.

206 *nine chapters:* Columbus has turned back from the *Elucidarium* to the
Vigintiloquium. See F. von Bezold, 'Astrologische Geschichtsconstruction im
Mittelalter' in *Aus Mittelalter und Renaissance* (Munich, 1918), 164–95, especially
pp. 185–8.

specialised: A. Deyermond, *A Literary History of Spain: the Middle Ages* (London,
1971), 195–200.

209 *new discoveries:* Text from Varela, *Cristóbal Colón*, p. 310.

210 *Hispaniola:* Genesis 10:4; Isaiah 23:12.

moon: cf. below, p. 223.

212 *self-revelations:* Text from Varela, *Cristóbal Colón*, p. 347.

charity: Navarrete, *Obras*, i, 471.

'provisions': Varela, *Cristóbal Colón*, p. 347.

213 *out there:* Or 'of the way the government is being run'.

214 *'Paria':* Le Historie, ii, 85.

216 *'great wish':* Ibid., p. 93.

218 *apparitions:* W. Christian, *Apparitions in Medieval and Renaissance Spain*
(Princeton, 1981), p. 211.

221 *one to another:* This was the common practice at sea. Cf. F. Fernández-Armesto,
The Spanish Armada (Oxford, 1988), p. 59.

my roof: These complaints must be treated cautiously: they are hardly compatible
with expectations Columbus evinced before his departure (above, pp. 209–13) or
with the sums in gold he received from Hispaniola during the period of the fourth
voyage (above, pp. 215, 220 and below, p. 237). They may be intended to suggest
a comparison with Job. Milhou, *Colón y su mentalidad mesiánica*, pp. 268–9.
Job 19:13–16.

222 *Cariay:* Quiribiri, according to Las Casas.

Ciamba: One of Marco Polo's names for part of Cochin-China. Čioranescu,
Oeuvres, p. 484, n. 15.

Caramburú: Perhaps Bahía del Almirante. Morison, *Admiral of the Ocean Sea*,
p. 605.

223 *Aries:* This was on 14 September 1494, according to a note made by Columbus in
the *Book of Prophecies:* 'and it was found', he says, 'that there was a difference from
there to the Cape of St Vincent in Portugal of five and a half hours.' There seems to
be a reference to this same measurement in his draft letter to Pope Alexander VI
(above, p. 209) where the difference is said to have been ten hours. Here yet another
figure – nine hours – is suggested. If this last figure is adopted in order to follow
Columbus's argument here, since each hour corresponds to fifteen degrees of
longitude at the equator, he must have traversed 135 degrees of the earth's surface.
Ptolemy assigned 180 degrees to the ocean: Columbus would therefore still have the
equivalent of forty-five degrees at the equator to travel before reaching the extreme
east of Asia. Marinus of Tyre, however, by Ptolemy's report, reduced the span of the
ocean to 135 degrees, placing China in the vicinity of Columbus's estimated
position. Varela, *Cristóbal Colón*, p. 288n., suggests that Columbus may have been
following Ptolemy in 1494 and defected to Marinus on later reflection. The evidence
for this, however, is a report of Columbus's findings at second hand. *Raccolta*, part
III, ii, 247.

degrees: The Cape of Good Hope extends to about 34°50′S.

water: Esdras IV, 6. Cf. above, p. 171.

stand here: above, p. 25.

Puerto de Bastimentos: Probably Nombre de Dios. Morison, *European Discovery,* p. 24.

224 *Retrete:* Probably Escribanos. Morison, *Admiral of the Ocean Sea,* p. 614.

Puerto Gordo: Perhaps Puerto Colón. Morison, *European Discovery,* p. 257; *Admiral of the Ocean Sea,* p. 620.

226 *to my help:* According to Alain Milhou (*Colón y su mentalidad,* p. 279), the phrase translated here as 'captains of your Highnesses' men of war' could be intended to echo the Vulgate's *magister militiae* (literally, 'commander of the host') in, for example, I Samuel 12:9 or II Samuel 10:16. The 'four corners of the wind' obviously derive from Christ's eschatological discourse (Matthew 24:31), which introduces the theme of Messianic prophecy, prominent in the language of the rest of the passage describing Columbus's mystical experience. See Milhou, op. cit., pp. 272–86 on the biblical sources generally.

God of all: Columbus's choice of Old Testament forerunners has excited the attentions of the advocates of the theory that he was a Jew (e.g. S. de Madariaga, *Vida del muy magnífico señor Don Cristóbal Colón,* Madrid, 1975, p. 261). The figures cited in the course of the message from the voice, however, were all thoroughly assimilated in Christian tradition; indeed, all were types of Christ Himself, and evoke the millenarian fervour typical of Columbus's later life. Milhou, op. cit., p. 230. 'Fools, slow to believe' are prefigured in Christ's own words to the disciples at Emmaus: Luke 24:25.

all the earth: Columbus has conflated two texts – perhaps Jeremiah 1:5 ('Before I formed you in the womb I knew you . . .'), which he also cites in a marginal note of his *Book of Prophecies,* and Romans 10:18. The implication is not only that God has rewarded Columbus with worldly fame, but also that He has chosen him to bear the message of the Gospel.

keys to you: These remarks are an implied rebuke to Ferdinand and Isabella. Columbus suggests that the monarchs' formal 'grant' to him of rights in the Indies masks a deeper reality: that the discovery was conferred on him personally by divine grace, which he generously passed on to the monarchs. This doctrine, which the monarchs are unlikely to have welcomed, recalls the arguments by which some members of the medieval Aragonese nobility claimed to hold their honours by 'divine right' no whit inferior to that by which the king held his kingdom (Fernández-Armesto, *Before Columbus,* p. 14). 'The keys of the Ocean' echo Job 38:8–10: this model sprang readily to the mind of Columbus, inclined to paranoia and convinced that he was the victim of a conspiracy of courtly enemies, whose machinations were diabolically inspired.

out of Egypt?: The deliverance from Egypt is a common topos in medieval literature for pilgrimage and crusade and should not be read as evidence of Columbus's supposed Hebraic affinities. The same image occurred to him during his first recorded mystical experience (above, p. 95). The standard text of the present passage (*Raccolta,* part I, ii, 192) reads 'al pueblo de Israel' ('to the people of Israel') but some editors, including Varela (*Cristóbal Colón,* p. 323) prefer 'al tu pueblo' ('to your people'), thus implicitly endorsing the theory that Columbus was a Jew. I read 'al su pueblo' ('to His people'): the obvious allusion is to the *Nunc Dimittis*, a text which appealed to Columbus, who liked to think of himself as enlightening pagans.

king in Judaea?: A closely similar allusion is made in a passage attributed to Columbus's letter to Juana de la Torre, but omitted from most texts: 'I am not the first Admiral of my line. Let them call me by what name they will. For, when all is said, David, that very wise king, was a keeper of sheep and afterwards was made king in Jerusalem. I am the servant of that same Lord who raised David to that estate.' *Le Historie*, i, 55.

a young woman: Seven sentences replete with well known biblical allusions here substitute the figure of Abraham for that of David. Both figures were strongly attractive to Columbus – in David's case as a type of the Messiah, in Abraham's because of the 'inheritance' due to his spiritual progeny (Romans 4:13–22). Abraham is also of interest to Columbus as evidence of God's willingness to favour ageing heroes. From the third voyage onwards, Columbus, though probably only in his fifties, habitually referred to himself as old and white-haired.

227 *compulsion*: The sources, if any, of this sentence are hard to identify and its meaning is obscure. Columbus's point seems to be that God only accepts voluntary martyrdom, whereas, by implication, he has had it thrust upon him by the Catholic Monarchs. The context – complaints of broken promises and contractual casuistry – is a reproach to Ferdinand and Isabella for failing to give Columbus the rewards he claimed under the terms of his original commission of 1492 (above, p. 30). The mention of Abraham may have inspired Columbus's comparison between royal knavery and divine fidelity to a 'covenant'.

'service of others': I follow Varela's reading (op. cit., p. 323) on the principle of *difficilior lectio*. The standard reading (*Raccolta*, part I, ii, 192) would yield, 'Now He has shown me the garland you have earned in all your endeavours and dangers in the service of others.'

'behind them all': The voice's final command is common to most Biblical visions, though it is usually uttered by an apparition at the opening of any dialogue. The tribulations etched in marble are reminiscent of Job 19:23–4, calling for the record of his woes to be 'cut into the rock for ever'.

Belpuerto: Probably Puerto Bello, which he had visited and named on 2 November 1502. Morison, *European Discovery*, p. 246.

faith is vain: I Cor. 15:14.

Mangi: Cuba. 'Mangi', borrowed from Marco Polo's nomenclature, is Columbus's usual preferred name for what he regarded as the easternmost province of China. Note that although Columbus is no longer alone, he persists in single-minded use of the first person singular.

228 *Lord God*: Columbus's prose is broken with the apparent force of strong emotion. 'Anchor' is naturally feminine in Spanish but seems intensely personified here.

leagues away: Columbus may have wished to stress that he was close to Hispaniola because it was flattering to his prowess as a navigator and because it implicitly justified his desire to return to an island from which he had been exiled. His claim to have 'seven thousand miles' of open sea to cross was more characteristic: a mystical number, embedded in an exaggeration of conventional proportions.

a miracle: There may be a hinted comparison here with Jonah 2:11, whose experiences closely paralleled Columbus's own: the flight to Tarshish, the voyage among hostile foreigners, the catastrophe at sea, the longing for the Temple, the trials of faith.

God knows: Columbus had tried to evade these orders on his outward journey and seems, from these excessive protestations, to have intended to try again on the way back.

229 *the mainland:* It is hard to follow this highly condensed account. The harbour Columbus used in Hispaniola was probably Azúa. The island of Las Bocas must have been one of the Bay Islands, perhaps Bonacca. See Morison's reconstruction in *Admiral of the Ocean Sea,* pp. 592–5.

where they said: Columbus means that when they left the mainland his pilots thought they were on the meridian of Puerto Rico, whereas he realised they were much farther west: in fact, off Cape Tiburón, near the modern Colombian/ Panamanian frontier, in what he persists in referring to as part of China. Morison, *European Discovery,* p. 253; *Admiral of the Ocean Sea,* p. 635.

prophets: Columbus's meaning seems to be that astronomical navigation, which involves scrutiny of the heavens, is a means of divining information which is celestial in origin. For his sources on the relationship between astrology and other forms of prophetic divination, see above, pp. 204 and 206nn.

harness of gold: The Massagetae, Scythians who, Columbus noted in his copy of the *Historia Rerum* of Pius II, 'had an abundance of bronze and gold' and lived near the Anthropophagi, whom Columbus mentions in the next paragraph but one. *Raccolta,* part I, ii, 300.

231 *fell silent:* Above, p. 223.

Paradise: The purity, durability and therapeutic properties of gold gave its name more than merely material resonances in Columbus's day. It could stand, in some contexts, for Christ, the Virgin (as it still does in the Litany of Our Lady) and the Church. Columbus's formula here may contain an allusion to the eschatological tradition that anticipated the 'enrichment' of the poor, through the release of treasure hidden in the earth, in the last days. Milhou, *Colón y su mentalidad mesiánica,* pp. 113–44.

232 *De Antiquitatibus:* VIII, 7.

reported: II Chronicles 9:13–17; I Kings 10:14–25.

Spain: Above, p. 223.

saintly woman: Presumably a reference to Jerome's services in guiding Paula, Eustochium, and their sisterhood around the Holy Land.

Christ: Above, p. 31.

233 *a joke:* Jeremiah 20:7–13 rather than Job 30:1 seems to provide the type of Columbus's suffering here: the suffering prophet, who incurred arrest (Jeremiah 26:8, 37:14, 38:6 – cf. the next paragraph) as well as incredulity and vilification.

his due: Matthew 22:21.

234 *royal court:* The danger was certainly credible: above, p. 209. In 1475 Antonio da Noli, another Genoese adventurer, had defected to Castile from Portugal from his base as lord of the Cape Verde Islands, and it was entirely possible for Columbus to make the same shift of allegiance in the opposite direction. C. Verlinden, 'Antonio da Noli et la colonisation des Iles du Cap Vert', *Miscellanea storica ligure,* iii (1963), 129–44.

235 *supplies:* In a note in the *Book of Prophecies*, he mentions his unsuccessful efforts to time the eclipse. *Raccolta*, part I, ii, 107.

236 *disingenuous:* Las Casas, *Historia*, iii, 315–22.

    March 1504: Ibid., pp. 315–16.

237 *3 August 1504:* Text from Varela, *Cristóbal Colón* p. 332.

238 *the Order:* Ovando had been elevated from the rank of Commander to Grand Commander of the Order of Alcántara.

    son: Text from Varela, *Cristóbal Colón*, p. 335.

240 *world began:* See P. Brown, *Augustine of Hippo* (London, 1967), pp. 403–7.

242 *influential parties:* Bustamante, ed., *Libro de los privilegios.*

    1 December 1504: Text from Varela, *Cristóbal Colón*, p. 338.

244 *Pinelli's sons:* Pinelli had provided finance for the monarchs' Granadine and Canarian wars before collaborating with Luis de Santángel and others in arranging the backing for Columbus's first voyage. He was a member of the Casa de la Contratación – the Board of Trade of the Indies. Fernández-Armesto, *Before Columbus*, p. 206; R. Pike, *Enterprise and Adventure* (New York, 1966), pp. 3, 99.

245 *follows:* Text from Varela, *Cristóbal Colón*, p. 341.

248 *at court:* Text from Varela, *Cristóbal Colón*, p. 358.

    'your Highnesses': J. L. Espinel Marcos, 'Cristóbal Colón y Salamanca' in J. L. Espinel Marcos and R. Hernández Martín, eds., *Colón en Salamanca: los Dominicos* (Salamanca, 1988), pp. 23–4, 31–2.

249 *Diego:* Text from Varela, *Cristóbal Colón*, p. 353.

250 *his will:* Text from ibid., p. 360.

    my successors: An earlier version of the entail survives, dated 1498. See above, p. 132.

252 *Vega de la Concepción:* This may be a reference to Columbus's campaign against the 'rebellious' Indians of Hispaniola, supposedly pacified at Concepción de la Vega in 1496. See C. O. Sauer, *The Early Spanish Main* (Berkeley, 1966), pp. 88–90.

    my soul: The date of Fernando's birth, November 1488, gives a *terminus ante quem* early in that year for the start of Columbus's liaison with Beatriz Enríquez. She was of peasant parentage, but, when Columbus met her, was the ward of a well-to-do relative in Cordoba. A meat business gave her income of her own, mentioned in the only other record of Columbus's solicitude for her: a letter to Diego, written in 1502, just before departure on the fourth Atlantic crossing, in which the explorer enjoins his son to 'take Beatriz Enríquez in your care for love of me, as you would your own mother'. Varela, *Cristóbal Colón*, p. 309.

253 *context:* Las Casas, *Historia*, iii, 325.

    following letter: Text from Varela, *Cristóbal Colón*, p. 357.

254 *Dr Villalón:* The existence of such overtures from England, France, and Portugal, and Dr Villalón's part in conveying them, is confirmed by Las Casas, *Historia*, i, 165–7. As far as we know from other sources, however, it was Columbus who took the initiative in approaching these potential rival patrons – in the English and French cases through the agency of his brother Bartolomé. Ibid., i, 153–5; *Le Historie*, i, 93.

255 *Laredo:* Text from Varela, *Cristóbal Colón*, p. 358.

INDEX